Contents

1. Equal Opportunities in the Curriculum

Preface

This book consists of a collection of papers given at a conference entitled *Equal Opportunities in the Curriculum* held at Oxford Brookes University in September 1997. The day attracted nearly one hundred delegates from all over the British Isles in an event which underlined the importance of this topic to the mainstream of HE teaching and research.

Higher Education, alongside the rest of the public sector has undergone significant changes over the past decade. Reductions in funding, greater competition for student numbers and more stringent methods of quality control have all contributed to a change in culture. Academics, so often accused of inhabiting ivory towers, have had to engage more in the realities of recruiting additional numbers to their courses and ensuring that their subsequent experience is a positive one. The concept of customer care has perhaps been slower to infiltrate academe than many other public services. However, the increasing numbers of students paying all, or substantial amounts of their tuition fees, together with the growing expectations of sponsoring employers, have established it as a concept to be taken seriously.

The effects of these changes have been manifold. However, one of the more significant impacts has been to force HE institutions to rethink their traditional expectations of student cohorts. Many, to their credit, have seen their role as widening access to higher education to as broad a base of the communities they serve as possible. Such institutions have needed no specific prompting to adopt a more open style of recruitment and selection for their courses. They have seen the development of greater diversity among both staff and students as an integral part of their mission statements. However, in the main, they have also tended to recognise that such objectives can only be achieved with hard work, usually accompanied by institutional change. The attitude in the majority of HE institutions has, however, differed markedly from this approach. Many other institutions have perceived the increase of diversity purely in terms of extending the market for their products. International students have become very attractive because of the higher fee income they represent.

However, irrespective of future expansion, the position currently facing most British universities, particularly the newer ones, is one in which student cohorts reflect a high degree of diversity. This picture has been endorsed by the Dearing Report *"Ever since the Report of the Robbins Committee was published in 1963, rates of participation in higher education have run ahead of most expectations and of expert predictions. The speed and the scale of the expansion have been unprecedented within the UK and some outstanding achievements deserve to be recorded and celebrated. For example, the statistics show that within one generation the UK has achieved equal proportions of women and men in undergraduate HE and most ethnic minorities are now, if anything, slightly over-represented. There is, however, no room for complacency as some marked inequalities in educational opportunity remain." (Coffield and Vignoles, 1997).* Diversity is for many of us, a fact of life. How best to accommodate it in a way which is positive for students as well as from an institutional perspective has therefore to be faced if the standards within higher education are to be maintained.

It is against this backdrop that Oxford Brookes University's Equal Opportunities Action Group have been working since 1994. A more detailed account of our work in developing equal opportunities in the curriculum can be found in chapter 1. It is sufficient to say at this point that by the end of 1997, we felt that we had built a significant momentum within the University in terms of awareness and interest in this topic. As far as we could tell from our research, the progress we had made between 1994-7 was as great, or greater than that achieved elsewhere. Indeed, in contacting other institutions, the response was usually a desperate request for assistance. The decision to hold a conference was therefore taken with two objectives in mind. The first was to share the information and expertise which we had developed over time, offering encouragement, but also some caution. The second was to provide an opportunity for academics and support staff from all over the country to come together and compare experiences, hopefully taking something away which might prove of practical benefit.

It was with these objectives in mind that we split the day between a small number of keynote addresses followed by a series workshops which focussed on four specific themes:

- developing materials and practice
- enhancing the learning environment
- making it happen
- the student experience

Each of the workshops comprised three papers and/or practical exercises. All of the presented workshop papers and most of the keynote addresses are contained in the following pages.

The event was an undoubted success. The feedback from virtually all delegates was positive and supportive. The wealth of knowledge and expertise displayed at the conference is replicated in the material contained in this book. Anyone interested in equal opportunities in the curriculum, either from a practical perspective or as an area of academic research will find a diverse and erudite body of information. Many of those presenting represent the leading edge in their field of study.

The keynote sessions included important contributions from Professor Diane Woodward, considering equal opportunities in relation to gay and lesbian students and Angela Glasner from HECFE, who covered the essential nature of equal opportunities in achieving quality (not included). Other sessions from Joanna Foster, ex-head of the CRC and current governor of Oxford Brookes University, addressed the importance of communications in ensuring equal opportunities. The final session was a paper by Martyn Pearl and Janette Ryan, which mapped the Brookes experience.

The papers by Jane Fearon from Sheffield Hallam and Merja Makinen and Peter Newby from Middlesex both describe in detail, the first hand experiences of those involved in implementing equal opportunities in leading Universities. The message is clear, that even those institutions endorsing an equal ops approach are vulnerable to obstruction. The vital area of monitoring, so as to identify areas in which performance may not be acceptable is tackled very analytically by Ruth van Dyke. In her paper she outlines measures which might be used to both identify and tackle underachievement, both institutional and student.

Pauline Noden offers a well tested and pragmatic approach to delivering the equal opportunities message. She is convinced of the need to ensure that the most vulnerable do not lose out through an insensitive approach to recognising and addressing their needs. This theme is further developed by Jeni Turner, who highlights the need to overcome alienation within educational institutions and develop safe environments for all students to contribute and learn. The paper by Sue Ledwith and Ann Lee examines the phenomenon of alienation for overseas students in the practical classroom experience of groupwork. The results are uncomfortable and give cause for concern.

Penny Wallace and Sue Randall describe a teaching and learning strategy which they have developed for a professional training programme, together with a critical reflection on their own experience from an equal opportunity perspective. Especially noteworthy is their attempt to highlight the significance of the diversity of learning experience in formulating a teaching strategy which relies upon self-learning as a key component. The paper by Hilary Yewlett offers an ample reminder that there are considerable obstacles to be overcome if we are to achieve a gender balanced approach in our institutions.

Barbara Bagilhole and Jackie Goode further explore the "gender dimension" of the curriculum in higher education. They highlight that in male-dominated disciplines like engineering, the curriculum is viewed in a "narrow sense" whereas in other disciplines, where women were present in greater numbers, curriculum is viewed in a "broad sense". However, they sound a note of caution that even when the broader informal curriculum is recognised, which takes into account the need for pastoral care of students, a disproportionately greater burden of this task falls on women lecturers.

Gayle Letherby and Jen Marchbank provide a lively and provocative account of their experiences based on their pedagogic work in developing a student-centred and feminist approach to teaching and learning. Their paper not only describes the positive and negative responses to their efforts from both students and staff, but also brings to light the hidden forms of hierarchies even among the oppressed and marginalised sections of the academic community.

Lewis Anderson's paper is an effort to raise awareness about the needs of deaf students in further and higher education, making the point that good practice for teaching deaf students is likely to be good practice for teaching hearing students also.

'Becoming a Nurse: the Experience of the Black Student' by Linda Waterworth explores the damaging impact of racism on the black nursing students. The paper describes different forms of racism which the black nursing students had to experience during their training programme.

In total, this book provides an important source of current thought and practice in the area of equal opportunities in the curriculum. The material is provoking, informative and interesting. These were certainly adjectives endorsed by the delegates attending the conference, the vast majority of whom would have preferred an extended event. It is with warm thanks to all of those who took part, either in organising, presenting papers or simply attending that this book is dedicated.

Martyn Pearl and Pritam Singh

2. Developing Equal Opportunities in the Curriculum - An Account of Oxford Brookes University

Martyn Pearl & Janette Ryan, Oxford Brookes University, Australian Catholic University

The principle aim of this Equal Opportunities in the Curriculum conference is to share knowledge, experience and expertise in the area of equal opportunity and the curriculum. For many higher education institutions, this has become increasingly important as a result of the growing diversity within student cohorts. The widening of access in recent years, coupled with the scramble for increased student numbers has resulted in many institutions recruiting higher numbers of international, mature and non-traditional students. A significant proportion of these have tended to make additional demands on teaching and support services, the nature of which may not previously have been evident. This has certainly been true of my own University, and one of the reasons for choosing to stage the event here at Oxford Brookes University is the belief that we have, as an institution, made steady progress in this area since 1994.

This slot in the programme is intended to offer an insight into one specific set of institutional experiences. Over the next thirty minutes we will outline the initiatives we have taken, focussing in particular on an in-depth study of good practice within Oxford Brookes University, launched earlier on this year as an intended cornerstone of expanding the programme of equal opportunities curriculum development.

Two years ago Brookes adopted a new vision statement, the "Agenda for Brookes" which committed the University *to create a diverse learning environment within which individual characteristics, such as gender, age, nationality, disability and ethnic origin are valued* (Agenda for Brookes). The document further promised a review of equal opportunities policies and practices following which the appropriate and necessary steps would be taken *to integrate equal opportunities policies and implement best practice.*

This has been part of a process which has attempted to change a largely white, middle class profile which a 1993 University of Central Lancashire report found to pay very little attention to questions of race and ethnicity in relation to either access or the curriculum. That particular report also identified a 'lack of awareness' at the needs and requirements of ethnic minorities and attributed a level of 'discomfort' at the need to address the issue.

This shift has obviously not been brought solely about as the result of a sudden widespread conversion to the principle of equality. High on the

5

agenda for all HE institutions has been the need to broaden their traditional cohort profile in order to attract more students. Many institutions have realised that one of the best ways of achieving this is by targeting a largely untapped market of non-traditional students. However, whatever the motivation, the effect has often been to pose a new set of questions, which has resulted in an awareness of the need to change.

Whilst there remains a long way to go, we feel that substantial progress has been made to properly facilitate diversity within this institution. Support from the top has been a notable feature of the process, most notably from the previous Vice Chancellor, Clive Booth. Thankfully, as we have already heard this morning, we can also look forward to this being sustained following the appointment of Professor Upton. I have to say that, in my opinion, this is an absolutely vital ingredient of any proposed programme of institutional change.

It is also fortunate that there is a well established culture within the University for pedagogic innovation and quality. The establishment of a Learning and Teaching Committee, bolstered by a supportive Dean has provided a fertile environment for constructive debate around curriculum issues.

While the EOAG has therefore not acted in isolation in promoting the development of good academic practice, we have been particularly focussed on identifying and addressing the specific issues generated by an increasingly diverse student body. This has been of considerable importance in raising the profile of equal opportunities within the University generally and more specifically providing a resource for both staff and students.

I would guess that Brookes differs little from many other HE institutions in terms of the level of support from staff for equal opportunity initiatives. We have those, and I include both teaching and non-teaching staff, who perceive it as crucially important to the way they work; we have those who are generally unaware of the main issues but are open to be convinced; and we also have those who are sceptical or even openly hostile to the concept. In reality the implementation strategy we have adopted has been based on a combination of subtle persuasion and the strength of sound academic evidence. We have recognised from the outset that of all the areas of activity tackled by the EOAG, influencing the curriculum was likely to be the most problematic. After all, it lies at the very heart of the professional integrity and status jealously guarded by academics at large.

We have therefore sponsored a range of research reports intended to unpick some of the issues relating to diversity and the experience of particular groups of staff and students. To date we have research papers relating to mature students, minority ethnic students, and disabled students all of which are relatively recent but will hopefully feed into the future policy and practice of the University. We have also been involved in evaluating the impact of IT within the University. We recognise that it can be a powerful and liberating tool, but, if underestimated can also marginalise students who have neither the skills nor access to the necessary kit required to participate adequately.

We have expected some resistance to our initiatives. We have taken the view that whilst we would not court controversy, neither would we avoid it where it needed to be confronted. However, on the whole we have preferred an incremental, consultative approach based on the dissemination of information, the provision of training and the achievement of consensus.

As the Vice Chancellor has already mentioned, our interpretation of *the curriculum* has been broad. We have taken the view that in practice activities such as field trips and placements are as critical to creating and sustaining diversity as are admissions procedures and recruitment practices. Similarly a research profile which promotes equal opportunities in both its execution and content is as valuable as representative course content and materials and sensitive teaching and assessment strategies.

The importance of the wider environment has been graphically borne out of work carried out by the group in investigating the impact of Harassment, Bullying and Intimidation within the University. A report published in 1995 indicated that extensive 'low level' harassment was experienced by both staff and students throughout the university. More specifically, over half of non-white students reported racial harassment; and around 40% of all staff and students reported sexual harassment. For students, the harassment mainly took place within lectures, seminars and tutorials.

Unsurprisingly, the indications from the survey was that harassment was a major influence on the performance levels of the victims, affecting *'work, personal relationships and emotional health (especially high amongst ethnic minority students)'*. We have therefore been made clearly aware that a considerable amount of work still needs to be done before Brookes can justifiably boast the existence of an academic environment which practically reflects the intent of the Agenda for Brookes.

However, we have made solid progress. There is now a requirement that equal opportunities forms a tangible element of the operational and strategic plans of all Schools and departments within the university. To facilitate this, members of the EOAG have provided training sessions to heads and deputy heads involved in drawing up these documents. By way of a further small incentive (but after all, every bit helps), Schools and Departments were invited during the course of this year to bid for a grant of up to ,500, specifically to further equal opportunity initiatives contained within their strategic plan. Continued support is provided by each member of the EOAG taking responsibility for liaising with identified schools and departments. In addition, schools and departments have been invited to nominate interested individuals, who have become links people between their work area and the EOAG.

7

In theory therefore, a structure exists which can take the University forward with an integrated commitment to equal opportunities. However, no matter what statements are contained within policy documents, the reality for most students exists in the lectures they attend and the assessments they receive. For staff, the pressures of delivering an effective and satisfying service to the University and its students is often hampered by a lack of resources and an ever onerous burden of performance criteria. However, if individuals are not signed up to, or equipped to deliver institutional objectives, the effect will be one of dilution and undermining. We have therefore considered it as important to provide detailed guidance on implementing good equal opportunity practice, as to create a sound policy infrastructure within which it might flourish.

Prior to commissioning the good practice research, we held a series of internal seminars with a variety of interested staff members to get a feel for the issues and concerns which might exist in 'diversifying' the curriculum. The most common message we received was that staff needed a clearer understanding of what they could do and how equal opportunities might relate to their specific area of work.

In the light of this, we felt that abstract guidance alone would not be totally effective in overcoming these concerns or inspiring new and innovative ways of working. We needed to be able to say that our goal was to some extent already part of the University culture, but generally rather ad hoc and patchy. We also needed to able to offer concrete examples of approach and practice, so that individual members of staff would be able to recognise the relevance for their own professional discipline and teaching/research environment.

We therefore undertook a project to document examples of good equal opportunities practice in the University's curriculum. We devised a research brief, allocated funds and engaged a researcher to devote the necessary time to interviewing staff and compiling their responses. The motivation for documenting examples of good equal opportunities practice was initially to profile the excellent work undertaken by teaching staff within Brookes. However, of equal importance was the need to broaden the message to the University community generally, to explain what is meant by 'good equal opportunities practice' in the curriculum and to promote its broader development.

The broad goals of the project were to:

- identify examples of good equal opportunities practice across all areas of the curriculum;

- identify examples of good equal opportunities practice across all departments of the University;

- obtain the views of staff and students about what constitutes good equal opportunities practice;

- identify gaps where examples should be sought from elsewhere;

- compile examples which cover various aspects of the curriculum and offer practical advice and guidance to staff.

As already mentioned, much of the initial, consultative groundwork had already been completed. This meant that there was less need to convince staff of the merits of the project, although it soon became evident of the need to develop a common understanding of the topic.

Information was collected from a range of sources including extensive interviews with staff and students, observations of lectures, seminars and student presentations, and an examination of course materials and assessment tools. Staff and students gave generous support to the project. Students from a range of 'disadvantaged' groups participated in the project in a variety of ways including individual interviews, group discussions and discussions during tutorials. Approximately fifteen percent of University staff, both academic and general, contributed either by providing their ideas or feedback, participating in a range of staff development exercises, or by allowing their work to be included in the 'Good Practice Guide'.

The initial stage of the project involved consultation with staff and students on the aims of the project, and a literature review. In defining the topic, the project drew heavily on the work of Dr Ruth Van Dyke for the Open University in 1991 on 'Equal Opportunities Guidelines for Teaching Materials'. The paucity of sources on the topic, however, reflected the fact that equal opportunities in relation to curriculum issues had received little attention in relation to the everyday workings of classrooms in the university setting.

It soon became evident from discussions with teaching staff and students that equal opportunities in the curriculum meant different things for different people. It became obvious that while there was broad understanding about what equal opportunities means in a policy sense, there was less clarity about its operational application. That is how it relates to curriculum content and design, pedagogy and assessment, across disciplines. Most importantly perhaps, how these impact upon different groups of students within the university community in terms of opportunity for access, participation, retention and success in their chosen areas of study.

Some of those consulted perceived equal opportunity in the curriculum to apply rather narrowly to gender issues in the main. Others held a broader view of curriculum and pedagogy, recognising the value of diversity in teaching theory and practice. Many staff simply did not relate their teaching methods and practices to good *equal opportunities* practice. They seemed instead intuitively to recognise that good teaching and learning practices work to the advantage of **all** groups of students.

Others were pushing the boundaries even further, questioning and broadening the conventional wisdom and accepted practices of their disciplines in critical and dynamic ways and reflecting on the very question of what constitutes good equal opportunities practice in the curriculum. This was often happening in areas where it would not normally be expected, such as construction and earth sciences, mathematics or biology and molecular sciences.

At best the examples collected were a 'snapshot' of the work being carried out, but by collating them we have been able to provide a range of examples across disciplines which illustrate the diverse interpretations and applications of equal opportunities. This has addressed staff concern that often discipline-specific issues or dilemmas were critical drivers in influencing practice, limiting their ability to adopt different methods of teaching, etc. Examples quoted included the low participation by women students in engineering, or the range of different cultural health and dietary practices relevant in the health care field.

Examples were also sought to demonstrate good practices across the range of curriculum, pedagogy and assessment issues. This involved gathering examples of content covered in courses to demonstrate the diversity of topics covered, the range of perspectives included in the course, or the ways in which course content catered for the particular needs of different groups of students. The inclusion and description of different pedagogical techniques was also important. Of particular interest were methods used by staff to encourage **all** students to participate and feel valued in the classroom, and how students were able to bring their own experiences into classroom discussions and have them recognised and valued. In the area of assessment, examples were sought of the range of assessment tools available to ensure that the broad range of student learning styles and backgrounds can be demonstrated and rewarded.

Essentially, the common elements of the examples sought were responsiveness to the diversity of students and also staff, and inclusiveness and diversity of the learning experience itself. Examples were sought which covered the range of different student groups, academic traditions, differing perspectives, values, needs and expectations.

For the purpose of collecting examples, a broad framework of the issues and areas to be examined was developed. In determining which broad topics to cover, existing work in the teaching and learning areas was utilised but discussions with staff and students filled in the detail of the range of topics of importance within these areas. The topics fell into three broad categories:

- Curriculum
  - course content
  - illustrative examples
  - case studies
  - range of perspectives
  - tailored to needs of students

- Pedagogy
  - teaching strategies
  - classroom organisation
  - ground rules
  - valuing of perspectives
  - reflective practitioner

- Assessment
  - diverse range
  - negotiable
  - explicit
  - values difference

The contents of the 'Good Practice Guide' are intended to given a range of illustrative examples of all of these areas across different disciplines. Most of the examples documented demonstrate in a practical way, how the lecture or seminar worked in practice, rather than simply describing what occurred. In some cases copies of OHPs or handouts are provided, reading lists or seminar topics have also been included to indicate the range of materials and perspectives covered, or examples of assessment topics or tools are given. Sometimes the comments of students from interviews, during seminars or via evaluations or journals are included.

Members of staff willingly gave their time to talk about and share their work, and were extremely generous in allowing their lectures and tutorials to be observed. The views and experiences of a range of different groups of students were also sought including women students, international students, mature age students, lesbian gay and bisexual students, ethnic minorities students and students with disabilities. Students were very open and honest about their own personal needs and expectations, and sometimes told of the very difficult experiences that university attendance could involve for them.

What was clear from discussions held with these students was that their experiences in higher education often differed significantly from the outcomes teaching staff believed they were delivering. This gulf in perception appeared to impact directly on students' learning and their perceptions of the way they were treated in assessment. Students with disabilities often reported difficulty in participating in classroom activities. Ethnic minorities students felt that they were sometimes viewed negatively by staff and that their contributions were not valued. International students sometimes felt disadvantaged by assessment methods that differed from those that they were used to. Gay, lesbian and bisexual students reported instances of discriminatory behaviour towards them by both staff and students. Mature age students felt that little attention was given to the extra demands on them. Women students sometimes felt unsupported and isolated in areas in which women are traditionally under-represented. Much of this went unnoticed by teaching staff.

What was also clear from students' comments was the extent to which they recognised and appreciated good teaching and learning strategies when exposed to them. Their formal and informal experiences with teaching and other staff at university, along with their experiences with their peers, play a major role in the development of self-esteem and enabling learning and ultimately, in their rates of retention and success.

Although common themes and issues emerged during the research, it was clear that different solutions suit individual lecturers and tutors depending on the subject matter, their own teaching style and the composition of their student cohort. Many staff recognised the importance of adopting a flexible and reflective approach to their teaching, being aware of disadvantage suffered by some groups of students and being prepared to respond to students' individual needs.

The intention behind the 'Good Practice Guide' was to offer staff a clear, 'hands-on' approach to embedding the principles of good equal opportunities practice within the teaching demands of their own disciplines. It offers practical and diverse ideas and suggestions to those seeking to develop new practices and approaches, while celebrating the work of those staff at Oxford Brookes who already demonstrate some expertise in this area. It also provides a checklist for good equal opportunities practice at different levels - individual lecturers, course developers, and School level structures. The examples showcasing the work of practitioners in various disciplines not only provide interesting and stimulating reading for those in their own fields, but provide lessons for those in other fields in how the same principles can be applied in all disciplines.

In producing the report, we have found there to be a number of essential elements which underpin the delivery of good equal opportunities practice in the curriculum:

- Approaches to curriculum that positively value and nurture the increasing diversity among staff and students

- A broad and diverse approach to the curriculum which is responsive to a variety of student needs and is open to new ideas and perspectives

- Teaching materials and environments that are representative and inclusive

- Assessment criteria that is explicit and fair

- Opportunities which exist for all students to be able to achieve their potential, and to be able to fully participate in the curriculum

Following its completion, the Good Practice Guide was circulated to all heads of School and Department throughout the University. Publicity was also distributed to make staff more generally aware of its existence. It is difficult currently to assess how effective we (and the Guide) have been in achieving our goal of facilitating a greater consistency of good equal opportunity practice throughout the University. However, it is likely that a considerable amount of continuous work will be needed, both in updating the guide to ensure currency and in reminding existing staff, and informing new staff of its existence. We are considering whether it is possible to convert the text into an electronic, intranet-based document. This, would, however require a considerable injection of resources, which the EOAG does not have.

In reflecting on this exercise, we have cause to be both encouraged and concerned by the position in Oxford Brookes University. We have been genuinely surprised by the extent to which a sizeable number of staff within the University have a clear and demonstrable commitment to student-centredness and equal opportunities. However, less positive is the gap that exists for many staff between their perception and the reality of the student experience. Whilst this is not solely an equal opportunity concern, those students who are less likely to fit the traditional model of a higher education student are most likely to suffer as a result. There is clearly much work to be done in this area.

As something of a post script, two significant events have taken place following the conference in September 1997. The first of these relates to the School of Planning (SoP) undergoing a teaching quality assessment by the Higher Education Funding Council. The SoP has been one of the most progressive parts of the University in terms of adopting a proactive approach to equal opportunities. The result was an outstanding achievement of 24/24, the maximum available score. Reference was made in the inspection team's feedback of the student-centredness of the staff team and the integration of equal opportunities into all activities. Perhaps the lesson to be learned is that good equal opportunities practice delivers both equality and *quality*.

The second notable point is less an event and more of a process. As part of the University's efforts to make ends meet financially, the budget of the EOAG was reduced from £60,000 to £5,000. This has effectively redefined the group as a voluntary, rather than a University-funded resource. The rationale behind this has been that the group has become a victim of its own success - equal opportunities is now embedded into the University and its main work is therefore done. There are those who would question this presumption.

The endurance of an equal opportunity ethos within Brookes remains to be tested in the light of fierce competition for teaching and research resources. However, the work of the EOAG and the production of the Good Practice Guide has been instrumental in creating an institutional culture and framework for those wishing to endorse equal opportunities and deliver quality within an increasingly diverse environment.

3. Sexual Orientation: the Hidden Inequality

Diana Woodward, Dean of the Graduate School – Cheltenham and Gloucester College of Higher Education

What is the issue?

Last Saturday, the day of Diana's funeral, was a very emotional day for me - and not just because I empathised with her concern for 'the constituency of the rejected', as her brother put it, which included abused women, the homeless, those with HIV/AIDS, and lepers; but also because it brought back powerful and sad memories for me of a close friend of my own age who died of cancer almost exactly ten years ago. At that time I had two young children, and was part of an outwardly normal but inwardly loveless marriage. Jackie's death gave me the courage to leave, and to set up home with the woman I loved. This act made me a kind of leper, to my own family and my partner's. However, professionally I was fortunate in that I had the protection of already being a Dean, with an established reputation and responsibility for over 100 staff, and with a strong network of women friends. I have since taken great delight in coming out to vice-chancellors at formal dinners, and in advising lesbian and gay students on how to navigate their way through the quicksands of higher education. But few gay men and lesbians in higher education have had the advantages that I did.

One of my first tasks as Dean was to handle a student appeal. The student was a lesbian, on a Housing Studies degree, who had been thrown off the course having failed her exams. The case looked fairly clear-cut. However, on further investigation, it emerged that she had suffered two years of mounting ridicule and hostility from several of her lecturers, particularly a law lecturer with a bow-tie (forgive the stereotyping here) who played up his 'traditional attitudes'. She had sought to counter his rampant and unrepentant mysogyny by writing 'hers' instead of 'his' throughout an essay, which he then refused to mark. Their continued harassment of her, after her complaints about them in Course Committee meetings were ignored, led her to feel more and more uncomfortable about coming to classes, and so her work suffered. We won the case, she repeated her year and graduated, and when I met her several years later she was by then established in her chosen career.

Let me begin by telling you about some other people whom I have met in the course of my career in higher education. The first three, all aged in their late twenties or early thirties, are currently my PhD students - bright, able people capable of going far in their careers. One felt from an early age that she was a lesbian. Growing up in a working class family, in a mining district, she was making very good progress at secondary school, enjoying particular encouragement from her class teacher and her English teacher (who were a married couple) until they saw her kissing another teenage girl in a bus shelter. Their support was instantly withdrawn, to be replaced by distance and hostility. Her family provided no empathy or support. This student left school early and experienced a series of major personal problems (including homelessness and an addiction problem) until she was fortunate enough, in her twenties, to get a place at an adult residential college, from which she entered higher education. She is now confident and outgoing, and is likely to become a social worker, putting her own experiences to good use in championing the needs of the elderly and disabled.

Another student is a young man who has recently come to believe that he is gay. Last week he was attacked by a man with a heavy piece of wood as he left one of Cheltenham's two gay pubs. Although he reported it to the police, he declined to give them his name, for fear of what would be done with this information. The previous year he became very distressed at his treatment in the laddish culture of a men's hall of residence. After he came out to the other postgraduates who share his office, his former dancing partner lost her enthusiasm to continue and began to ask rather intrusive, judgmental questions about his new status.

The third student already held a responsible post as a university lecturer when she began her PhD on a part-time basis. She has been suspended from work for the past seven months for alleged gross professional misconduct, following complaints from two colleagues, after her long-term partner, who was already lecturing part-time at that institution, applied for a permanent post. My student had already voluntarily declared this relationship, in accordance with institutional procedures about consensual relationships, and was careful to avoid any part in the appointment process. She is now appealing against the decision to demote her, and can show that male colleagues found guilty of serious breaches of contract have been much less harshly treated. She has received enormous support from her colleagues, both locally within her institution and nationally within her professional association.

A decade ago, a male colleague died of AIDS. He was a member of one of the caring professions, as was his long-term partner, who had nursed him through his decline. Because of this, neither had felt able to disclose their relationship, or the nature of Don's illness, to other than a very few close friends. You can imagine the problems of nursing a dying partner, trying to manage with minimum time off work, and grieving for them after their death, all without the informed support of one's colleagues. The lesbian partner of a former colleague had just had a miscarriage when I first met her, which had left her clinically depressed. She is a primary school teacher and would have made a wonderful mother, supported by her and her partner's extended families. Her head assumed that because she was not in a relationship with a man, this had been an unintended pregnancy. Far from it. On hearing about the miscarriage, her response was 'Perhaps it's all for the best' -an unimaginably hurtful comment.

All of these people have experienced terrible isolation, and their behaviour has been judged to their detriment in a way that heterosexuals can barely imagine, both at work and at leisure, in private and in public places, purely because of their sexual orientation. This is particularly pernicious when it happens within higher education, as we claim to offer insight and enlightenment, opportunity and support.

'Equal opportunities should affect all areas of school life. It is vitally important that it is not just seen as a set of rules - a list of dos and don'ts - it must celebrate the diversity of lifestyles, languages and cultures in a school as well as empowering young people to develop an understanding of both the origins and practice of oppression and to enable them to act upon those understandings. Unless all issues of equal opportunity inform the curriculum such an aim cannot in my view be realised.' (Bob Hodgson, deputy headteacher of a south London mixed comprehensive, quoted in Paul Patrick and Susan A. L. Sanders, 1994, p.118).

I believe that this mission applies in higher education just as much as in school education. Within the last decade the promotion of equal opportunities has become a major objective for some (but by no means all) British universities and colleges, especially in the post-1992 sector where the planned expansion of student numbers required new efforts to recruit and retain students from social groups with little history of entering higher education. Some major changes have been achieved, for example women now comprise over half of the student body, compared with just over a quarter in the 1960s (Anderson, 1992; HESA, 1997). However, other aspects of the student profile have proved remarkably resistant to change, for example social class, which has barely changed since the Robbins Report of 1963. Recent research commissioned by HEFCE for the Dearing Committee (using census data) found that children in 'very high income' professional neighbourhoods had a 73 per cent chance of entry to higher education before the age of 21, compared with only 7 per cent of children from council homes in areas of high unemployment (The Guardian, 19 April 1997). Even these limited achievements are remarkable, given the history of higher education in this country, as the exclusive preserve of upper class Anglican men until a century ago, and the recency of women's admission to this privileged elite. (Women were only accorded the right to graduate from Cambridge University in 1948, the year of my birth, and when I was a postgraduate student there in the early 1970s women students were outnumbered 9:1 at undergraduate level, worsening to 100:1 at postgraduate level in the department where I studied.)

Although they are important and fascinating issues, it is not my brief today to assess what progress has been made in relation to the various aspects of equal opportunities, and at the gap between management rhetoric and student reality in many institutions. Instead, I will focus on sexual orientation as a neglected issue in higher education by posing the questions "Why has sexual orientation been largely ignored as an EO issue in higher education?" and "What can be done to address this inequality through the medium of the curriculum?" What follows is a wimpy, liberal analysis of the issues; I look forward to being pushed towards a more radical stance by critical questioning from an impatient audience.

The invisibility of sexual orientation as an issue in the Equal Opportunities agenda

I have been speaking and writing about gender issues in education and employment for over 25 years, but this is my first presentation about sexual orientation. In trying to prepare for it, I was struck by the paucity of relevant material and information - although perhaps it was naive of me to be surprised. Other equal opportunities issues - notably gender, 'race', maturity and educational disadvantage - have become topics for discussion, policy development, implementation and monitoring, to the extent that some battles have now been won, and if not, then at least the rhetoric of 'political correctness' is now evident in many universities and colleges. Progress lags behind in the area of disability, in my view, with still far too much evidence of a 'charitable' approach based on individual cases, and not enough politicised discussion about equality of access and esteem, and entitlements. But in relation to issues about sexual orientation, few institutions appear to have developed policies or procedures for students or staff about freedom from discrimination or harassment. I believe that this is partly attributable to the lack of pressure to do so from social institutions in the wider society and the law, such as exists in relation to discrimination on grounds of sex and race, and (to a lesser extent) disability; in this country, it is not illegal to discriminate on the basis of sexual orientation. But also, lesbian and gay students and staff are often unidentifiable and invisible, making it difficult to identify and respond to their specific concerns. And these concerns can be life-threatening: research by the London Lesbian and Gay Teenage Group found that one in five young gay men and lesbians had attempted suicide (Susan A.L. Sanders and Helena Burke, in Epstein, ed., 1994) and lesbians' incidence of alcohol abuse is several times higher than the national average for women.
A television programme broadcast last week about gay-bashing included some interviews undertaken in a Belfast Working Men's Club. All of the people interviewed said that they had never met a gay man or lesbian. Since

18

it is estimated that perhaps 10 per cent of the population are lesbian or gay, it is a pretty safe bet to say that they **have** encountered gays and lesbians, who were too frightened to be out. The same applies in higher education. 'Out' students and staff are a small, brave, politicised minority. The rest keep their heads down, denying to others and often to themselves that they are deviant, because of rampant homophobia, which they have often internalised. Pressures to seek acceptance by conforming to the norms of the lesbian and gay subcultures lead to uniform dress codes and appearance: it was de rigeur at this year's Pride for lesbians under 30 to have army haircuts, D Ms and camouflage trousers. But this means that lesbians who do not fit this stereotype may not be identifiable by straight society unless they choose to advertise their sexual orientation in a different way, for example in academe by writing and publishing on lesbian topics. Other equal opportunities issues concern groups who are fairly readily identifiable, either visually or through data held on them, or by self-identification - although there are clearly issues about whether students and staff choose to identify themselves as from a minority ethnic group or having a disability, lest there be unforeseen negative consequences of this revelation. But lesbian and gay students and staff may be anywhere on a spectrum from being fully 'out' and hence readily identifiable; or being out only in certain settings and contexts; or closet but acknowledging this identity to themselves; or they may well be struggling to establish a stable sexual orientation. Institutional policies, practices and systems need to be very sensitively developed to reflect this diversity of their/our situation.

In some disciplinary and professional fields it can be acceptable or even seen as a mark of exotic individuality for members of staff to be publicly identified as lesbian or gay - for example, in the creative arts and humanities. These people provide role models for students, but often within a narrow range of stereotypes. My son once said to me 'Why do pictures of gay men always make them look like wimps with beards?' It is far harder to find 'out' staff in traditionally male disciplines, where there is less emphasis on the creative process and on the results of work, than on its subjective aspects and relationships. (I was told of a male academic who attended conferences in a branch of engineering wearing a leather mini-skirt, but I am not sure whether any of his colleagues ever actually asked him if he was gay.) To be an 'out' engineer may pose problems for relationships with professional peers, but is unlikely to result in formal exclusion or dismissal. In contrast, it can be dangerous and threatening to be 'out' in other fields, especially those associated with the professions, such as school-teaching, health care and social work, where working with the vulnerable or children may be seen as incompatible with overt homosexuality by the kind of ignorant people who think that all gays want to have sex with small boys. An acquaintance who is headteacher of a private secondary school is currently enduring a whispering campaign started by one of the parents, about her alleged 'lifestyle' problem, although nobody is suggesting that she is anything other than fully competent in her job.

I am not saying that it is impossible to be an 'out' teacher or nurse, as that is clearly not so; merely that to do so carries potentially far greater risks, which many people understandably feel unable to countenance. In other fields same-sex friendships are tacitly condoned, but only so long as people are 'discreet' about them; they are never openly discussed. This is a more liberal, tolerant position (akin to 'don't ask, don't tell', to cite President Clinton's policy on homosexuality in the US military), but still forces people into self-censorship of what they tell colleagues and of their behaviour (no overt physical expressions of affection are permitted), and leaves people isolated in times of trouble from understanding colleagues. Examples of this organisational culture include the police and the military and, in higher education, women's colleges before most went co-educational in recent years.

But being closet of itself entails firstly, acknowledging the force of homophobia, and second, deciding not to mount a personal challenge to it. The best protection against criticism is to be out; then your opponents lose their best weapon. This is easy to assert for a confident, established middle-aged academic like me. The world looks very different for young and older students who are struggling with their sexual orientation, and hence their whole sense of self. Here are two accounts of how women coped with their lesbianism when they were students:

'I came out at college by having a large poster of two women locked in an embrace on my wall. It worked a treat. To start with I had come out to individuals but no-one was too freaked out, especially as I had a girlfriend, so they weren't worried I was going to pounce. Because I've never had a severely negative reaction to my face, I've not held back on coming out since I've started college. It's not so much 'coming out' as just being me, and part of being me is that I'm a dyke, take it or leave it. I've always been out at work. I've never said clearly 'By the way, I'm a lesbian,', but I just let it be known. I talk about my partner or girlfriend and if people are too horrified they'll steer clear of me next time. But then I work in a nice intellectual atmosphere where most of my colleagues read *The Guardian* and it would be most improper of them to react otherwise. I think some of them actually think it gives them credibility to have a lesbian couple as friends. But I am fully aware that a large section of the population would happily beat me up and/or rape me if the situation permitted it. (National Gay and Lesbian Survey, 1992, p. 83)

'I had my first lesbian relationship at university. It was a very agonising period in my life as the relationship was conducted secretly and sporadically, with a lot of hurting on both sides as a result. We both felt totally isolated as lesbians, although a lot of our contemporaries must have known what was going on. Because of the secrecy and self-doubt, the relationship was doomed from the start.... I take no pleasure in living a secret life and keeping my lesbianism a secret has always been a burden to me. I have never come out to my 38-year old brother since he is very family orientated and ridicules gays, nor to my father because I was too frightened; he is now dead. ...at that stage I began to work up to telling my mother. It was very difficult as I feared being rejected, but in the end it wasn't as bad as I had imagined. She said that, although she was surprised, she was not shocked. It took her a long time to accept, but now she is fond of my girlfriend, and gets a lot of support from us emotionally.....

'I have come out at work when my workmates have started ridiculing gays. I tend to keep quiet unless someone is being anti-gay.....1 think I have chosen a line of work which is independent of others, in the world of entertainment where attitudes are a bit more 'liberal' than in the establishment. I believe that being out at work would lead to problems for most people and I would never blame them for keeping quiet about it. I feel a little resentful that some avenues seem to be closed to me precisely because I have stopped myself from pursuing a career in the mainstream.' (op. cit., pp. 87-88).

What can be done?

This afternoon I am speaking to the converted: to activists who are committed to the cause of promoting equality of opportunity, but who are currently likely to have varying levels of familiarity with what are the main issues facing lesbians and gays in higher education, and what steps can be taken to address their concerns. I have tried to indicate the wide diversity of circumstances and outlooks of people who are lesbian and gay, or who are struggling to determine whether they are or not. Let me now propose some measures to address these issues:

I. Tackling homophobia
This is arguably the most important single measure in addressing the demonisation of homosexuality. Over the past twenty years the academy has been forced to acknowledge that women, blacks and the disabled are people too. Sexist and racist jokes and examples are now widely (if not yet universally) regarded as unacceptable; it should be possible to establish an institutional ethos, backed by mandatory staff development, in which the same applies to homophobia. This entails addressing both the formal, specified curriculum but also the 'hidden curriculum' of messages conveyed through the way in which information is presented, and the privileging of certain ideas over others. Years ago I used to be invited by the all-male team teaching social theory to do one guest spot on feminist theory, which

invariably fell on the final week of the autumn term, the night after the Christmas disco. The messages conveyed by that formed part of the 'hidden curriculum'. Munt (1997) asserts that the same applies to so-called minority issues ('race', class and lesbianism) within Women's Studies courses.

Course committees and students' evaluations can be used to monitor negative references to lesbian and gay issues, both within the formal curriculum and in informal interactions between staff and students, but the relevant questions need to be posed explicitly, and the assessments made by students who are well informed about the issues. Training to educate staff will need to be accompanied by awareness training for students undertaken by the Students' Union, so that evaluation and 'policing' is not left to a few activists.

2. Making the invisible visible
There are few 'out' lesbian and gay staff to provide role models for students, but they take their responsibilities seriously. Munt (a lecturer at the University of East Anglia who describes herself as a working class butch lesbian) writes:

'I believe that romantic precept. that education is one proven way to dissipate prejudice. I get such a kick out of standing in front of 200 18 year-olds, and being able to tell them about lesbian history, women's history. I know that, for significant numbers of them, this is the first time they have knowingly encountered a real live lesbian. For the one or two gay or lesbian looking students out there, my lecture is for them. I love the way, sooner or later, they all make it to my office. We pass in the corridors and smile. The way we recognise our need for that acknowledgement is a statement of community.' (1997, p. 98)

Far too much teaching assumes, in its content and examples, that the world is heterosexual, that everybody is part of a family, and that the nuclear family is the norm. More and more students are finding that one or more of these assumptions does not apply to them, making them feel marginalised and excluded. Again, staff development can help to identify approaches or topics which address this. Instead of relying on hackneyed, stereotyped themes and images, teaching and learning can be brought up to date by (say) designing a hostel for abused women in architecture; contrasting the experience of being gay in an urban and a rural area, and evaluating the services provided in each community, in health and community studies, rural and urban studies, geography, sport and leisure studies, etc.; analysing the value of the 'pink pound' in economics; examining the history, art and literature on same sex friendships; and so on.

3. Making the stigmatised acceptable
Staff members' and students' ignorance, as well as their homophobia, must be addressed, and the classroom is probably the most appropriate site for this transformation. (I am taking it for granted that institutions will have policies in place to control the display of offensive images, but discriminatory oral presentations such as debates and presentations by external speakers may need particular consideration.) Some people will feel that their homophobic values are entirely acceptable (for example, those with certain religious convictions). Social work staff, who are highly experienced at educating students for non-discriminatory professional practice, may be available themselves, or with their students, to provide sessions for other groups of students and staff to address this. Staff members must be educated in their responsibility not only to monitor their own speech and behaviour, but also to challenge homophobic comments by students.

Marigold Rogers studied lesbians' experiences in a mixed comprehensive school for her MA dissertation, finding that many of her informants felt ignored and isolated (Rogers, 'Growing up lesbian: the role of the school', in D. Epstein, ed., op. cit., pp.31-48). The same is true in higher education. 'I think the worst aspect of my schooldays was the complete and utter absence of any mention - at school, at home, in literature, in the media - of lesbians and gay men. I felt, to use the cliché, as if I was the only person in the world to love other women. This is not to say that there was no mention of lesbian and gay issues anywhere in the media but there wasn't any in what I read, listened to, watched.' (Helen, p.38)

Her chapter quotes Julia Melia as saying 'These young people are quite clear about what they want from education: an acknowledgement of their existence and a right to a self-defined identity' (Julia Melia, 1989) This applies equally to higher education, and Marigold Rogers' recommendations to schoolteachers about this can be achieved (presented here with my amendments in italics) offer plenty of ideas for us to consider (op. cit., p.46):

- open discussion of homosexuality in class, where it is not treated as a problem; open discussion of the oppression of lesbians and gays;

- incorporation of lesbian and gay theories, examples and perspectives into the curriculum *(my addition)*;

- the identification of role models *(both local/actual and in course materials)*;

- talks by former students *(or external speakers); critical* discussion of plays, books and other materials;

23

- ensuring staff acceptance of their responsibility to defend students and to challenge homophobic comments and behaviour, rather than seeking to be even-handed or abdicating this responsibility;

- establishing lesbian and gay students' right to be taken seriously;

- ensuring that all tutors and providers of support services have been educated/trained to be sensitive to issues associated with students' sexual orientation, and identifying and if necessary appointing lesbian/gay members of the support staff

- publicising internal and external sources of support and advice for lesbian and gay students including, if necessary, supporting the establishment of student societies.

Some of these do not appear at first sight to constitute part of the formal curriculum, but they do merit consideration if we conceptualise the student experience as a whole, where the 'hidden curriculum' conveys its own powerful messages, both intended and unintended, which may support or undermine formal institutional objectives. And unless we address issues in the wider environment which marginalise and alienate lesbian and gay students, they will never get to the point of engaging with the curriculum.

My written paper includes a list of sources of further information and references, which I have used here. I would also like to take this opportunity to solicit case study examples of equal opportunities issues of all kinds (not just concerning sexual orientation) for a handbook, which I am compiling on the management of equal opportunities in higher education for the Open University Press.

References

Anderson, RD. (1992) *Universities and Elites in Britain since 1800,* Basingstoke: The Economic History Society/Macmillan.

Epstein, Debbie (ed.) (1994) *Challenging Lesbian and Gay Inequalities in Education,* Buckingham: Open University Press.

Higher Education Statistics Agency (1997) *Students in Higher Education Institutions 1995/6,* Cheltenham: HESA.

Melia, Julia (1989) 'Sex education in schools: Keeping to the norm', in C. Jones and P. Mahoney, (eds.), *Learning Our Lines: Sexuality and Social Control in Education,* London: The Women's Press.

Munt, Sally R. (1997) 'I teach therefore I am': Lesbian Studies in the liberal academy, *Feminist Review, No.56,* Summer, pp. 85-99.

National Gay and Lesbian Survey (1992) *What A Lesbian Looks Like: Writings by Lesbians on their Lives and Lifestyles,* London: Routledge.

Patrick, Paul and Sanders, Susan A. L. (1994) 'Lesbian and gay issues in the curriculum', in Debbie Epstein (ed.), *Challenging Lesbian and Gay Inequalities in Education,* Buckingham: Open University Press.

Rogers, Marigold (1994) 'Growing up lesbian: The role of the school' , in Debbie Epstein (ed.) *Challenging Lesbian and Gay Inequalities in Education,* Buckingham: Open University Press.

Sanders, Susan A. L. and Burke, Helena (1994) 'Are you a lesbian, Miss?', in Debbie Epstein (ed.), *Challenging Lesbian and Gay Inequalities in Education,* Buckingham: Open University Press.

Useful sources:

UK

Directory of Lesbian and Gay Studies available from Ford Hickson, DOLAGS, Unit 64, Eurolink Centre, 49 Effra Road, London 5W2 1BZ.

NUS Lesbian, Gay and Bisexual Campaign: Cath Fletcher, NUS HQ, 461 Holloway Road, London N&6LJ. *0171-561-6517.*

Stonewall: 16 Clerkenwell Close, London EClR OAA. 0171-336-8880.

FFLAG (Families and Friends of Lesbians and Gays): PO Box 153, Manchester M60 1 LP.

USA

The Govemor's Commission on Gay and Lesbian Youth, Room 111, State House, Boston, Mass. 02133, USA. Publisher of 'Making Colleges and Universities Safe for Gay and Lesbian Students', Principal Author:Warren J. Blumenfeld (available free from this address). Warren is founder and first director of the National Gay Student Center, now the National Queer Coalition of the United States Student Association, e-mail: blumenfeld@educ.umass.edu

Queer Studies List e-mail address: QSTUDY-L@LISTSERV.ACSU. BUFFALO.EDU

Acknowledgement

I would like to thank Fatih Ozbilgin and Mike Milne-Picken for helping me to locate useful materials for this presentation.

4. Equal Opportunities and the Higher Education Curriculum

Jane Fearon, Policy Research Centre – Sheffield Hallam University

Abstract

This paper is based on the findings of a primarily qualitative research project "Equal opportunities in the Sheffield Hallam University Curriculum", which was initiated by Sheffield Hallam University (SHU) Equal Opportunities Coordinators in SHU Business School and funded by the University's Learning and Teaching Institute. It will contribute in particular to the conference theme concerning the development of an equal opportunities research profile and touch on issues of delivery methods, assessment strategies and the development of appropriate teaching materials.

The initial intention of the research was a) establish what activity is currently undertaken by lecturers in SHU Business School to ensure that equal opportunities issues are (viewed as) an integral part of the curriculum; b) to develop a broader picture of the current situation re: equal opportunities in the SHU curriculum; and c) to produce an equal opportunities resource pack for teaching staff, including summary statistics, teaching materials and examples of good and bad practice.

However, during the course of the fieldwork it became apparent that in spite of the existence of a plethora of equal opportunities-related activity at the levels of policy making and implementation, it was widely felt that the institutional environment in which the curriculum was delivered at best diluted the effects of delivering a broad and balanced curriculum and at worst rendered the task impossible. In particular, the climate of virtually continual change which has prevailed for the last decade, resulting primarily from (response to) changes in government policy concerning most aspects of HE activity, has meant that equal opportunities has slipped down the institutional agenda. Further, the research highlighted the difficulty of reconciling multiple conceptualisations of equal opportunities in terms of policy and practice. Although the policy is clearly specific to SHU, the findings will be of interest to anyone concerned with the development of effective equal opportunities measures in higher education.

Introduction

This paper is based on a primarily qualitative research project 'Embedding Equal Opportunities in the Sheffield Hallam University Curriculum' which was initiated in Summer 1996 by Sheffield Hallam University (SHU) Equal Opportunities Coordinators in SHU Business School. The research was funded by the University's Learning and Teaching Institute with the initial intention of discovering the extent to which equal opportunities issues were addressed, both implicitly and explicitly, in the business and management curricula delivered by the Sheffield Business School (SBS)[1]. Based on these findings, we had hoped to produce an equal opportunities resource pack for teaching staff including summary statistics, teaching materials and examples of good and bad practice. Another aim was to develop a broader picture of the current situation re. equal opportunities in the SHU curriculum as a whole using the SBS findings as a basis for preliminary investigation.

However, during the course of the fieldwork it became apparent that in spite of the existence of a plethora of equal opportunities-related activity at the levels of policy making and implementation (see below), it was widely felt that the institutional environment in which the curriculum was delivered at best diluted the effects of delivering a broad and balanced curriculum and at worst rendered the task impossible. In particular, the climate of virtually continual change which has prevailed for the last decade, resulting primarily from (response to) changes in government policy concerning most aspects of HE activity, has meant that equal opportunities has slipped down the institutional agenda. Further, the research highlighted the difficulty of reconciling multiple conceptualisations of equal opportunities in terms of policy and practice.

The paper begins by briefly setting the study in context and outlining the methodology. It then goes on to discuss a selection of the findings[2]. Finally, potential approaches to improving the quality of the curriculum in terms of equal opportunities are highlighted.

Background

Although not enjoying a high profile across the university as a whole, equal opportunities activities such as training courses (largely staff development) and a variety of in-house projects looking at, for example, gender and the curriculum (see Lawrence et al 1995) have kept equal opportunities issues

---

[1] As of August 1st 1997 Sheffield Business School has been split into a graduate school known as Sheffield Business School and a School of Business and Management which is primarily concerned with the delivery of undergraduate programmes. This paper refers to *old* SBS and the research therefore considered both post- and undergraduate programmes.

[2] As the study was undertaken in SHU, some of the findings are SHU specific. However many of the issues raised and the problems and opportunities pertaining to equal opportunities are relevant to other HEIs. It is largely these findings which are presented here.

relatively high on the institutional agenda with a flurry of activity following incorporation in 1992 (SHU (no date), SHU (1995a), SHU (1994), SHU (1992), Survey & Statistical Research Centre (1994), SHU (1995), Willcocks, D et al (1995)). Although it is beyond the scope of this paper to comment in detail it is worth noting that the fact of incorporation has undoubtedly had a significant impact on the policy's evolution in so far as the need to avoid litigation has featured in more recent discussions about how policy and practice should be developed and/or modified. Just as theories about concepts and causes of unequal or discriminatory treatment can shape the kind of equal opportunities policy we adopt (Blakemore and Drake 1996), the anticipated consequences of inadequate policy and practice can determine the emphasis of an institutional policy. Evidence for this can be found in the relatively recent concern with issues surrounding disability and the focus on targets in the areas of recruitment and promotion which characterises many equal opportunities policies.

University-wide activities are supported by a School based structure with 22 Equal Opportunities Coordinators (EOCs) in each School or Department who are 'appointed' on a voluntary basis. EOCs activities are not prescribed, with the exception of a requirement to establish a local Equal Opportunities Committee to respond to concerns raised in that area of the university. This has resulted in varying amounts of activity with some areas having well established groups who produce newsletters, organise seminars and become involved in research projects and others with groups in name only who rarely meet[3]. There is also a university-wide EOCs group but at the time of the fieldwork, this had not met for over a year.

Centrally, until 1996 when a senior post was created to take overall responsibility for the area, equal opportunities policy fell under the remit of a member of the Senior Management Executive, a situation which contributed to the lack of consistency mentioned above. It was also difficult to feed local opinions and problems into the decision-making structures at the centre.

Of most relevance to this research, it appeared that no single individual or group had responsibility for equal opportunities and the curriculum. This in spite of the existence of revitalised course validation procedures and quality assurance mechanisms.

---

3 Given the importance of equal opportunities and the centrality of the curriculum to a university's activities it is ironic that the most active groups were based in non-teaching areas and made up of non-teaching staff.

Methodology

Data collection was carried out in two distinct but overlapping stages: a survey of teaching staff in SBS and interviews with selected Equal Opportunities Coordinators university-wide. A short questionnaire was sent to undergraduate and post-graduate Programme, Route and Subject Group Leaders in SBS requesting information on the curriculum areas on which they teach and aspects of equal opportunities present in these areas. A response rate of 45% was achieved and about half of these indicated a willingness to participate in further research in the future. Those who declined future involvement cited workload as the reason.

To provide a context for, and to complement the survey of SBS members, the views of some of the 22 Equal Opportunities Coordinators throughout SHU were also sought through a series of semi-structured interviews. In the context of time/resource constraints, purposive sampling was carried out and only those EOCs with a direct involvement in curriculum delivery were interviewed.

In addition, the current chair of the Women's Committee, the Registry EOC and a senior lecturer from the School of Health & Community Studies were interviewed in response to information gained from other interviewees relating to their significant involvement with equal opportunities issues. University-wide responsibility for the coordination of equal opportunities issues now lies with a post in the Human Resources Department and this individual was also interviewed. In total, 12 interviews were carried out.

In addition to lecturing staff, Registry and Chaplaincy, the following areas of university work are represented by the Equal Opportunities Coordinators: Library and Learning Resources, Technical Staff, Students Union, Administration and Clerical, Computing Information Services and Finance. Coordinators from these areas were informed about the research and invited to participate if they wished: none did.

Findings and discussion

Aspects of equal opportunities in the SBS curriculum
Many respondents commented that where there were no or very few aspects of equal opportunities included in their course syllabuses this was largely due to time pressures on teaching which has been exacerbated by semesterisation. In this context it was felt that the emphasis is inevitably on covering the syllabus and assessing students' knowledge in relation to specific learning outcomes rather than developing a broad based knowledge of an area. In some cases equal opportunities was simply not perceived to be relevant. In other cases, respondents stated that equal opportunities does not

29

form part of the core subjects and as such there was no time or money to teach it.

Overall there was a high degree of awareness of the need to deal with equal opportunities as part of the syllabus on business courses, particularly in relation to the significance of power and influence in the workplace and covert methods of perpetuating and exacerbating existing inequalities. Respondents also mentioned ethics and environmental issues as equally important but neglected areas. In some cases equal opportunities was seen as somehow 'in competition' with these issues in terms of finding space for them in the curriculum.

University-wide Curriculum Issues: teaching and learning

This section will briefly discuss aspects of curriculum delivery raised by respondents, acknowledging where appropriate the considerable overlaps between each of the following activities:

- curriculum design;
- teaching methods; and
- assessment strategies.

Curriculum Design

Some programme areas outside SBS cited by respondents do clearly include aspects of equal opportunities. For example: modules of applied social studies (social policy, sociology and psychology routes), social work, post graduate teacher training, physiotherapy, research methods and of course the BA and MA in Women's Studies. Each of these curriculum areas incorporate aspects of equal opportunities. In some cases there are modules which specifically focus on issues of discrimination and inequality in relation to policy and practice. In others, it is through the careful selection of appropriate case study materials and/or through the inclusion of a variety of theoretical approaches that equal opportunities issues are addressed.

Where equal opportunities are addressed in the content of a course, the inclusion of multicultural teaching materials and a global perspective on theory and practice is specifically intended to counter the dominant influence on the curriculum of the white, middle class and in some areas, male, view. Respondents stated that this is done at an individual level with the intention of delivering a curriculum which reflects more closely the experiences of the student population. Respondents were aware that this has become increasingly important in recent years as the 'traditional' student, i.e. white, middle class and post A level, represents a lower proportion of the university's intake.

Some respondents made the point that in terms of securing market share in the future, it is in the university's interest to ensure that the culture of the institution is inclusive and non-discriminatory. It is clear that the 'traditional' student is in short supply and in order to maintain student numbers, the university will increasingly have to attract students from currently under represented groups.

The largely individual nature of curriculum design activity means that there is considerable variation as to the inclusion/treatment of equal opportunities issues even within courses. Further, there is no discernible 'local' policy on this issue. Respondents suggested that a lack of emphasis on equal opportunities has meant that the university curriculum has become increasingly irrelevant to many sections of the student population.

In addition to courses which *include* aspects of equal opportunities, there are also courses which focus solely on issues of inequality or discrimination. However, even in these areas there is some concern as to the status of these modules: many are options. For example a module on equal opportunities used to be a core subject on the Applied Social Studies programme but is now an option. Modules on 'gender and inequality' and 'race and racism' in the same programme are also optional. Although respondents acknowledged that this is in part a result of modularisation, many expressed concern as to why these were not core subjects, particularly in areas where equal opportunities are central to a sound understanding of the subject. However, an Equal Opportunities option offered at level 3 in the Business School has attracted an increasing number of students.

In other areas such as the natural sciences it is apparent that it can be more difficult to incorporate teaching and learning on equal opportunities issues without it being perceived as an 'add on' or tokenistic. This can be attributed in part at least to the perceived history of the subjects as the domain of white, middle class males. Respondents commenting on this pointed to the potential of a historical approach to the subject as a way of ensuring a pluralistic approach. This can include consideration of the different contributions made by different individuals and groups to the development of the discipline. According to many respondents this approach to equal opportunities is particularly relevant in the context of growing trends towards multidisciplinary and globalised learning and research.

However, the compartmentalisation of learning resulting from modularisation, which in turn reinforces the view that knowledge is neutral and therefore value free, means that adopting this approach on all courses would be a difficult task requiring considerable resource input and commitment from individuals involved in course delivery and assessment. A few respondents expressed the view that in Cycle 1 courses this would be neither possible nor desirable due to the (necessarily) 'introductory' nature of the courses and the varying abilities of students.

Teaching Methods

Many respondents were aware of research which suggests that certain methods of teaching and learning are more appropriate to different population groups and as a result, course delivery is planned accordingly.

The importance of teaching methods was highlighted by many respondents in the course of discussions of curriculum content. A key point is that whereas it is relatively easy to give people teaching materials which reflect a non-discriminatory, inclusive ethos, it is much more difficult to get them to change their methods of delivery. Particular concern was expressed in relation to the use of non-discriminatory language. Respondents were also concerned about the increase in the use of 'mass lectures' as a teaching method, particularly in the context of reduced contact time. In a similar vein there was widespread concern about the use of IT with many focussing on their own lack of skills and confidence in the face of the need to develop IT based learning materials. It is interesting to consider this in the context of recent research on computer aided learning and equal opportunity in HE.

In common with other HEIs Hallam is exploiting IT in all its forms to develop new and hopefully improved delivery methods and modes of study. Although this can be seen primarily as a response to increasing student numbers in a climate of competition and dwindling resources, a main focus is on the changing nature of the student population. In the wake of the post 1992 expansion, the proportion of 'non-traditional' students has increased significantly with, as the Terms of Reference for the Dearing Review pointed out, over 50% of students now entering HE over the age of 21. Although computer assisted learning is a key part of the new mass education system, the relatively early stage of its development provides an opportunity to ensure that equality is central to its development as a tool for teaching and learning. Henry and Rafferty (1995) assert that through a rigorous process of 'equality proofing' (ensuring the parallel and complementary development of IT and equal opportunities strategies) the new teaching and learning environment created by the use of learning technologies will avoid the pitfalls of the old system and contribute to a more equitable education system. Indeed mature students along with women staff and students, students with disabilities, students with English as a second language, students with low level IT skills and no access to a computer or network at or from home will NOT benefit from new technology if the new system merely replicates and emphasises existing patterns of discrimination and inequality (Henry and Rafferty 1995).

Assessment Strategies

One of the recent attempts to reduce discrimination in assessment - anonymous marking - is widely regarded as a double-edged sword.

Although the system *does* remove the possibility of bias resulting from personal knowledge of the student, many respondents pointed out that it also means that they are unable to differentiate between students who are simply careless with spelling, grammar etc. and those who have 'genuine' literacy problems as a result of either a learning disability such as dyslexia, or having English as a second language.

A further anomaly exists in relation to these two groups. Although the university has a formal policy governing written examinations for dyslexic students (they are allowed extra time) there are no equivalent procedures for students for whom English is a second language/non-mother tongue. Several respondents made general comments about the increased use of unseen, time-constrained examinations as a method of assessment: this was widely viewed as an inevitable but undesirable corollary of the mass teaching methods mentioned above. Many were concerned that courses are assessed using this method alone and that this will disadvantage some groups, particularly mature students who often have been away from education for some time and/or those who have qualifications which do not use this method of assessment. This was attributed to a) the growing problem of plagiarism and b) pressures on teaching staff: time-constrained examinations can often be less time consuming in terms of marking which is important in the context of the inter-semester time period allocated for assessment and moderation.

Some respondents also expressed uncertainty concerning the assessment of equal opportunities aspects of a course: when we assess an equal opportunities aspect of a course what exactly are we assessing? Is it the quality of the work in an academic sense, the conduct and attitudes of the student, or both of these? This was raised in the context of notices throughout the university which say that individuals may be excluded from the Students' Union, for example, for acting in ways which are discriminatory. Respondents felt that it was unclear as to whether this applied only to 'social' (rather than 'academic') aspects of university life.

The problems of equal opportunities in relation to course delivery and assessment are also related to the concept of academic freedom. Many respondents pointed out how difficult it can be to assess objectively work in this area which is expressing a view which is clearly contradictory to one's own personal beliefs. A good illustration is the policy and values of the so called 'new right' which are an anathema to a majority of those who believe in an inclusive model of equal opportunities for all underpinned by 'positive freedom'. It was agreed, however, that the work of students who argue logically and can support their arguments in an academic manner can be differentiated from those whose conduct and course work are simply not acceptable in the context of the university as an environment which claims actively to promote equality of opportunity.

In general terms, the above issues were considered to be of secondary importance compared with the growing problem of plagiarism.

Placement year/work experience

Several respondents mentioned placement as problematic in terms of equal opportunities. It raises the question of what are the parameters of an institution's equal opportunities policy? Is it the university's 'responsibility' to ensure that staff and students do not experience discrimination whilst involved with placement organisations and/or external contractors?

SBS staff have produced guidelines for placement which cover harassment and discrimination in the workplace. These do not, however, confer any obligation on the employer either to have their own equal opportunities policy or to adopt a model of equal opportunities which is in line with SHU's. There is an unwritten - but widely spoken - rule governing placement: if a student experiences discrimination whilst on placement, in certain circumstances, they may be removed from that placement. However, the degree of discrimination which has to be experienced before such a decision is taken, and what kind of 'evidence' is required in support of the claim, is obviously impossible to quantify and will vary by individual case.

There is also a formal agreement that a student has the right to protection/support from both the placement employer and SHU, although the form which that takes and the accessibility of the system will inevitably vary between workplaces.

Several respondents were concerned that simply removing the student is not sufficient - a university 'ought' to take action, perhaps to the extent of removing the organisation from the list of placement providers. This, however, is unfeasible in the current climate - it is already difficult to place all students[4]. Therefore, tutors tend to adopt a 'preventative' approach, using their knowledge of the placement organisation to make a judgment as to whether, for instance, a female would experience discrimination and/or harassment in a given work environment. One respondent considered placement experience to be beyond the concern and jurisdiction of the university. This was based on the notion that placement is work experience and should as far as possible be 'a real job' in the 'real world' where, of course, discrimination and harassment do occur. For the majority this is an unacceptable view: students are still 'with' the university even when they are on placement and should be protected from harassment and discrimination as they would be in other years of study.

---

[4] A current SHU project looking at the integration of placement into the curriculum of sandwich courses in UK HEIs has found that this is a widespread and increasing problem in the area of Business and Management courses.

A good illustration of problems with placement concerns blind physiotherapy students. Local Hospital Trusts have said that they will not accept these students yet placement experience is a requirement of their course. As these Trusts are sole providers of the opportunity for placement experience for the physiotherapy course, it is clear that in this case, SHU's stance on equal opportunities cannot be enforced.

In relation to all the above areas of teaching and learning, respondents felt that course validation procedures and quality mechanisms should incorporate 'equal opportunities audit'. Although it is acknowledged that this would effect only course design and assessment strategies (not delivery methods), it would ensure that equal opportunities issues were addressed as part of mainstream curriculum-related activity.

Other Equal Opportunities Issues

Although the focus of this research was equal opportunities in the curriculum, all respondents involved with curriculum delivery made the point that the centrality of the curriculum in an HE institution meant that it was not possible to consider equal opportunities in relation to this alone. That is to say, perceptions of and concern about equal opportunities in the curriculum were entangled with broader issues of equal opportunities relating to the day to day functioning of the institution. This section will therefore focus on institutional issues identified by respondents as relevant to embedding equal opportunities in the university's curriculum.

Equal Opportunities as a definition/concept

When speaking about their departmental/school role as Equal Opportunities Coordinators, many respondents pointed out that, perhaps inevitably, their perceptions of equal opportunities activities and priorities were often determined by the make up of their staff, i.e. the gender, race, and age of workers and the role that they undertook, i.e. course delivery, administration, technical support, etc. A good example of this is a focus on equal opportunities in relation to staff development found in several departments; this is of course partly a result of recent (devolution-related) changes in the allocation of and rules governing access to staff development monies. It is no surprise then that views concerning what the priorities for the University should be, varied considerably. However, respondents were aware of the potential compartmentalisation that this situation may lead to, and as a consequence, a related dilution of the force for change on a University-wide basis. It was widely felt that devolution will exacerbate the situation further.

Another area of concern was the tendency of the University to translate equal opportunities policy into practice through a focus on issues of recruitment and selection. Further, the focus here is on gender and race to the almost total exclusion of age[5] and sexual orientation. Respondents were also critical of the increasing lack of support for some groups AFTER they have entered the institution[6].

It is apparent that for many, equal opportunities is constructed around the positive and negative experiences of particular population groups in the University, another factor which will increase the degree of 'compartmentalisation' mentioned above. It was pointed out by many respondents that a (perhaps) unintended consequence of prioritising activity in this way has led to a focus on factors which are 'visible' and relatively amenable to solution such as setting targets for recruitment, and a neglect of more complex and 'invisible' areas such as teaching and learning.

The perceived 'failure' of equal opportunities policy was attributed in part to the fact that equal opportunities is seen to signify 'everything that is wrong with the institution'. This in turn has rendered activity in this area vulnerable to the charge of 'wanting to change the world'. A related issue here is the question of demarcation concerning the rights and responsibilities of the staff, students, employees' groups (including Unions) and the institution in terms of equal opportunities; i.e. what is a Union issue and as such a 'genuine dispute with the employer', and what is 'an equal opportunities issue'? Also, is this a useful distinction which may clarify the situation or a complicating factor which may lead to 'burdening' equal opportunities policy with unsolvable problems? Respondents expressed uncertainty in this area with the following exceptions: pay and conditions, which is a union issue, and the curriculum, which is clearly *not* within the remit of (employees') unions' duties.

Evidence in support of the view that equal opportunities is indeed about 'wanting to change the world' - or at least the culture of the institution - came from a majority of respondents who raised a number of points which they considered to be equal opportunities issues. They highlighted the adverse effects of many of the recent changes in the University - and indeed the HE sector as a whole - which make a commitment to equal opportunities difficult to sustain in terms of either policy or practice.

---

[5] During the course of the research the departure of staff under SPEES brought age in the workplace to the fore but it was seen very much as part of a wider, socio-economic change rather than something the institution 'ought' to or was able to influence.

[6] Interestingly, however, SHU's 'share' of Access students from colleges in the region has increased steadily and although localisation will be a factor here it begs the question of whether the concept of 'adequate support' is constructed by teaching staff or students.

Examples given included:

- the reduction in academic support for Access and other 'non-traditional' students, e.g. study skills sessions;

- the reduction in 'social' support for mature and 'non-traditional' students, e.g. failure to expand crèche provision in line with the expansion of student numbers;

- inequalities in generic student support re. the availability of personal tutors: in some schools they were entirely absent (this was attributed to cutbacks in lecturing staff);

- the increased use of temporary contracts (this was perceived as compromising the equal opportunities of both staff and students: the former suffering uncertainty and the latter, declining standards of teaching);

- the increased tendency for 'consultation' to be a cosmetic exercise, i.e. after decisions have been taken;

- the reduction in Staff Development opportunities[7] (both in terms of availability of funding and time available to attend courses etc.); and

- the recent decision to charge students deposits on some post-graduate programmes[8].

In the context of the above it is easy to see why many respondents felt that an analysis of curriculum issues in isolation from other (institutional) factors would not constitute a thorough analysis of the current situation. A final point made by many respondents about the nature of the University's equal opportunities policy relates to the intended policy outcome: is equal opportunities policy a means of avoiding litigation or does it represent a genuine commitment to an institutional environment in which people are free of discrimination and harassment?

---

[7] Respondents were particularly concerned about this in the context of Investors in People (IiP) activity. Although the IiP philosophy *appears* to be based on equal opportunities in relation to staff development and training, that is not the way it has been received by respondents. The failure to either make explicit or to exploit the fact that IiP and equal opportunities policy are natural allies, was felt to be a mistake.

[8] Since this research was conducted there has of course been the decision to charge all but the poorest students ,1000 per annum, a further factor which, it is widely believed, will reduce equality of access to HE.

The role of Equal Opportunities Coordinators

Although a majority of respondents stated that the current remit of Equal Opportunities Coordinators does *not* include curriculum issues, a number of factors relating to the role and effectiveness of the existing university-wide Equal Opportunities Group were identified as having a significant impact on the institutional status of equal opportunities and therefore curriculum content and delivery[9].

There is no discernible consensus on the overall role of Equal Opportunities Coordinators in the University. Broadly they are there to deal with 'equal opportunities issues' in their department whenever they arise. Although there is a high degree of flexibility inherent in this situation, which could have positive implications in terms of the variety of issues which may be addressed, the broad and non-consensual conceptualisations of equal opportunities cited above suggests that this is more likely to result in different degrees of activity in different areas of the University and a general lack of impact.

There was, however some agreement regarding their role amongst present EOCs: perceptions of the role vary in relation to the following factors:

- location in the university;

- nature of post, i.e. lecturing, technical, administrative;

- length of time in post, i.e. familiarity with the university in general terms and policy/practice in the area of equal opportunities in particular;

- degree of involvement with other individuals and/or groups/ structures concerned with equal opportunities; and

- personal views on the nature and desirability of policies intended to promote equal opportunities.

Three interviewees were also Harassment Officers and this system - instituted following the change to University status - was widely praised. However, the demand for this service is increasing and there was some concern as to whether the existing posts were sufficient to meet this need.

---

[9] In spite of the above, curriculum issues had been raised in school/departmental Equal Opportunities Committees, but no action has been forthcoming.

The impact of Equal Opportunities Coordinators

In addition to the all-encompassing and unprescribed role described above, EO Coordinators cited the following factors by way of explanation for the perceived lack of impact on University life:

- Lack of direct reporting mechanism to central policy-making mechanisms;
- Lack of women, people with disabilities and ethnic minorities in senior positions;
- Lack of resource commitment; and
- Status of representatives.

The status of the University-wide Coordinators group is ambiguous. Although in theory it is a means whereby important institutional equal opportunities issues are raised locally and fed into the central decision-making mechanisms (or vice versa), there was considerable scepticism on the part of respondents as to whether this worked in practice. The group has no formal status and there is no direct reporting mechanism.

A further complicating factor here is the school based devolution of the University. Respondents were unclear concerning exactly what constitutes a University-wide policy in this context. There was concern that equal opportunities issues would be at best marginalised and at worst be vulnerable to the personal views and preferences of individual Directors of School and senior staff at a local level. It is in this context that point 2 above is particularly important. An illustration of this is inconsistency in that the agendas of some School Boards regularly include equal opportunities issues and some do not.

The lack of resource commitment referred to by respondents has two dimensions: a) the voluntary and unpaid post of Equal Opportunities Coordinator, and b) the (low) position of equal opportunities in the hierarchy of priorities in the University.

All respondents felt that their role was not given a high priority and pointed out the limitations inherent in taking it on in addition to other work. Several said that they only took it on because no-one else would and there was some concern that there was implicit (and sometimes explicit) pressure on women to take on the role as if it were somehow more appropriate. This was cited as one explanation for the marginalisation of equal opportunities issues throughout the institution and is clearly related to the point about the under-representation of women in senior positions in the University.

The relatively low status of equal opportunities issues has meant that much work in this area has been 'lost', e.g. workshops took place in 1994 looking at gender and the curriculum yet a majority of respondents were unaware of these. A number of articles and reports ensued but they were not widely disseminated and knowledge of these appears to be restricted to those who took part.

The way forward: steps towards embedding equal opportunities in the curriculum

The activities described in this section are currently being undertaken as part of a University wide review of equal opportunities policy and practice: a majority can be seen to link directly with the findings of this study. Although it is beyond the scope of this paper to go into detail it is worth noting that although progress *is* being made, the University's approach to equal opportunities is much closer to the 'liberal' rather than the 'radical' model.

A Teaching Resource

All respondents - in the survey and the interviews - were informed that one of the intended outputs of this research was a teaching pack of materials which would aid the incorporation of equal opportunities issues into the curriculum. Respondents were asked to contribute relevant materials which they were willing to share. The results of this exercise were varied: for some curriculum areas, notably sociology, placement preparation and mathematics, many learning materials were forthcoming. However, in other areas, many respondents pointed to the Unit Learning Scheme which, when examined, contained implicit references to an overarching assumption that equal opportunities were relevant to a consideration of the course content. To an extent it could be argued that this is what 'embedding' means - it certainly avoids accusations that the subject is tacked on or artificially incorporated into a syllabus.

Further, it became clear during the course of the research that it would not be possible to produce a generic pack aimed at all curriculum areas as the 'needs' of each area in relation to embedding equal opportunities are diverse. The resource implications of effectively re-writing each course specification to embed equal opportunities are prohibitive. Some respondents also felt that this could be viewed as an attempt to curtail academic freedom.

Finally, the potential benefits of producing a teaching pack are also limited in so far as people will not be compelled to use such a pack and anyway, the use of anti-discriminatory material can neither preclude the use of potentially discriminatory methods of delivery and assessment nor compensate for an inequitable and discriminatory learning environment. However, there is a commitment to pursuing this course of action in some schools at least using internal funding to develop appropriate resources. Professional Development for staff will complement such activity.

Curriculum Design

In spite of the difficulties described in this paper, the findings of this research suggest that there *is* broad support for the re-design of the SHU curricula to incorporate aspects of equal opportunities, in particular in relation to more 'routine' aspects of assessment such as methods of and regulations governing assessment discussed above. Indeed, there is evidence to suggest that in some areas of the University these issues are already being addressed, albeit on an individual basis, with some success.

However, the resource implications of taking each curriculum area in turn and effectively re-writing course submissions render this course of action impossible. It is also clear that previous attempts to raise awareness of the importance of equal opportunities in the curriculum have not been entirely successful to the extent that respondents did not indicate any significant progress in this area. There were exceptions such as the growing popularity of level 3 Equal Opportunities modules in two programmes and the inclusion of sections on equal opportunities in some PG modules. However, for a large part of the University's curriculum, equal opportunities is either entirely absent or an 'add on'.

Methods of Assessment

Whereas there are formal university procedures for dyslexic students with respect to additional time allowed in written, time-limited examinations, no such specification currently exists for students for whom English is not a first language. This, combined with anonymised marking presents problems when assessing scripts. However, it is acknowledged that this may be difficult in the absence of diagnostic mechanisms/opportunities in the context of the wide variation in language abilities of students for whom English is not a first language/mother tongue.

However, some progress is reported in this area in terms of the use of more sophisticated learning outcomes in relation to student assessment and feedback.

The Personal and Professional Development System

As a compulsory but non-assessed aspect of students' studies, the Personal and Professional Development (PPD) system has replaced a taught placement preparation unit for SBS sandwich course students in the year preceding their of period work experience and incorporates the personal tutor system for other years of study. PPD was recently instituted in SBS and presents an opportunity to introduce elements of teaching and learning relating to equal opportunities into the curriculum. Students are required to complete written self-development exercises throughout the year which require them to identify their strengths and weaknesses through reflection on their experiences whilst studying. A personal tutor is allocated to each student to support them through this process. Any necessary amendments to the PPD materials could be carried out as part of the responsive process of refining and improving the system which will occur anyway as the system is fully integrated. If this is successful, it could provide a model for a university-wide system.

A Tutor's Guide and an RVL Support Pack

Another way in which equal opportunities could be embedded in the SHU curriculum is to modify or add to the recently produced *Regular Visiting Lecturers* (RVL) *Pack* (SHUCFHE&LTI 1996). This is a substantial information pack developed by the SHU Learning and Teaching Institute and circulated to all part-time lecturing staff[10]. The RVL Support Pack contains a wide variety of useful information for lecturers ranging from practical points on room bookings through to guidance on how to develop and deliver a unit. Indeed, the practical aspects of equal opportunities such as seeking appropriate accommodation and facilities for disabled students are mentioned along with where to seek general support and advice.

In the case of these practical aspects the information is adequate. However, there is scope for including equal opportunities in the University's *Handbook to support your teaching activity* which is circulated to all teaching staff and represents an increased emphasis on skills as part of a commitment to maintaining high standards of teaching in the University. For example, the information on lecture planning mentions the different 'needs and experiences of students', and *implies* the need to select materials and employ methods which are suitable for and reflect the experience of the audience. It does not, however, include any discussion/research evidence concerning the ways in which different groups are favoured or discriminated against by the use of different teaching materials, methods and assessment strategies.

---

[10] It is the intention that this and more importantly access to relevant professional development courses is available to all lecturing staff as part of a commitment to maintaining high standards of teaching in the University.

Monitoring Progress towards Equal Opportunities

A key aspect of any effective awareness raising strategy is the regular and targeted dissemination of relevant information. The University has developed computerised recording systems which hold demographic information on staff and students which could be used to make this information publicly available. Although there are targets relating to recruitment of under-represented groups - a key aspect of SHU's equal opportunities strategy - there is currently no mechanism to ensure visible/public monitoring of our progress towards the achievement of these.

Review of Posts with an Equal Opportunities Remit - the need for a supporting cast

Many of the points raised in this research could be - and indeed are - seen as Union issues, e.g. those which relate to pay and conditions and recruitment and selection. This overlap is something which can be usefully addressed in a review of the respective roles of individuals throughout the university who have equal opportunities as a specific part of their remit. At the time of writing the role of Equal Opportunities Coordinators including the future of the University-wide Coordinators Group is currently under consideration by the Senior Management Executive.

Conclusion

Although the issues raised by this study paint a somewhat gloomy picture, the research proved to be an effective awareness raising strategy with well received dissemination on a university-wide basis. The positive developments described in this paper in the context of the University-wide review of equal opportunities policy and practice demonstrate a commitment to addressing at least some of the issues raised here.

It should also be noted that some of the issues raised in this report are beyond the control of the University, e.g. student finance, pressure to increase students numbers, different levels of IT provision between Schools, the income implications of the concentration of research activity in certain HEIs etc.. As such these difficulties are faced by a majority of UK HEIs at the present time. However, there are issues raised by this study which are the proper domain of the University. For example, it is clear that no individual or group currently has overall responsibility for curriculum issues in the context of equal opportunities. Although this study has shown the complexity inherent in the relationship between the institution and its curriculum, it is apparent that understanding this more clearly is a necessary step on the road to embedding equal opportunities in the curriculum.

References

Blakemore K & Drake R (1996) Understanding Equal Opportunities Policies, (series Contemporary Social Policy), Prentice Hall, Harvester Wheatsheaf

Henry MS & Rafferty J (1995) *Equality and CAL in Higher Education* Journal Of Computer Assisted Learning V.11 pp72-78

Lawrence L et al (1995) Enhancing Awareness of Gender Issues in Curriculum Planning, paper to Women's Studies Network (UK) conference, University of Stirling, June 1995

Lawrence L (1993) *Teaching Equal Opportunities* JFHE 17 (2) Summer 1993

Merrieman J & Lankford M (1995) Setting Equality Targets (presentation to the Senior Management Group, Sheffield Hallam University)

SHU (no date) Disabled Students Handbook

SHUCFHE&LTI (1996) RVL Support Pack SHU

SHULTI (1995) Tutor's Guide SHU

SHU (1995a) Equal opportunities Action Plan (draft)

SHU (1994) Staff Charter

SHU (1992) The Code of Practice for the Implementation of Equal Opportunities

SHU, Survey & Statistical Research Centre (1994) The Experiences of Black Students at Sheffield Hallam University

SHU (1995) Ten Years On: the position of women employees in Sheffield Hallam University (1984 -1994) SHU

Willcocks D et al (1995) Sheffield Hallam University Equal Opportunities Review

Other materials used in the course of this study include unpublished SHU internal documents: data from interviews and questionnaires; minutes from Departmental Equal Opportunities meetings; School/Departmental-level Policy documents; and teaching and learning materials from some undergraduate and postgraduate courses.

5. Monitoring the Curriculum: Problems & Solutions

Merja Makinen & Peter Newby – Middlesex University

Abstract

At Middlesex University in 1995/96, Campus Equal Opportunities Committees and Faculty Academic Development Committees were jointly asked to monitor 3 to 4 courses per year as part of a rolling programme. The experiences of the campus committees that did this, outlined some of the problems that can arise from such monitoring (particularly anxieties in relation to academic freedom) and the solutions for shared problem solving that evolved. The experience culminated in a one day seminar on equal opportunities in the curriculum, which created a space for colleagues to think through and question their practices in relation to equal opportunities and the curriculum. In the morning workshops were set up on course delivery. The workshops were given the University's code of practice on EO and the curriculum and asked colleagues to identify how they ensure the curriculum they deliver, or have responsibility for, takes into account the needs, perspectives and experiences of the diverse society and avoids being discriminatory in terms of access, content, pedagogy and assessment. In the afternoon workshops were set up to consider language and the criteria for monitoring equal opportunities in curriculum design, syllabus construction, teaching and learning situations and assessment methods. This paper will explore some of the practical difficulties that arose out of monitoring courses in relation to equal opportunities and put forward the solutions devised during the monitoring and the ideas that came out of the one day seminar both for monitoring and for course delivery.

Introduction

The pattern of scholarship in any area reflects the concerns, interests and agendas of academics. The issue of equal opportunities is long established as a field of legitimate concern to educationalists. Yet the issues that have commanded our attention in higher education are substantially different from those that our colleagues concerned with school education grappled with. Put simply, while we in higher education have conceived of equal opportunities in terms of student access and staff employment, the debate in schools has joined with the societal role of education and the extent to which it can support or break down the barriers that facilitate inequality of opportunity. Thus, for example, if we take the work of Farish et al (1995) as expressing the current interest of British academics in this area we would note their (entirely legitimate) focus on equal opportunities as a human resource issue. In the school system, researchers are concerned not just with the management of this process but with impact of the educational process itself. One of the recurrent themes in this work is the linkage between equality of outcome as an objective in multicultural societies and the need to reflect student diversity with multiple teaching strategies and assessment frameworks (see, for example, Bollin and Finkel, 1995). It was this contrast between the full and rounded way in which equal opportunities is addressed in schools compared with higher education, together with a realisation that the process issues which researchers at school level were seeking to explore were equally applicable to higher education that led Middlesex University to take its first steps in exploring equal opportunities as a curriculum issue. This paper describes the extension of the equal opportunities policy into the curriculum and assesses its impact.

Background

Middlesex University is divided into seven main campuses dotted across 150 square miles of North London, and at the time under discussion had six faculties each based on one or two campuses. Each campus had its own Campus Equal Opportunities Committee and the Chair (with remission of half a post) also formed part of the University Equal Opportunities Committee, the main policy and monitoring body, chaired then by the Vice Chancellor. It has an Equal Opportunities Policy and associated Codes of Practice together composing a 23 page document.

In December 1993, the Academic Deputy Vice-Chancellor sent to the University Equal Opportunities Committee a draft Action Schedule for implementing the University's Equal Opportunities Policy - in particular the Codes of Practice related to: Education of Students and to Curriculum, Pedagogy and Assessment.

Middlesex University's Equal Opportunities Policy states, in relation to **Teaching and Learning,** that:

- Deans, campus heads, directors of studies and heads of services are responsible for implementing the University Equal Opportunities Policy and for taking action on decisions relating to equal opportunities in the staffing and operation of the academic programme and in all other activities on campuses under their control.

- The general policy relates to all aspects of employment and academic life, including advertisements, recruitment, pay, terms and conditions of service, training, secondment, redeployment, benefits, promotions, grievance and disciplinary procedures, curriculum, pedagogy and assessment, course validation and admissions strategies. It also applies to contractual relationships with other agencies such as in purchasing and collaborative programmes of study involving other institutions.

Its Code of Practice 6, (Appendix 1) relating to **Curriculum, Pedagogy and Assessment,** states that:

- The University is committed to an education for all students on all sets and programmes which does not discriminate against students on the grounds of age, colour, ethnic origin, family responsibility, gender, marital status, nationality, 'race', religion, sexual orientation, socio-economic status or special needs. The policy embraces freedom of speech and thought in the context of scholarly dialogue.

- Staff development and retraining will be provided for all aspects of the implementation of the Equal Opportunities Policy, for example to promote awareness of the limitations particular ethnocentric approaches.

The Action Plan was a five page document that considered recruitment and publicity, support systems and monitoring procedures, and facilities as well as the taught programmes, but it is the taught programmes that we will consider here, in particular the plan to

- audit annually at least 10 module syllabi (three per Faculty on a rolling programme) including handbooks, teaching materials, assessment materials and book lists to identify good practice and to ensure they are not discriminatory.

The responsibility for this Action was the Deans', the monitoring to be done jointly by the Academic Standards Committee and representatives of the Campus Equal Opportunities Committees.

The Process

Once it had been finalised and sent round, the Humanities Faculty was the first to implement it. The Chair of the campus Equal Opportunities Committee was asked by the Dean to present the action plan to Faculty

Management Team, to Academic Standards and to the Faculty Academic Development Team. Both the Chair of Academic Standards and of Equal Opportunities were aware this was a new initiative and were keen to start gently, so rather than choosing which modules to audit, each of the four Schools in the Faculty chose which module they wished to put forward. While it was appreciated that they might put forward their 'best' one, ie their most equal opportunities friendly one, this was not seen as a problem because it would allow the University to begin compiling good practice and would get the auditing started quietly. It would also send a signal that as this was an ongoing programme. Once their ideal one had been monitored, they would need to start looking at the others and thus begin to review their modules themselves.

The four schools submitted their modules. Two schools did submit their 'best' but the other two did not. One was selected only by the Head of School, and submitted because he was unhappy with it for academic reasons (which was not our remit). The other was put forward as a challenge 'let's see what they will make of that'. The auditing panel met in June 1995 and was made up of the Chair of Academic Standards (who chaired it), the Chair of Equal Opportunities and the four school members of the campus Equal Opportunities Committee, plus one other invited for her expertise. The panel agreed that the agenda was to begin to raise staff awareness of difficulties students might have in learning because of race or gender or belief. It voiced some unease at not having clear criteria for the **auditing.** However, the **members found that in** practice they were unanimous in their views of the four modules. The modules were audited. The Chair wrote up the general findings and sent them to the Dean and to the School Boards. Each school was sent the general findings and the specific comments on their module only.

The general findings of all the **faculties who audited modules** were the same as the **Humanities:** a focus on terminology, names and stereotyping. **Terminology** in **every faculty pointed** to finding other words for 'man' as a generic term (ie using 'people') and to examples not always being 'he' when 'they' or a balance of 'he' and 'she' would be more inclusive. Names when used in examples need not be all male nor all Anglo-Saxon, but should reflect a wider gender and ethnic mix. **Stereotyping** was to be avoided wherever possible, whether casting women or ethnic groups in stereotypical roles or (when it came to class) that the deserving poor were always good and that beggars were always bad. The Humanities faculty was also concerned with the context within which modules were presented. So that, for example, where a module was Eurocentric the first lecture needs to explain this and to discuss why historically such a canon had developed, in order to allow students to situate the course and to question its assumptions.

Problems arose with two of the modules. The one sent by a Head of School, ie not by the choice of the whole school, pointed to the need for the whole school to have some say in the process. The panel had given 15 lines of praise and suggestion ending with the observation that two of the assessment questions had 'implications of gender stereotyping'. The member of staff who coordinated the module, even though he had not devised it, felt very protective towards it. Without reference to any other of the 12 staff, he wrote a two page denunciation of the suggestion of gender stereotyping and of the silliness of equal opportunities and read it out to the students assembled for a lecture. The module which had been sent as a challenge, 'let's see what they will make of this' - assuming that the content was 'value free' - had overlooked the fact that all the examples used were male except for two which were pejorative views of women. The panel's report was met with complaints to the Dean, written complaints to the Vice Chancellor and threats to go to the newspapers and to sue, on the grounds of academic freedom. Since the Vice Chancellor was also the Chair of the University Equal Opportunities Committee, the panel and the process had support but members were all surprised by the strength of the opposition to very mild criticism. On two aspects of our process, the experience in Humanities influenced the programme as it moved to other Faculties. First, both the general and the specific findings went to the Board of Studies of the specific School; second, and more important, the staff were given a right of reply on the report. Given that this was a new and exploratory enterprise, it was agreed that the general findings of the auditing should go to the School Boards but that the specific views would only go to the module tutor whose views would be reported back to the monitoring group. And this is what happened when the Business School convened its auditing group, to which the Chair of Equal Opportunities in Humanities was invited because of her experience of having been through the process.

The Business School's experience was much more positive, partly because as a Business School with more interaction with the outside world staff members had already taken on board a number of equal opportunities issues in relation to gender and ethnicity. Their general findings also focused on terminology, names, stereotyping and in addition visual images (Do all of our computer packages display the instructor only as white male in a suit?). Even so during the meeting the members of the group reported feeling surprisingly defensive when their School's module was being looked at (even though it was not their own module) and one member became extremely defensive about some suggestions for a well received module and ignoring the mechanism for reporting back, broke the confidentiality of the group and told the module tutor that the module had come in for the most criticism. This was wrong. The group had talked about it the most because it was, on the whole, the best in its presentation of gender issues. Comment

49

had mostly been praise. The module tutor was reassured by the Equal Opportunities Chair for the Faculty, but once again the monitoring procedure brought out the intense sensitivity that is involved in monitoring the curriculum even when everyone is in agreement about its value.

The Social Science and Education Faculty was the third and final Faculty to audit the modules and, learning from the experience of the other two faculties devised what seemed the best method. It too consisted of Faculty Academic Standards Committee members and the School representatives from the campus Equal Opportunities Committee but it also invited the module tutors to the meeting so that rather than the process being a *monitoring* exercise it became a staff *development* exercise where they all developed the criteria for assessment in relation to the modules under discussion. No repercussions arose from this meeting because the module tutors had been able to explain their views and to gain ownership of the whole auditing process and the general findings that came out of it.

The main thing that has struck all the Equal Opportunities and Academic Standards staff involved in the process was how patchy the responsibility for, or ownership of the policy and codes of practice on equal opportunities in the curriculum was. In all the Faculties, there were plenty of areas where extremely good work was being done, especially in the newly devised modules. However, all Schools also had some tried and trusted modules that had been going for a long time and that had been devised when such issues were less prominent. In order to highlight the importance of equal opportunities within the curriculum and to overcome some of the reactions to it, the Equal Opportunities Chairs decided to seek the help of the Academic Vice Chancellor who had set the whole initiative in motion. It was suggested that the Academic Vice Chancellor might like to focus one of his day-long seminars for Senior Managers on **Equal Opportunities in the Curriculum** to signal to the senior managers (Deans and Heads of Schools across the Faculties) their need to take ownership of the policy. The Academic Vice-Chancellor readily agreed.

It was further agreed that the one-day seminar on Equal Opportunities in the Curriculum, should create a space for colleagues to think through and question their own practices in relation to equal opportunities and the curriculum. In the morning workshops should be set up on course delivery. The workshops would ask colleagues to identify how they ensure the curriculum they deliver, or have responsibility for, takes into account the needs, perspectives and experiences of the diverse society and avoids being discriminatory in terms of access, content, pedagogy and assessment. In the afternoon workshops would be set up to consider **language** and the **criteria for monitoring** equal opportunities in curriculum design, syllabus construction, teaching and learning situations and assessment methods. This programme went to the Equal Opportunities Committee in February 1996 and was accepted.

The Purpose of The Seminar

The introduction of equal opportunities into the course review process was seen not just as a test of compliance with University statements on equal opportunities but also as an awareness raising and staff development process. The organisation of a seminar and staff conference on the same topic provided an opportunity to broaden the engagement of staff with the issue and to further raise awareness of problem areas and solutions. The target audience for the seminar was carefully chosen. Since the concern was equal opportunities in the curriculum, it was essential that the bulk of staff who attended were directly involved in managing and directing the students' learning experiences. While most of those attending were classroom teachers, they were selected because of their responsibility for course and programme management, curriculum development, teaching resource allocation and campus academic management. In other words, these were the people who shaped and determined the overall environment and context in which teaching and study took place. The intention of the seminar was to use this level of academic management as the bridge between the rhetoric of policy and the commitment of good intentions on the one hand and practice that benefited the student on the other.

The Structure of The Seminar

The seminar was organised so as to maximise individual involvement in the process of considering the issue while drawing together a collective understanding of the way forward. The theme of equal opportunities had been championed by both the Vice Chancellor and Deputy Vice Chancellor and both made keynote presentations, one at the start of the morning session, and one at the start of the afternoon session. The remainder of these sessions had a common format - a consideration of specific issues within workshop groups, followed by a plenary presentation, discussion and session summary.
  It is not our intention in this paper to report what was said. Instead, while focussing on the main themes we wish to consider them in terms of attitudes to the topic, implications for the management of an action programme and for the actions themselves. The workshop groups considered the following issues: in the morning, they explained how they, as academic managers, could ensure that the curriculum took account of academic issues; in the afternoon they considered the implications of language for equal opportunities, the criteria by which one might judge the effectiveness of equal opportunities practice in a curriculum context and how others might

be encouraged to take equal opportunities issues on board. Equally, the statements and debate showed that there was not uncritical acceptance of equal opportunities and that while many were committed to the ideal their pragmatism led them to question not only whether the ideal was realisable but also whether it was worth realising given the level of resourcing, tensions between personal interests and institutional goals and a sense that merely recognising the issue was to start skating on thin ice.

Big Issues

While equal opportunities is, ultimately, about the treatment of individuals, it raises concerns and issues of a more general yet (in terms of institutional values and processes) more fundamental nature. These fall into the following categories: the link between equal opportunities and academic freedom and the implications of resource reductions.

Equal opportunities and academic freedom
The heart of the concern in this case was how far the freedom to express a view might conflict with policies on equal opportunity, racism, sexism and so on. Many held the view that the prevailing values should be those of academic freedom arguing that once a view was exposed it was easier to confront. Equally, there was a sense that compliance with notions of political correctness and standard solutions could be disadvantageous to the whole equal opportunities initiative. We should, colleagues argued, acknowledge not just individual values but also cultural differences between subjects and campuses. What was important was that members of the University should feel that they could argue against aspects of equal opportunities practice without being harassed as being opposed to equal opportunities principles. For a university this balance between the freedom to speak out on the one hand and an institutional position and policy on the other is potentially problematic. There is no universal answer and each difficult situation is likely to be confronted and determined in the context of a specific set of circumstances.

Does equality of opportunity require more resources?
The concern of staff was that the University would enter into commitments on equality of opportunity which, without additional resources, could lead to academic staff shouldering the burden. This concern was itself nested within a belief that a lack of resources in general, reduced the range of and number of opportunities. The concern was particularised in terms of the recognition of the need for individual support for students to be provided via the University's Academic Adviser System. However, staff also recognised that increases in SSR would lead to reductions in time available for such

support. While there was an undoubted commitment to equality of opportunity, it was clear that staff expected some structural response to provide an appropriate targeting of resources, leaving them to deal with those aspects of equality of opportunity that could be internalised in their normal working practices.

The Agenda

The starting point for the day's discussion was that the University had a policy on equal opportunities in the curriculum but there was no guarantee, beyond the liberal principles of many staff that it was having a significant impact upon academic practice. In this section we identified those areas where there was degree of consensus about issues and actions.

Is it an issue?

Until this seminar there was no general feeling that this was an issue. The policy commitment had been debated at the higher levels of the University and within the equal opportunities committee structure but it had not impacted in any significant way on the day to day activities of staff. Academic managers were prioritising the research assessment exercise and where changes in teaching and assessment occurred they were driven either by the introduction of different models of learning and purpose or by budgetary cuts. The sense of the discussion was that until staff believed it was an issue, there would not be ownership of the problem and without this, commitment would be at the level of lip service.

The first task which many staff felt should be addressed was to raise awareness and make equal opportunities in the curriculum an issue. The following themes were identified:

- Training should help staff get a perspective on the issues. This would do two things. First, it would demonstrate the types of problem which can exist and it would help staff consider whether these problems existed in their teaching. Second, it would provide a 'map' of the problems. This is important because without it one can create an impression that all of the problems are down to individuals. If the responsibilities of committees, groups and resource allocators are not acknowledged then placing the burden on individuals is a sure way to create frustration, despair and probably inaction.

- Training should begin at induction. Equal opportunities as a curriculum issue should be developed as being partly the culture of the institution and the individual. If individuals accept it, then as their number grows the institutional culture begins to shift.

- Training should address the difficult issue of how to get academic staff (still predominantly white and still predominantly male) to understand, and feel what it is like to be a student whose finances are stretched, to feel that your home and schooling background has not prepared you for the independence which higher education expects, to feel what it is like to be a black or a woman student. The concern of staff was that we had to find alternatives to instructional modes of training in order to deepen staff understanding. Role plays and case studies were suggested but no models or examples could be provided.

Identifying Student Need

Equal opportunities should be a partnership between institution, tutor and student. The fact of this seminar could be read as the institution taking a lead to build the partnership with the staff who are actively engaged with the students. Without active student involvement we cannot be sure that we have identified the right issues. The following emerged as action points:

- We did not need better ways of identifying need, we needed to use existing ways better. There is an equal opportunities question on the module monitoring questionnaire which students complete and the University has frameworks for consultation and discussion with students (for example, Boards of Study) but these have traditionally not addressed equal opportunities issues. Where equal opportunities issues may have arisen, because they have not been considered within an equal opportunities framework, they have been "resolved" according to different criteria. Some staff felt that the solution might be found in getting the Students' Union to play a more active role and in incorporating equal opportunities curricula themes in a training programme for student committee representatives. There was a belief also that we should extend our processes of identifying specific student needs. Students with a physical disability or special learning needs self-report and are assessed by the Director and staff of the Able Centre (a unit operating within the University that supports students who have special needs). Other students' needs only become apparent after staff have sight of first assessments, by which time the lack of language support, writing support, learning support may have impacted adversely upon their self-perception, their progress and their ability to progress. Even where such needs are identified, there was concern about the University's ability to meet them. If the support resources were not available, was it worth pursuing the practicalities of an equal opportunities policy?

- Any identification of need and diffusion of awareness should be culturally sensitive - to students, to staff and to the institutional and academic cultures which they inhabited. Students may be reticent about admitting disadvantage and their cultural background might intensify this. Understanding need is not another student questionnaire but a sensitive probing of issues on an individual or group basis. As a start, it was suggested we need to be clear about what different groups find offensive and respectful, about what conditions, situations and language they find inclusive or exclusive and so on.

- Where did responsibility for identifying and meeting needs lie? In a complex multi-campus organisation it was all too easy to see responsibility falling between campus management (the student's geographical home), which provides infrastructure support to the academic programmes and Faculties and Schools (the student's academic home) where the problems may first come to light.

- Even when a student was known to have particular environmental or learning requirements this knowledge was not transmitted to all tutors. Yet the mechanism for making this information known is available via the University's student data base system which could flag a student's circumstances on the personal record.

Practical Issues in Teaching and Learning

This is a central issue in relation to the theme of equal opportunities in the curriculum and as the discussion unfolded during the day the range and detail of the practical classroom and learning implications became clear. It is not possible to report them all in a short paper but the most significant are as follows:

- The relationship between the teaching arrangements (such as timetabling for parents of school aged children and expectations for out of class learning), the influences that drive those arrangements (the need to create research time, personal staff preference for a consolidated timetable) and the consequences of the arrangements for specific groups of students should be actively considered at the planning stage. For example, off-campus learning (field trips, travel abroad) is recognised as being valuable for deep learning, yet it is problematic for part time students, for mature students and for students with domestic responsibilities. While many students can rely on the support of the extended family, this is not guaranteed, particularly if a student in these categories comes also from an ethnic minority group and is a first generation migrant. It may be difficult to change the teaching arrangements (and equally it may be desirable that they are unchanged), in which case it is a fundamental requirement of the teacher's 'contract' with the students that off-campus learning, study outside of the normal working day and so on are made explicit and are known to students before they join courses and modules.

- Student intolerance was identified as a concern that might be growing. While it might be anticipated in the form of white racial intolerance, the University reflected society and intolerance was possible between any groups. The problem for teaching staff was that they did not know how to confront or react to any incident. While they are likely to find any expression of intolerance abhorrent, they do not know whether the best strategy is one of confrontation and the sanction of removing the student from the class (or the University) or of attempting to defuse the situation. There was a view that the best way was to act pre-emptively, first by the member of staff making his/her own position perfectly clear and, second, by introducing the topic of discrimination and equality of opportunity into the syllabus. The lecturer was seen to play an important role in promoting tolerance within the framework of a multicultural institution and a multicultural world. It was felt that few would object to this as a general goal. However, dealing with it as a syllabus topic was far more problematic because of lack of time. This brings the issue of equal opportunities directly into contact with the prevailing academic culture and the dominance of the subject curriculum.

- The management of the learning situation is another area which can generate apparently trivial but for individuals deeply hurtful equal opportunities issues. Things which we take for granted, such as pointing, may be offensive behaviour in other cultures. As the manager for classroom activity the lecturer can promote, encourage and facilitate gender and cultural interaction. The lecturer also has a role to ensure that individuals are not excluded from any learning situation. Discussion and argument may be problematic for some overseas or minority group students - first, in terms of command of English and second, because confrontation is alien to their culture. However, since so much of our assessment is based upon justification and the exercise of judgement, it is necessary for staff to include all students in the learning process and not to allow some to exclude themselves.

- Finally, assessment should not be ignored within this context of teaching and learning. Assessment is, of course, inherently discriminating. The work students do is either correct or incorrect, it falls along a continuum from good to bad. Assessment has become anonymised wherever possible (for example in examinations) to remove the effect of ingrained expectations by markers. We cannot change this. For one thing the world outside expects us to have standards. More importantly, however, we learn from confronting our deficiencies. What should not be acceptable, though, is that some students should fail to achieve their best because they do not adequately understand the rules. In many ways this is not just an equal opportunities issue. The assessment process must be open and openness begins by creating a criterion-based assessment structure. In this situation all students know how standards are judged and those students who, because of their linguistic or cultural background or because of a disability, underperform can have the reasons for their under-performance addressed. One issue that ties assessment directly to equal opportunities for ethnic minority students is command of English. The question posed by some staff was 'whether allowances should be made?' There was widespread recognition that academic standards should not be compromised, nor students patronised. The solution was seen as effective literacy support in the first year that builds on the existing provision of workshops, individual support and computer based learning.

Strategy and Action

The move from knowing that there is an issue, to practical steps to understand its form and character and to deal with it requires action, both in terms of a guiding framework and specific activities. What emerged at the seminar were some principles and examples that could form the basis of an institutional approach.

- Equal opportunities needs to form part of our culture and values, so that what we do and how we do it have equal opportunities concerns embedded within them. One discussion group referred to this as 'a new form of politeness'. This would include equality of respect, equality of comfort and equality of inclusion (in, for example, communication)

- It was felt that it would be impossible to move the institution as a whole and that progress should be incremental - a strategy referred to as 'drip, drip'.

- Action should occur both 'top down' and 'bottom up', the former forcing change and the latter cultivating it. Formal mechanisms for consideration of a harassment case, for example, could be parallel led by discussions of principle and practice with colleagues. Formal structures and processes (Boards of Study, annual monitoring, school review, validation) could be supplemented by informal discussions with students. The purpose of these discussions would not be to validate our actions and behaviour as staff but to find out whether students share our perceptions of ourselves.

- The quality assurance system was generally felt to be an important mechanism for producing change as well as ensuring compliance. First, it had to address equal opportunities within the discussion. The issue had to be much more than a matter of ticking boxes. Second, the system should force equal opportunities into the curriculum design and review process. Third, because those who operate the quality assurance process are as much at sea as the rest of the academic community, we should develop a set of 'touchstone' questions which would allow review teams to get to the heart of the matter from an equal opportunities perspective. Fourth, the University has the capacity to monitor the progress of different groups of students and it should do so.

- Staff felt out of their depth with equal opportunities and they wanted benchmarks of both good and bad practice in order to understand the targets they should set themselves. As one participant expressed 'the best is the enemy of the bad'.

Conclusion

The process which we have been through has been illuminating and at personal, individual and institutional evels helpful. The first point we would make is the difficulty we encountered in engaging academic staff with the issues. This took a variety of forms. In module audit people could be defensive because the process felt threatening. With the seminar, many heads of school and other senior managers sent deputies - an action which could be interpreted as signifying that, for them, equal opportunities was not a priority issue. Those who attended the seminar, while committed, were sceptical in terms of resourcing and where the burden of action might fall. Our conclusion from these activities is that the issue should be explored within a framework of individual and institutional development (rather than audit and inspection or through an imposed training model) and that at each stage judgements and actions should be owned by those directly involved.

While the evidence from the Social Science and Education Faculty was that it is perfectly possible to pursue module review on a partnership and inclusive basis, at the institutional level the process will raise questions of a different order. In particular it will force an institution to address the question of its role and purpose in forming social values. Discussion of this will create a tension between individual rights and institutional social responsibilities. On the one hand, the former must be safeguarded but on the other a university (perhaps more than any other body) has the duty to promote an inclusive society (or at least to discourage an exclusive society). Expressed in this way, a university's commitment to equality of opportunity is a subset of a broader commitment to ensuring that its members are responsible and effective citizens. The issue then for a university is how, within the curriculum, it can find ways of achieving this. We cannot teach 'correct' values and attitudes but we can create situations which allow students to find, develop and understand their values. If a university takes its position on leadership seriously then it must find ways of ensuring that its graduates are committed to citizenship.

This implies, of course, that the curriculum designers and teachers believe in this purpose and are capable of delivering it. In our seminar one group expressed the view that to be multi-cultural in education practice was to be professional. This certainly has implications for training especially for the institution to ensure that the issues of citizenship and equality of opportunity do move up individual agendas. We would see benefits from using equal opportunities as the point of entry into a discussion of curriculum purpose and learning attainment. Just as we saw in our brief review of assessment, equal opportunities will impact on teaching style and learning quality and will deliver outcomes far greater than an equal opportunities curriculum.

While all of these actions are important, it would be unwise not to believe that some change still lies in the future. In order to ensure that the momentum and commitment is not lost, the enthusiasts must form networks within and outside institutions to sustain the pressure for institutional action, to publicise activity and to compare practice.

References

Farish M, Mcpake, J, Rowney J, and Weinber G (1995) Equal Opportunities in Colleges and Universities

SRHE and Open University Press, Buckingham

Bolin 66, and Finkel J (1995) Equity and Excellence in Education 28(1) 25-30

Appendix 1 - Monitoring the Curriculum: Problems and Solutions

Middlesex University's Code of Practice on **Curriculum, pedagogy and assessment** in 1994

Policy

The University is committed to an education for all students on all sets and programmes which does not discriminate against students on the grounds of age, colour, ethnic origin, family responsibility, gender, marital status, nationality, race, religion, sexual orientation, socio-economic status or special needs. The policy embraces freedom of speech and thought in the context of scholarly dialogue.

1.Course Development

1.1   The process of review and validation shall include an examination of the extent to which sets and programmes draw upon the experience of; and address the needs of; people with diverse cultural backgrounds, those of different sex and sexual orientation, and those with special needs or disabilities, and different political, social and religious viewpoints.

1.2   The Academic Development and Quality Assurance Unit and faculty academic development committees shall establish appropriate procedures for monitoring course submissions to ensure compliance with the Equal Opportunities Policy.

1.3   The development of non-discriminatory syllabi and teaching materials shall be required of all University programmes and modules including those commonly argued to be 'value-free'.

1.4   The teaching and learning strategies of all programmes should provide opportunities to discuss the formation of judgements and the criteria used to assess value.

2. Set and Programme Delivery

Within all areas of teaching and in the provision of learning resources and other student support, the University will:

- recognise and support models of good practice in this or other institutions;

- use materials which recognise the cultural diversity and special needs of society and individuals, developing such materials where necessary;

- promote teaching which is anti-racist, anti-sexist and free from other forms of discrimination;

- encourage and support staff to review all learning support materials over time to ensure that their provision does not contravene the Equal Opportunities Policy;

- avoid the use of concepts or language containing disparaging or patronising connotations;

- develop sets, programmes and new modules designed especially for disadvantaged groups;

- establish a comprehensive range of programmes of study for disadvantaged groups to gain access to courses;

- ensure that assessment procedures avoid stereotyping the abilities and potential of students and take account of special needs;
- where appropriate use anonymised examination scripts for marking;

- monitor the delivery of sets and programmes with respect to this policy.

3. Staff Development

Staff development and retraining will be provided for all aspects of the implementation of the Equal Opportunities Policy, for example to promote awareness of the limitations of particular ethnocentric approaches.

4. Complaints Procedure

The Equal Opportunities Policy Complaints Procedure should be invoked in case of any complaint.

(The whole policy and Codes of Practice have since been reviewed, amended to take into account the Disability Discrimination Act, and our own restructuring, but remains much the same)

6. The Use of Monitoring Data on Student Progress and Achievement as a Means of Identifying Equal Opportunities Issues in Course Provision and Developing Appropriate Remedial Action

Ruth Van Dyke – South Bank University

Abstract

In this paper I want to explore how equal opportunities monitoring of student progress and achievement can be used to identify curriculum, assessment strategies and student support services that may hamper or enhance the learning experience and outcomes of different student groups. While universities have diversified their student bodies in the past ten years, course provision has not necessarily been adapted to reflect the needs, experiences and expectations of these new groups. Research conducted in London on the progress and achievement of students by ethnicity and gender suggests that the current form of service delivery in higher education does not ensure equal outcomes for all groups of students. Thus the paper will discuss how more systematic monitoring of student outcomes can be introduced by universities' departments/courses, and more importantly, how emergent differences can be explained and possible tackled through changes in student support, assessment regimes and curriculum.

Introduction

Groups of students do not have equal success in higher education in Britain. According to data on degree results collated by the Higher Education Statistical Agency, minority ethnic students are much less likely to gain firsts or upper second class honours degrees than white students (see Table 1). Women students are also less likely to gain first class honours degrees than men students. In 1995, 20.8 per cent of men at Oxford obtained a first class degree compared to 13.5 per cent of women. Nationally the figures are 9 per cent for men and 6.9 per cent for women. This gender gap in degree results was reported by *The Independent* newspaper in 1997 because Oxford University was finally beginning to ask why women 'don't get their *fair share* of top degrees' (my italics).

Table 1: Proportion of Home Students who Achieved a First or Upper Second Degree at Selected Universities between August 1994 and July 1995 by Ethnicity

University	White Students		Black Caribbean Students		Black African Students		Indian Students		Pakistani Students	
	%	No.	%	No.	%	No.	%	No.	%	No.
Univ of Central England, Birmingham	40.7	1,736	18.2	77			27.3	139	31.5	73
Coventry Univ	44.2	1,979					23.8	126		
University of East London	57.6	935	33.3	141	27.6	127	32.3	127	30.8	78
Manchester Metropolitan Univ	46.9	3,532					29.1	103		
Middlesex Univ	57.8	2,047	33.0	106	21.6	116	38.8	139		
De Montfort Univ	49.2	2,618					32.8	268		
South Bank Univ	53.0	1,006	24.0	125	12.9	170	26.5	113		
Kings College	63.4	793					41.4	128		

Source: Higher Education Statistical Agency

National data on degree results disaggregated by sex and ethnicity highlights an equal opportunities issue - inequality in higher education outcomes - that the higher education establishment and its constituent providers must address.

The intention of this chapter is to put the goal of 'equality of outcomes' on the agenda of staff with a course or curriculum responsibility. It is also to suggest a method - equal opportunities monitoring - which can forward this goal. Equal opportunities monitoring of student progress and achievement is a continuous process which can:

- reveal patterns of group inequality;

- identify barriers or obstacles that might account for the differences between groups of students;

- help identify remedies to such problems. (see CRE, 1992)

Equal opportunities monitoring challenges two key assumptions that underpin higher education, that these institutions are 'fair' and that they operate on meritocratic principles where student success is based on ability (see Williams et al., 1989). Moreover it can call into question the assumption

63

that they provide an 'appropriate' education. In other words equal opportunities monitoring holds these assumptions up to scrutiny. It asks: How do universities know that students are treated fairly or that they have an equality of opportunity to succeed if they do not monitor the progression and achievement of groups of students? How do universities know that the topics taught or the approach adopted by academic staff to their subject are of interest and value to all groups of students? How do universities know that particular styles of teaching or assessment are fair and appropriate for all groups of students? Finally, how do universities know that support strategies are adequate for all groups of students?

The Higher Education and Equality document, published and disseminated by the Equal Opportunities Commission, the Commission for Racial Equality and the Commission for University Career Opportunities in 1997, raises similar questions. Monitoring student experience and outcomes features as a key strategy for implementing equal opportunities goals as part of higher education policy.

Equal opportunities monitoring has become much easier to institute because of the data that the Higher Education Statistical Agency (HESA) requires higher education institutions to collect. For example all universities collect information about students' characteristics: age, sex, ethnicity and entry qualifications. They also have to collect data on subject performance, degree results and student progression. Universities thus have the data necessary to monitor the performance of groups of students defined by their age, sex, ethnicity and entry qualifications.

If this data is analysed and inequalities in group achievement and progress emerge, then explanations need to be sought, and where appropriate, remedies devised. The collection of additional information is necessary to shed light on the obstacles which affect the success of particular groups of students. Three kinds of information can be collected: data on students' characteristics, students' views about the factors that affect their academic performance; and research on students' study habits and the curriculum.

A self-completion questionnaire is one method for collecting explanatory data about students' characteristics which might impact on their performance, for example, socio-economic class, responsibility for children or other dependants, first language, disability status and hours of employment (see Gunaratnam and Van Dyke, 1997).

Listening to students is another way of finding out about barriers to academic success. Course directors might want to ask different groups of students about their experiences on a course. Does the evidence suggest that they all felt they were 'treated equally' (in the orientation of the curriculum, by academic staff, in the support they were offered, in the way the course was taught and assessed)? If not, is 'unequal treatment' something that needs to be tackled in order to improve some groups' academic success? Course directors might also want to find out what factors students feel enhance or hamper student success on their course. Moreover, they might want to ask if these factors are equally distributed between groups of students or if some groups are disadvantaged in their opportunities for success? This qualitative data might help explain inequalities between groups of students and it also might suggest strategies that universities/courses could adopt to help reduce inequalities in educational outcomes.

Focus group interviews are a useful method of collecting information from students (Gunaratnam and Van Dyke, 1997) The equal opportunities monitoring research conducted by Van Dyke and Gunaratnam identified several factors that students felt had an impact on their achievement and which advantaged certain groups of students: knowing the rules of the higher education game, adequate childcare, skills in standard English, and discrimination.

Uri Teisman's research (1992) suggests that students' study/learning habits and the curriculum are both factors which can help explain differences in student success. Teisman looked at why African American students failed college calculus. He found that Chinese students met as a group to study as well as studying on their own, and it was the group interaction and sharing of information that made them more successful than their equally able and motivated African American peers. When the calculus course was redesigned with an emphasis on group work, African Americans adopted the interactive approach to learning and their academic success significantly improved.

Teisman (1992) also found that the way that calculus was taught also had a negative impact on student success. He found that the courses had become so compressed, so 'devoid of life and spirit' that students failed. 'The problem wasn't the students', it was higher education practices (p. 370). Teisman's research therefore suggests that inequalities in student failure should prompt an audit of curriculum and teaching and learning methods, rather than a scrutiny of students' characteristics. The problem as he defines it is within institutional practices rather than within the student body.

What equal opportunities issues has equal opportunities monitoring of student progression and achievement identified? What possible remedies might course directors and universities want to consider in order to tackle inequalities between groups?

Student Progression

Student progression can be measured at the end of every year by identifying the proportion of students who withdraw, are referred, defer their studies, transfer to other courses or are deemed to progress to the next level. It is the last figure which higher education institutions are particularly concerned about, since finances are dependent on retention figures.

Student progression can also be measured by tabulating the graduation rates for groups of students. The data presented in Table 2 sets out the graduation rates of two cohorts of 1995 graduates. It indicates that there are similarities and differences in the progress of groups of students. For example, the graduation rates were similar for men and women social science and business studies students, but students with Access qualifications, on both degrees, were less likely to graduate within the normal time period than students with A levels or BTEC qualifications. This data suggests that some groups (older students and students with Access qualifications) have benefited from 'widening participation to higher education initiatives', as they have gained access to universities, but do not at this point have an equal opportunity of graduating in the normal time period. Explanations for inequalities in graduation rates (a key higher education outcome) should focus on the first year since retention is largely a first year issue. Monitoring students' status at the end of the first year is the most effective way of identifying whether the problem to be tackled has to do with differences in student failure, deferral, withdrawal from the course or transfer to another course/institution.

Table 2: Graduation Rates within the Normal Time Period

Groups of Students	BSc Social Science	BSc Business Studies
Male students	66.0	54.8
Female students	70.1	58.3
18-20 year old students	84.4	67.9
21-24 year old students	80.0	50.0
25-30 year old students	50.00	33.0
Students who are 30+	76.0	50.0
Students with 12+ A level points	87.5	66.0
Students with <12 a level points	81.0	64.3
Students with BTEC qualifications	87.5	60.0
Students with Access qualifications	69.9	16.7

Equal opportunities monitoring of student progress on three courses in two London universities revealed inequalities in student progression and graduation rates. If equal opportunities monitoring is instigated on a wider scale it is likely that these findings would be replicated. How can these group differences be explained? The extra demands (domestic and financial) faced by mature students may be one explanation for the higher withdrawal rates of Black students who tend to be older than white students

(Richardson, 1994, Gallagher et al., 1993). A mismatch between universities' expectations of students' skills and those actually brought by students with qualifications other than A levels, on the other hand, may account for differences in failure rates. Research findings suggest the following three factors are important : (i) 'unfriendly curriculum'; (ii) units that act as a bottleneck; and (iii) student isolation or harassment. As discussed below these factors have a negative impact on only some groups of students. Thus in order to increase student retention and to equalise opportunities to progress, course directors would have to tackle these problematic higher education practices.

1. Curriculum is not 'friendly' for particular groups of students
At the university level, where education is not compulsory, students may vote with their feet against a curriculum that is exclusive or that is perceived as sexist, racist, classist or homophobic.

In her report 'Women in Science and Technology: Strategies for Practitioners', Ann Bridgewood (1992) states that curriculum that 'addresses women's participation in science and technology, and possible difficulties which they may encounter have been shown to be instrumental in improving retention'. In other words, to enhance the progression of women students on courses which remain dominated by men, the curriculum needs to be adapted to ensure that women's participation and contribution to the discipline and to employment in the field are addressed.

Incorporating a 'Black' perspective and making courses less Eurocentric may enhance the retention of minority ethnic students on courses that have been shaped by traditional knowledge and practices, and by a white student body. For example, does history only treat 'Black' people in the context of slavery or Empire? Is literature largely confined to white authors? Do Marketing courses look at the way in which minority ethnic groups can be included or excluded in marketing strategies? (see Van Dyke, 1991)

2. Units that act as bottlenecks to student progression
Another reason why groups of students may fail to progress is that specific units on a course may act as bottlenecks to progression. Failure in this one unit presents a serious obstacle to advancement. Table 3 shows that quantitative methods, a first year unit, on a Business Studies degree can have this affect as some groups of students are more likely to fail then others. Black students, older students, students with BTEC qualifications and women students were less likely to pass this unit and thus less likely to be able to progress.

Table 3: Mean Marks for Quantitative Methods by Ethnicity, Entry Qualifications, Age and Sex

Groups of Students	Quantitative Methods Mean Mark
White Students	47.3
Asian Students	54.6
African-Caribbean Students	36.1
African Students	35.3
Male students	47.5
Female students	42.9
18-20 year old students	48.8
21-24 year old students	43.6
25-30 year old students	41.4
Students who are 30+	35.0
Students with A level qualifications	49.7
Students with BTEC qualifications	38.1
Students with Access qualifications	40.7

If units have quite adverse affects on student progression, radical action might be called for. For example, the Business Studies course team might want to consider the following:

- introduction of diagnostic tests followed by pre-entry courses to bring applicants up to the standard necessary to succeed on the course.

- develop mathematics support classes, but this action will not benefit students who do not want to be singled out for 'remedial' help (minority ethnic students may feel they are singled out as academically weak and do not want to provide what they consider as ammunition to support staff prejudice)

- revamp the way in which the unit is taught to make it more student friendly, based on research that documents why students fail. This approach would aid all students, but in particular might ensure that quantitative methods is no longer a bottleneck to progression

- review of the mathematical requirements of the course, are they a requirement because staff want to teach the subject in the way it has traditionally been taught?

3. Groups of students who are in a minority on a course, or in a university may be more likely to withdraw. They may feel isolated or they may experience harassment

Ann Bridgewood (1992) reported that sexist remarks and sexual harassment occurred within male dominated science and engineering courses. These had negative consequences for women students as it interfered with their work. (Just as sexual harassment leads to women leaving jobs, it may lead to women 'voluntarily' withdrawing from a course).

Racial harassment will have similar consequences for minority ethnic students. This is likely to be a pertinent issue where the numbers of minority ethnic students are small, as white students may feel confident about expressing racist views and stereotypes. It is likely that some critical mass of minority ethnic or women students on a course is necessary before the majority groups' power to express racist/sexist/homophobic views can be challenged (Gallagher et al., 1993).

Support groups/mentoring groups for students who are in the minority on courses, may break the isolation these students feel and thus increase the likelihood that these students will stay on the course. Ann Bridgewood documented the strategies devised at the Polytechnic of North London in 1990 to support women students on science and engineering courses. Second and third year women students mentored first year students. Confidence building sessions helped students learn how to tackle the problem of male students interfering with their work or male staff doing work for them.

Paul Allen's research on black students in a white higher education institution also documents the importance of a student support system (1998). In this case it was an informal system set up by students. Nevertheless it illustrates the point that universities need to provide support mechanisms for students who are in a minority on courses/within institutions in order to enhance the progression of this group.

Working towards more equal rates of progression/graduation is just one aspect of 'equality of outcomes', student achievement is another. Equal opportunities monitoring should encompass student performance, which is more than the results students obtained for their degree. Students' performance across all aspects of course assessment needs to be examined in order to understand group differences in degree results.

Student Achievement

The monitoring system for student achievement requires two levels of analysis. The first is a comparison of how groups of students perform on units as a whole. The second is a comparison of their achievement on the specific types of assessment that go to make up the unit mark (e.g.

coursework, oral presentation, case studies, examinations). Monitoring has to be undertaken at this level for the factors that hamper success to be identified and consequently for appropriate strategies to be developed.

Equal opportunities research conducted in two London universities has identified both similarities and differences in group achievement. In general it was found that women and men students had similar attainment outcomes. For other groups, defined by age, ethnicity or entry qualifications, the findings were much more variable. Data has been selected from this research to indicate how the following factors: discrimination; type of assessment; criteria of assessment; and the curriculum, help explain inequalities in the achievement of groups of students:

1. Discrimination as an explanation for inequalities in achievement
Discrimination and perceived discrimination may be factors that hamper the success of minority ethnic students in higher education. Table 4 shows the mean marks that white and Asian students obtained on first year units on an electronic engineering course. It clearly documents that Asian students performed better than white students on all units.

Table 4: BSc Electronic Engineering: First Year Mean Marks by Ethnicity

Units	White Students' Mean Marks	Asian Students' Mean Marks
Electronic Principles 1	50.4	68.6
Digital Logic	50.9	64.6
Ancillary Mathematics	51.0	69.1
Information Technology	55.8	58.9
Computer Aided Engineering	67.6	70.6
Electronic Principles 2	53.5	68.9
Communication Principles	52.1	54.6
Manufacturing Principles	36.0	56.3

Coursework on this course is not anonymously marked whereas exam scripts are anonymously marked. Non-anonymously marked work provides an opportunity for staff prejudice to express itself. By disaggregating the unit mark it is possible to assess whether there are differences in the pattern of student achievement on anonymously and non-anonymously marked work, which might suggest that discrimination is in operation. The one anomaly found related to the unit communication principles (see Table 5). On all other units, Asian students' mean marks were consistently higher than white students for both coursework and examinations, but on this unit Asian students performance was worse than white students, but only for work that was not anonymously marked. Is discrimination by academic staff the cause of these differences?

Table 5: Mean Marks for Non-Anonymously Marked Coursework Compared to Anonymously Marked Examinations by Ethnicity

Communication Principles	White Students' Mean Marks	Asian Students' Mean Marks
Coursework	54.9	49.8
Examination	48.7	59.8

Since perceived discrimination in assessments is the biggest complaint that the Commission for Racial Equality receives from higher education students, discrimination may be a possible explanation for this finding (Connolly, 1998). An informal chat with Black students provides greater weight to this explanation, as they cited a case where a white student had received a higher mark for an assignment than a black student who helped him understand the key principles. In these students' view discrimination in marking was practiced by a small number of staff which hampered the academic success of black students. However they were not going to raise the issue because they felt they would be victimised.

Monitoring student achievement provides a means of identifying discrimination in marking by academic staff. This is an illegal practice and universities can be liable for prosecution since it contravenes the Race Discrimination and Sex Discrimination Acts.

Even if staff do not discriminate, the perception of discrimination in marking remains a problem for universities because it may affect student behaviour. If minority ethnic students judge certain staff as discriminatory they may adjust their study strategies to take this into account. They may not be as motivated to read, to spend sufficient time on their assignment (this is what students told the researchers), or to attend all the practicals/lectures if they are not going to get credit for their effort. Once a student becomes demotivated it might become harder to remain enthusiastic about other aspects of the course. Perceived discrimination may be another factor hampering the success of Black students.

2. Type of Assessment
The assessment regime is the second factor that can affect student performance. Thus student achievement must be monitored by type of assessment because some groups of students may succeed at certain kinds of assignments but perform poorly on others. The monitoring data collected

from London universities suggests that minority ethnic students and students with access qualifications perform less well on examinations than coursework. Table 6, based on data drawn from a second year Business Studies course, clearly documents that African students outperformed white students on coursework but that they did significantly worse on examinations. If equal opportunities monitoring had focused on the analysis of unit marks, type of assessment would not have been identified as an explanation for inequalities in group performance.

Table 6: Mean Marks for Two Second Year Units on the Three Year Business Studies Degree

	Management Accounting			Human Resource Management		
	Unit	Coursework	Exam	Unit	Coursework	Exam
White Students	53.9	64.6	49.9	55.5	57.8	54.3
Asian Students	45.7	64.0	39.5	43.3	47.9	41.5
African Students	48.9	70.9	37.6	53.4	60.1	43.1

Examinations also had a more adverse affect on the achievement of students with Access qualifications than students with A levels. Table 7 illustrates this point with data drawn from a Social Science course.

Table 7: Mean Marks on First Year Social Science Units by Entry Qualification

First Year Units	Students with 12+ A level qualifications	Students with Access qualifications
Social Divisions (coursework)	53.5	53.2
Economics (coursework)	55.8	54.7
Psychology (exam)	56.5	45.2
Politics (exam)	57.2	49.9

Poor examination performance significantly undermines students' academic achievement since degree results are strongly influenced by examination marks which are given greater weighting than coursework marks.

There are a variety of strategies that could be adopted to tackle the disadvantage posed by examinations to some groups of students. Acquiring revision and examination skills through practice might be one method. Cheryl Gore's research (1996) on academic success in secondary schools suggests that schools with 'good' GCSE and A level results ensure their students have experience of examinations. Teachers had students practice taking old exam papers. Perhaps all Access courses need to introduce examinations in order to give their students some practise in examination skills prior to higher education.

A strategy recommended by Ann Bridgewood (1992), for enhancing the academic success of women students in science and technology, but which is applicable across all disciplines and for other groups, is to broaden the range of assessments. Not only will this enable different kinds of knowledge and skills to be tested (instead of those traditionally tested by examinations), but a broader assessment regime would give students with differing profiles of strengths and weaknesses the opportunity to perform well.

Current assessment practices in higher education may indirectly discriminate against some minority ethnic students, students with Access qualifications, and in some places like Oxford and Cambridge, against women students.

Oral Presentations may enable other groups of students to shine. For example, on a Media and Society course, working class students achieved slightly higher marks than middle class students when they were judged on oral skills, but performed slightly worse when they were judged on written assignments (essays and examinations). The same applied for students with Access qualifications, when compared with 'good' A level students. Changes in the assessment regime which enhance the contribution of oral presentations might have positive consequences for the overall achievement of working class students and students with Access qualifications.

3. Criteria of Assessment

But it is not always the case that oral presentations will enhance students' academic success, because the criteria used by staff might be biased against certain groups of students. In focus groups interviews, Black students described the way staff responded to oral presentations. They felt that white groups were often praised whereas Black groups seemed to be met with silence. The distinct pattern of responses made Black students less confident about their abilities, and made subsequent presentations more difficult. They also indicated that their style of speaking wasn't as acceptable as the speech of white students. They felt that too much importance was attached to 'standard English'.

> *'I feel that we should be marked according to the content, not according to our writing styles, because we come from different backgrounds...I thought it was an Economics assignment, not an English assignment. It's not that we want extra favours. It's just that my writing style is a bit*

different from an English guy, my expressions are different and I want them to mark me on my facts not on my writing style. So I feel that, that is the main way we are penalised...But we are different and it has to be taken into account.'

'It's like this oral exam we've got now for Business policy. I tell you I'm not being pessimistic but a lot of black people are not going to do well because they expect us to speak good grammar, yeah. The way you approach everything is got to be different from the way a white person is going to put their (ideas)...because we have different backgrounds you know'

'and it's a second language too.'

Minority ethnic students may be raising legitimate concerns that apply to other groups of students as well. Have course teams thought carefully about the emphasis placed on standard and academic English. Are the ideas that students are expressing ignored because of grammatical mistakes or non-standard English? Have course teams done enough to help students develop their written communication skills, and given them sufficient motivation to develop their skills in standard English?

The BEd. at the University of North London has developed a programme of English language workshops for students who are bilingual or Caribbean Creole speakers to enable them to make the transition to standard English. It was recognised that this process was necessary to enhance the students' academic success (Neophytou et al., 1995). These language workshops are now available to all students who make use of appropriate workshops because the benefits have been demonstrated.

Staff development workshops on language diversity and oral presentations may be a strategy some departments might want to adopt, so that they can scrutinise their assessment criteria - is it clear, can it be measured and is it fair? Another strategy would be to devise an assignment that valorises language diversity. For example, why not ask Business Studies students to present a business strategy to different kinds of groups: a consortium of Bangladeshi businessmen, a women's co-operative, a group of market traders, a black workers group.

Informal assessment criteria can also hamper students' success by undermining students' self confidence. Andrea Spurling's (1990) study of teaching and learning methods at King's College, Cambridge indicated that in tutorials male students aggressively asserted their opinions. This style of academic interchange was viewed as a positive indication of intelligence by Cambridge dons whereas the active listening and considered responses given by women students were judged as less intellectually worthy. Spurling wondered if empty rhetoric was being over-valued.

4. Curriculum

Finally I want to suggest that monitoring can identify aspects of the curriculum that enhance or hamper groups of students academic success. For example, on the Social Science degree, all minority ethnic groups outperformed the white students on only one unit - Developing Societies. It may be that curriculum that is less Eurocentric will prove more interesting to Black students. Curriculum that acknowledges all students' experiences, aspirations and needs may have a strong role to play in enhancing students' academic success. Will students be motivated to learn if the curriculum ignores them, or pathologises them?

One of the strategies that Ann Bridgewood (1992) promoted in order to makes Science and Engineering courses more women friendly was to alter the curriculum to include subjects of interest to women students. She linked the curriculum to women's academic success.

But there are also subjects which may hamper students' academic success. Quantitative methods on a Business Studies degree has already been mentioned as a subject that disadvantages specific groups of students. Equal opportunities monitoring data also revealed that white students do better than all groups of minority ethnic students on a Politics unit on a Media and Society course, and a Social Science course in 1997. Are these differences a reflection of the fact that white students have more grounding in this subject (through induction in the political process at home, through friends, at school) which they can build on? Do minority ethnic students have to make a greater knowledge leap to attain the same ends as white students? (Black students were more likely to talk about being 'lost' in politics than white students.)

I am not advocating that units which some groups of students find difficult should be abolished, but I am suggesting that differences in the outcomes between groups of students should be used to ask questions about course content, teaching and learning methods or forms of assessment. The Higher Education and Equality document (Powney et al., 1997) also advocates scrutinising the curriculum as a means of implementing equal opportunities goals. It suggests that the curriculum should reflect diverse experiences and needs and should incorporate new scholarship concerned with gender, race and disability.

Conclusion

Equal opportunities monitoring provides a tool for evaluating the curriculum, teaching and learning practices, and methods of assessment with respect to student diversity and for identifying strategies that may help promote greater equality in educational outcomes as well as greater 'equality' in the curriculum on offer.

However monitoring must be seen as an ongoing process, as a single snapshot may not provide an accurate picture of how groups of students are progressing and achieving on a course. Moreover it must entail an analysis of a variety of data drawn from students' records, rather than focus on retention figures or degree results. Identifying the obstacles to group progression or to underachievement is an essential part of the monitoring process. It requires a commitment to look at and beyond students' characteristics as higher education practices may well have adverse affects on some groups of students. Talking to students about their experiences on a course or in the university as a whole may reveal some of the factors that hamper or that enhance groups of students' performance. This evidence can then be used to devise 'remedial action' to reduce inequalities in group progression and achievement.

Equal opportunities monitoring that feeds into course planning and evaluation provides a strategy to forward the goal of 'equality of educational outcomes'. It challenges universities to scrutinise their traditional practices in order that they can become fairer institutions.

References

Allen P (1998) Black Scepticality in a White Institution', in Modood T and Acland T (eds) *Race and Higher Education.* London: PSI

Bridgwood A (1992) Women in Science and Technology: Strategies for Practitioners. Moorfoot: Employment Department

Commission for Racial Equality (1992) *Ethnic Monitoring in Education.* London: CRE

Connelly N (1988) *Ethnic Record Keeping and Monitoring in Service Delivery.* London: PSI

Connolly C (1998) Higher Education: Student complaints under the RRA, unpublished paper, London: CRE

Gallagher A, Richards N, and Locke M (1993) *Mature Students in Higher Education: How Institutions Can Learn From Experience.* London: Centre for Institutional Studies

Gore C (1996) The Relationship Between "School Effectiveness" and the Achievement of Pupils of Different Ethnic Origins, paper presented to Racism and Welfare conference, University of Central Lancashire, 2nd April 1996

Gunaratnam Y and van Dyke R (1997) Some Reflections on Methodology: looking at the progress of black and minority ethnic students in higher education, unpublished paper

Lyon E S (1988) Unequal Opportunities: Black Minorities and Access to Higher Education, *Journal of Further & Higher Education*, 12, 21-37

Lyon E S (1993) The Experience of Black Minority Students, in Calder J et al. (eds) *Disaffection and Diversity: Overcoming barriers to adult learners.* London: The Falmer Press

Modood T (1993) The Number of Ethnic Minority Students in Higher Education: some grounds for optimism, *Oxford Review of Education*, 19, 167-182

Neophytou E M, Chan S M and East P (1995) Encouraging Access: Language Across the ITT Curriculum, in Showunmi V and Constantine-Simms D (eds), *Teachers for the Future.* Trentham Books

Page T, Pearce G, Pearl L and Tam C (1994) An analysis of student performance by age, gender, entry qualifications and ethnic group, SHRE Conference Paper, December 1994

Powney J, Hamilton S, and Weiner G (1997) *Higher Education and Equality: A Guide.* London: Commission for Racial Equality, Equal Opportunities Commission and CVCP

Richardson J T E (1994) Mature students in higher education: academic performance and intellectual ability, *Higher Education*, 28, 373-386

Rosen V (1993) Black students in higher education, in Thorpe M et al. (eds) *Culture and Processes of Adult Learning.* London: Routledge

Singh R (1990) Ethnic Minority Experience in Higher Education, *Higher Education Quarterly*, 44, 343-59

Spurling A (1990) *Women in Higher Education.* Cambridge: King's College Research Centre

Taylor P (1992) Ethnic group data and applications to higher education, *Higher Education Quarterly*, 46, 359-74

Taylor P (1993) Minority ethnic groups and gender in access to higher education, *New Community*, 19, 425-440

Treisman U (1992) Studying Students Studying Calculus: A Look at the Loves of Minority Mathematics Students in College, *The College Mathematics Journal*, 23, 5, 362-372 van Dyke R (1991) *Equal Opportunities Guidelines for Course Material.* Milton Keynes: Open University

Williams J, Cocking J and Davies L (1989) *Words or Deeds? A Review of Equal Opportunities Policies in Higher Education.* London: Commission for Racial Equality

7. From Equal Opportunities to Anti-Oppression - Developing and Maintaining the Educational Environment.

Jeni Turner - Leeds University

Abstract

This paper will look at the needs of the Adult Learning Environment, and the needs of Adult Learners, in relation to the arena of equal opportunities teaching and practice. It will examine the difficulties inherent in the present system and will propose the use of the theory of Anti-Oppressive Practice as a means of moving things forward. Two models are described in the paper; a model for the development of Anti-Oppressive Practice within the institution, and a model for use in the classroom. The on-going process of achieving the eQuality Standard award is discussed.

Introduction

In the fields of Further and Higher Education many people from diverse backgrounds are thrown together, as students, lecturers and support staff, in a variety of disciplines. This is a population all aged over 16 with the majority being 18yrs and over. Thus it is primarily an environment created by adults for adults. Because of the diversity of disciplines, students will follow very different curricula, will attend at different times of the day/year and may have little contact with students from other courses, apart from social/communal arenas. It is easy to imagine, therefore, that the topic of 'Equal Opportunities' will have minimal impact on this situation, whereas the reality is that 'Equal Opportunities' has a very major part to play in this environment if the educational experiences of the students are to be maximised.

In many courses 'Equal Opportunities' is a timetabled part of the curriculum. Teaching staff often find this to be a stressful and difficult aspect of their work; it is viewed by many as a 'minefield' of potential conflicts, (Clements and Spinks 1994.), perhaps more so in areas where the student population is ethnically diversified. Staff, and people outside of these educational institutions, not directly involved in delivering this section of the curriculum, often find it difficult to understand the problems; after all, this is an 'adult' environment and 'adults' should be able to deal with all these issues in a mature, 'adult' fashion!

In reality, it is often the very fact of the 'adult' environment which causes many of the stresses and strains around this topic. Adults do not come to education 'new' or 'fresh'. They come with a lifetime's worth of experiences and knowledge, including attitudes and interpersonal skills, (Rogers 1986.). All of this affects their learning and the learning of others in their environment. People are not islands and events are not isolated. All individuals and all situations react and interact and an Adult Education Institution is a boiling cauldron of mixed lives, experiences, knowledge and attitudes. Some of these will be apparently 'positive' and others less so.

If the topic of 'Equal Opportunities' is to have meaning in such a context, it must lie within the answer to the question: 'What is the purpose of education?'. If education is just about the transmission of knowledge in the form of facts or concepts, then 'Equal Opportunities' has a limited meaning. If, however, education is about the advancement of society through the enhancement of individuals, as I believe it to be, then 'Equal Opportunities' occupies a central position.

For many people 'equal opportunities' begins and ends with a knowledge of the relevant legislation: The Race Relations Act; The Equal Opportunities Act; The Equal Pay Act and now the Disability Discrimination Act. This is factual knowledge and is seen as essential for those in 'service industries' and management. It can be taught in a very factual way and some teaching methods lend themselves to such a transmission of knowledge. Distance Learning strategies, where students are learning by themselves from specially prepared texts, can be used to effect with this topic. Lectures, where information is presented to large numbers of students at one time with little, or no, opportunities for questions or discussion, is another valuable technique. New educational technology, such as Computer Assisted Learning, multi-media packages and so on, achieve the same objective. In fact, any strategy which permits the student to gain factual knowledge, whilst at the same time, minimising the potential for interaction, can be employed here with good effect. For those who see this as the only point where 'Equal Opportunities' has any relevance and the only time when related issues might surface, this is probably the best approach. For the rest of us, there are other aspects to this work.

As mentioned earlier, our students come to education with a wealth of knowledge and experience. If that is not acknowledged by the teaching staff, then there is often a detrimental effect on the student's ability to learn and develop. This is where many teaching staff face a real dilemma. For many adult students the essence of learning comes through, and from, an interaction with others. This usually involves some exchange of ideas and experiences between the various members of a class, (Rogers 1986). The ideas may be developed out of personal experiences, or from things which have been heard of or read about, often in the media. Some of these ideas and experiences are very positive in the context of 'Equal Opportunities', but others would appear to be the exact opposite, (Thompson 1993.), conjuring up, in the minds of some people, the potential for allegations of 'incitement to racial hatred' or even 'incitement to riot'. No wonder then, that staff are wary of teaching these topics.

The essential issue is to find that delicate balance between acknowledging the validity of each students experiences and ideas and developing an environment which will allow every student to obtain the maximum benefit from this part of their educational experience. This is not a small, or a simple, undertaking. It is, I would suggest, the most important thing that any educational institution can do. It will have impact on every aspect of the institution and on every aspect of every person, both staff and students, within that institution. Its effects will be far-reaching in terms of both time and distance. It is a difficult task to attempt; there are many pitfalls and potentials for failure and there is likely to be resistance, (Gibbon 1992), sometimes from unexpected quarters and in unexpected forms but the results of success, for those committed to the wider vision of education, are more than worth the effort.

Studies have demonstrated that, when a student is in the minority in any group, they are often reticent about joining in discussions, (Allen et al, 1988; Astone et al 1990.), this may create a negative image of that student in the eyes of some lecturers, setting up a self-fulfilling prophecy situation. More importantly, where a student feels unable to contribute to discussions because they feel unsafe in that environment, it is very likely that the student will begin to withdraw from the learning situation. This may be a physical withdrawal, so that the student increasingly fails to attend classes, or it may be intellectual, where the student is physically present but takes no part in the class and makes no attempt to attend to what is going on, (Astone et al, 1990).

Feelings of 'being unsafe' can arise from a variety of sources. For people who are visibly in the minority in any group, it may be about a fear of being 'targeted' whenever issues affecting 'their' group are discussed. It may even be the case that overt discrimination, even abuse, maybe directed at the individual, (Clements and Spinks 1994). Such individuals may recognise occasions when the 'majority' view is misguided or incorrect and is based on inaccurate or insufficient knowledge; such moments are key learning points for us all: but only if the person who possesses the knowledge feels empowered to share it. If the student feels unsafe, then the knowledge will not be shared; individuals in the group will not have their learning enhanced; ignorance will prevail and discrimination will continue, (Clements and Spinks 1994). Students, or others, who are members of invisible minority groups, will have exactly the same problems and anxieties as their more visible counterparts, but their anxieties may be compounded by a need to maintain 'secrecy', at least within the educational environment. This may result in a person leading a dual existence; being one person on campus and another person elsewhere. The tension created by this cannot be overestimated: few of us are cut out for a life of espionage, juggling one identity with another, keeping one set of friends apart from another, worrying every time we go out whether we might be seen by someone from the 'other life' or might do or say the wrong thing and 'blow our cover'. So much energy and time goes into maintaining such a lifestyle that there can be little left over for learning.

To summarise thus far it is essential to understand one basic point: members of minority groups who feel alienated from education, or feel that their minority status must be kept secret, are reacting to an environment in which they feel 'unsafe'; people who do not support the minority groups fail to support because they do not feel safe; people who abuse or discriminate against others do so because *they* do feel safe in that environment. If you have a situation where some people feel threatened or unsafe, where others who want to offer support feel unable to do so, whilst still others feel able to demonstrate their prejudices, it is because there is *a perception that the institution supports discrimination*. It is here that the most difficult and most serious work must be undertaken. An individual lecturer can have control in one class, but if the overall ethos of the institution is perceived as being oppressive, (Thompson 1993.), then some people will feel unsafe and their learning will suffer as a result.

In essence, the problem has 2 strands to it; the classroom itself and the wider institution; both of these need to be addressed. Developing an ethos of Anti-Oppression is the most important long-term objective for the institution, but it is long-term and takes a lot of time and commitment to achieve - it will not happen overnight.

Many people are unclear as to interpretation of Anti-Oppression and the meaning of Anti-Oppressive Practice. Essentially, it is about valuing each individual. It is about recognising the intrinsic worth of each person and their contribution to the present situation. In an educational or managerial setting, it is about identifying the potential within each person and then facilitating that potential to develop to its limit. It is about empowerment, autonomy and respect. It is about the advancement and enhancement of individuals, of situations, of institutions and of societies, (Dalrymple and Burke 1995).

In the organisation where I work, we are just at the beginning of this process. We are applying to be awarded the Quality Standard, a TEC award which incorporates the CRE standard, but is much broader, encompassing all aspects of discrimination throughout all aspects of the institution. The first stage is to carry out a survey with all employees, which we have completed. Aside from the content of the questionnaire itself, the ways in which it is disseminated, received and returned can be very revealing. In my organisation the questionnaire was sent out with a date for return; when that date arrived, less than 25% of the forms had been returned and the deadline had to be extended, along with a second request for return of the forms; this achieved a final response rate of less than 50%. You should consider how this might differ in your organisation and what it might say about the position of Anti-Oppression in an organisation. We are awaiting the detailed analysis and the Action Plan which will emerge from this survey and an examination of our policies and procedures relating to Equality Awareness and Practice. An essential component of achieving this award is to commit some staff to be trained as eQuality Trainers, an award equating to NVQ Level 3, and for the organisation to undertake training for all of its staff, on Equality issues, policies and practices. For some people, and for some organisations, this will be hard learning.

Once some movement has begun in the organisation, the momentum must be developed and maintained. The obvious areas of recruitment and promotion must be monitored regularly, but less obvious areas are usually the ones where the problems are more likely to emerge. This brings us back the original point about the importance of personal interactions, both inside and outside the classroom and the ethos of Anti-Oppressive Practice.

An area that is often a crucial barometer to the level of oppression within an organisation, and the stage that the organisation is at in its response, is the area of harassment. This is a topic that is often poorly understood and frequently misinterpreted. It must be appreciated that harassment is a very personal thing, so comparisons between people are not helpful. If something is happening to an individual, or to a group of people, which is causing distress, this will affect the ability of that person, or that group, to achieve their full potential in any arena. Thus, harassment is damaging to the individual(s) on the receiving end of it, but it is also damaging to the organisation in that the performance of staff will be reduced and the end result, the academic achievement of the students, will be diminished. A harassment policy is a good first step, but it needs to be supported by the use of specially-trained harassment counsellors who will act as the 'front-line' for people to access and discuss their situations and concerns. It is important that these counsellors are specifically trained and appointed in this role, there should be counsellors available of both genders and from a variety of ethnic backgrounds. Clear information about the policy and its implementation should be prominently displayed, along with the contact numbers for the counsellors. A method of monitoring the success of this, and other policies, must also be in place: merely recording the number of complaints is not adequate since, in organisations which are perceived as being oppressive, people may not feel sufficiently 'safe' to actually make a complaint.

One way forward for an organisation, may be the development of the role of an Anti-Oppression Officer or Manager; a person whose job it will be to develop and implement policies and monitor their effectiveness, (Blakemore and Drake 1996). Providing appropriate staff training, on a continuous basis, will also be an aspect of this role, along with contributing to the development of a research-base for Anti-Oppressive Practice. This should be a Senior Appointment in order to reflect the commitment of the organisation to the development and maintenance of such an ethos. It is important that the title which this person holds reflects the fact that Anti-Oppression is about much more than Equal Opportunities, since this is an obstacle to understanding for quite a lot of people. This person will, ideally, be part of the team which is responsible for the delivery of related topics within the student's curricula, where this is appropriate, since they will have considerable knowledge and expertise.

The overall organisational model, therefore, is to develop an umbrella of Anti-Oppressive Practice, supported by the relevant legislation, incorporating essential skills to protect an ethos of Anti-Oppression within all aspects of the organisation itself. (See Appendix 1.).

Classroom work is where lecturers have the greatest concerns. How to balance the needs of adult students to have their own experiences heard and valued, whilst protecting the minority groups? Where minority groups are visible, this is both a greater and lesser problem. In most situations, the visible presence of minority groups will act to restrain others from raising very sensitive issues or making prejudicial comments. This, however, may only result in some students feeling frustrated that their own learning is not being acknowledged and is counter to what is being taught, (Rogers 1989), and the extent of judgement and prejudice may not be identified or addressed. Where minority groups are not visible, issues may be raised, or comments made by students wishing to contribute their own learning to classwork, which can, if not handled very carefully, be damaging to some students. A model is needed which addresses these problems.

The classroom model which we have begun to develop contains three elements already common to educational practice. These elements are:-

*   Respect and value of self and others;

*   An investigative approach to learning;

*   The importance of evidence-based knowledge.

Each of these 3 elements is important and can stand by themselves as valid principles in education; but to overlap them, (see appendix 2), creates a centre where much work on difficult issues can be achieved with safety.

In our classroom environment we usually begin our work on these elements with the development of some ground rules. It is important that the students themselves devise these with as little input from the lecturer as possible. However, the lecturer may facilitate the discussions and development of the rules by having some key words and phrases for the students to see and consider. We use words/phrases like Confidentiality; Respect; Listening; Being Heard; Learning; Questioning and Non-Judgmental to spark off the discussions. Quite often the students will use the same words in their Rules, but more often they will use their own words to mean the same thing. The Rules are written on a large poster and pinned to the wall. Especially in locations where the use of the same room for each session cannot be guaranteed, we print the rules onto a sheet of paper, and all the students get their own copy - as does the lecturer because the rules apply to the staff as well as to the students. Occasionally, it may be necessary to remind students of the ground rules and, in some circumstances, students may wish to revise what they have agreed.

Most of the students that I work with are nursing students. This does not indicate any reduction in the levels or types of prejudices that may be brought by the students into their education, as recent studies have demonstrated, (Beishon et al 1995; Gerrish et al 1996). Nor does it mean that they are any more willing, or able, to identify and deal with prejudices within themselves. What it does mean is that, as eventual members of a professional body, (UKCC), they will be expected to operate under a Code of Conduct, (UKCC 1992). Other professions/organisations of which your students will eventually be members, may have similar standards/codes. It is essential to become familiar with them since they can be used to good effect.

It may be necessary with some groups, (and a lot will depend here on the stage of their education that the students are at, and the work already completed with them on academic skills.), when you begin to work with this model, to discuss the importance of evidence-based knowledge and its relevance to their own experiences. It is sometimes helpful to encourage students to see their own experiences as just one piece in the overall jigsaw of knowledge and to understand that evidence-based knowledge enables them to see, if not the whole, then certainly much more of the picture. It may even be, when more of the picture is revealed, that the student comes to realise that the one jigsaw piece that they are holding, does not actually fit anywhere, may not even belong to this puzzle at all and the student may then decide for him/herself, to reject that piece in favour of another.

The acceptance by the students, of the importance of evidence-based knowledge, forms an essential aspect of the model, in that it is the most obvious 'working' part. It is useful to provide students with a detailed list of the topics to be covered in this part of the curriculum, though not necessarily the dates or order, since individual groups may identify issues or strands to their learning which dictate, for them, a logical progression which would not apply to other groups. Since effective learning on these sensitive areas is so very important for students, institutions and society, it is crucial that the students do feel that they have control over the direction of their learning and that things which are important to them are adequately addressed. As much time as possible should be allowed for students to explore topics and to develop autonomy in creating, within the curriculum framework, an order and timescale which is meaningful to them, (Rogers 1989).

Each student should be encouraged to locate, and bring to the appropriate session, at least one article/book/chapter on each of the programmed topics; (the lecturers should bring as many as they can!); this ensures that there is, within the classroom, a wealth of information on each topic being examined.

Examination of the topic of 'Human Rights' has been found to be a good starting point. It helps to 'ground' the principle of 'value and respect for self and others' and makes later understanding of some 'Equal Opportunities' issues much easier. It usually enables a logical progression into debating the Equity vs. Equality problem; (relating this to a 'real' problem such as access to tutorial support, helps the student to see the relevance of the debate - this will be useful later when the notion of 'Positive Action' is considered.).

If a 'Professional Code' exists, it may be useful to explore ways in which the topics under discussion 'fit' into the Code and the implications that this may have for the student as a qualified member of that profession. Newspapers, T.V. News Bulletins and other T.V. Programmes, can be useful in helping the students to explore the ways in which the things that they are learning are reflected, (or not, as the case may be.), in everyday life.

The principle of an investigative approach to learning is used to allow students to explore their own experiences/opinions. This can be organised in a specific way or it can be used as a way of dealing with issues as they arise. If the lecturer, from knowledge of the group, feels that there are issues for group members which are not coming to the fore but do need to be dealt with, a specific strategy can be organised. Students can be encouraged to write down their experiences/opinions/feelings anonymously and in the form of a question. These 'questions' can then be presented by the lecturer and the students enabled, from the information available to them, to find out the answer. The acceptance of the importance of evidence-based knowledge then helps the students to validate their own experiences and consider for themselves, their own jigsaw piece.

Using this model in this way allows students to feel that they are able to contribute, from their own experiences, to the learning of the entire group, (Rogers 1989). It enables the expression and examination of 'difficult' feelings/opinions and topics in a way which can enhance learning and it protects individuals and minority groups from feeling 'targeted' or exposed.

The model is in its early stages and further development is desirable. The two most important requirements for the successful implementation of this, or any other model, are that the institution is committed to the actualisation of an ethos of Anti-Oppression and that individual lecturers are well-trained in Equal Opportunities issues and in Anti-Oppressive Practice. It will demand visionary management, innovative teaching and considerable commitment, determination and stamina over a prolonged period, sustained against any resistance, if these topics are to receive the attention that they require.

Appendix 1.　An Organisational Model for Anti-Oppression.

Appendix 2.　A Model for Effective Teaching of E.O. Topics.

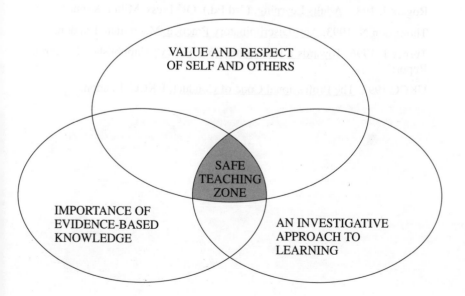

References

Allen M. et al, 1988. Recruitment and Retention of Black Students, Journal of Nursing Education. Vol. 27 pt. 3. p107-116.

Astone B. et al, 1990. Pursuing Diversity - Recruiting College Minority Students. The George Washington University, Washington D.C., U.S.A.

Beishon S. et al, 1995. Nursing in a Multi-Ethnic NHS. P.S.I. London.

Blakemore K; Drake R. 1996. Understanding Equal Opportunities Policies. Prentice Hall, London.

Braham P. et al, (eds). 1992. Racism and Antiracism. Sage Publications, London.

Clements P; Spinks T. 1994. The Equal Opportunities Guide. Kogan Page, London.

Dalrymple J; Burke B. 1995. Anti-Oppressive Practice. OU Press, Bucks.

Gerrish K. et al, 1996. Nursing for a Multi-Ethnic Society. OU Press, Bucks.

Gibbon P. Equal Opportunities Policy and Race Equality, Braham P. et al, Op cit.

Rogers A. 1986. Teaching Adults. OU Press, Milton Keynes.

Rogers J. 1989. Adults Learning. (3rd Ed.). OU Press, Milton Keynes.

Thompson N. 1993. Anti-Discriminatory Practice. Macmillan, London.

Turner J. 1996. Towards a Fair Admissions Policy? Unpublished Research Report.

UKCC 1992. The Professional Code of Conduct. UKCC, London.

8. Equal Opportunities: Delivering the Curriculum in An Anti-oppressive Way

Pauline Noden - Buckinghamshire College

Abstract

This paper is concerned with oiling the wheels in Equal Opportunities. Policies tend to focus on stating that everyone will have an equal opportunity and telling them how they can complain if they feel they are not being given one. Equal Opportunities may or may not appear on the curriculum in various subject areas. This paper is concerned with the middle ground of delivering the curriculum in a way which endeavours not to add any more discrimination or oppression to the student's life; which may redress some of the disadvantage the student has already suffered and may equip the student to demand and give a more equal service in future. It focuses on communication, course management and group interaction.

The Context

The Diploma in Social Work has an intake of 40-50 per year. The students are all mature, with numbers peaking around late 20s, early 30s and going on until the 50s. The vast majority are women and the majority of both men and women have family responsibilities. About one fifth of the students are black, with a handful from other ethnic minorities. The number of students with disabilities is small & variable but usually includes a couple of students with dyslexia in each year. Some of the students have 'A' levels, but most come via the Access or GNVQ route & have experience in the caring professions.

The Diploma in Social Work is unusual in that it specifically assesses Anti-discriminatory Practice. The Central Council for Education and Training in Social Work (CCETSW) states:

> "Social workers need to be able to work in a society which is multi-racial and multi-cultural. CCETSW will therefore seek to ensure that students are prepared not only for ethnically sensitive practice but also to challenge institutional and other forms of racism .. CCETSW will also seek to ensure that students are prepared to combat other forms of discrimination based on age, gender, sexual

orientation, class, disability, culture or creed." (CCETSW paper 30, 1989)

The value base of social work education is therefore closely allied to Equal Opportunities and the students come with a vague concept of discrimination at institutional, cultural and personal levels (Thompson 1997) and a willingness to do something about it.

Discrimination, oppression and multiples thereof

In order to deliver the curriculum in an anti-discriminatory way it is helpful to have workable definitions of discrimination and oppression. Bob Pease, in discussing social work education, gives the following definition of oppression. "Oppression involves the violation of personal integrity and the obstruction of people's ability to develop their full potential." (Pease-Spring 1992). Thompson defines oppression as, "Inhuman or degrading treatment of individuals or groups; hardship and injustice brought about by the dominance of one group over another; the negative and demeaning exercise of power...." (Thompson 1993). To avoid oppressing students we must therefore seek to avoid raising any additional obstacles to them developing their potential, remove obstacles where possible and avoid a negative exercise of power.

Thompson defines discrimination as, "Unfair or unequal treatment of groups; prejudicial behaviour acting against the interests of those people who characteristically tend to belong to relatively powerless groups within the social structure (women, ethnic minorities, old or disabled people and members of the working class in general)..." (Thompson 1993) In addition to minimising oppression then, we need to promote fair treatment for characteristically powerless groups.

We now need a theoretical framework on which to base anti-oppressive and anti-discriminatory practice. Pease suggests that such a framework must, "recognise that different oppressions are distinct, but also acknowledge that they are interrelated and mutually reinforcing." (Pease - Spring 1992). He also points out that anyone can be both an oppressor and oppressed at the same time. Thompson also favours viewing discrimination and oppression as "aspects of the divisive nature of social structure" and advocates that they should be viewed "as facets of an overall edifice of power and dominance rather than separate or discrete entities". (Thompson 1993). Whilst acknowledging that various discriminations need to be tackled separately at the legislative and policy levels, this integrated approach seems very appropriate for delivering the curriculum in an anti-oppressive way.

This paper details three small aspects of course delivery which aim to minimise oppression in general, paying particular attention to the additional effects of particular (multiple) discriminations and recognise that each participant may be both an oppressor as well as oppressed.

The "who" and "how" of discrimination and oppression in adult education

In relation to discrimination I found plenty of Sociology books quoting research that various groups are disadvantaged in the education system; women (Stanworth 1983), working class children (Lawton 1968), black children (Dominelli 1988) and disabled children (Barnes 1991) to name but a few. This ties in with who are generally found to be disadvantaged groups in society.

However, in reviewing the literature on theories of adult learning, I found two areas remarkable by their absence; the effects of discrimination on learning and creating an environment to promote equal opportunity. So one of the answers as to how discrimination occurs in Higher Education must be that Equal Opportunities are not embedded in the theories of adult learning.These theories all seem to focus on psychological issues. Rogers (1983), coming from a humanistic perspective seeks to promote "learner centred" models, which maximise choice, self-direction and self-actualization. Knowles (1978) has written about students taking responsibility for their own learning. This approach is much favoured on professional courses, including our own. These, and other writers have contributed much in terms of teaching methods, which improve learning for all and some of which, such as valuing the students' own experiences, must contribute to equal opportunities in valuing knowledge from a person's own perspective. However, Coulshed (1993) states that "Humphries (1988), .. argues that Knowles' insights have been offered in a political, social and historical vacuum: no account is taken of black people's experience of oppression within the education system nor of class and gender differences as regards individual's aspirations and opportunities for self-direction."

There are certainly factors which should be taken into account. Firstly, there are cultural differences in what is valued in intelligence. "..cultures and subcultures differ in the relative extent to which they emphasize memory versus reasoning in their notions of intelligence. In some cultures, the 'intelligent' child is one who can memorize perfectly those texts that are believed to be important in the education of the child. In other cultures, rote memorization is more or less frowned upon, and the 'intelligent' child is viewed as the one who can reason well." (Sternberg in Richardson, Eysenck & Piper 1987). A student who has been raised to regard memorization as very important may find being reflective a difficult notion and may take longer to "tune in".

Secondly, students who have been disadvantaged earlier in the education system for reasons of class, race, gender or whatever, may experience low self esteem & feelings of powerlessness in relation to their own development. Simply being told to "value their experience" or "audit their skills" may not be enough. For example, girls are socialised not to regard their experience or achievements highly, so a woman student may not include skills she has learned from child rearing or household management in an audit of skills. Girls are also socialised to put the needs of others first, so the concept of "identifying learning needs" may trigger the thought that personal needs are not important and should not be allowed to inconvenience others.

Thirdly, Nell Keddie wrote about comprehensive schools in 1971 that abstract knowledge, which was more highly valued than concrete knowledge, "tended to be offered to those considered bright enough to benefit from it." (Holland 1988). In short, not all students are at the same starting point in terms of self-esteem, skills, opportunity or understanding regarding "taking responsibility for their own learning".

In addition to these problems, we must also take into account that being discriminated against is tiring, time consuming and mentally draining. Take for example a wheelchair user, whose impairment may be painful and make movement slow, who must also organise their life to take a longer journey round the campus, because one particular doorway has a step. Or take the case of a black student who had chosen to investigate the discrimination against black children in the education system who remarked that it had made her feel depressed in a way that reading about social problems that did not personally effect her, did not.

There is another problem with adults "taking responsibility for their own learning" on a professional course. We have to ensure that they reach a certain standard in a wide range of prescribed activities in order to obtain their professional qualification. Even where they understand the concept and have the skills and confidence to audit their skills, knowledge and values and set learning goals, their learning goals must be in line with those of the course and must be attained in a tight time frame.

It seemed to me that a system which values responsibility for self, but has a very rigid end goal could be a recipe for very unequal opportunities, if the role of discrimination in educational achievement was not recognised.

I was anxious that the injunction to "take responsibility for your own learning", did not become synonymous with the command to "get on your bike" to find work, when the person had no bike, no map reading skills and no idea of the selection criteria for the job. I have initiated some improvements; in communication systems, group interaction and course management.

Communication Systems

Every course has communication systems such as; hand books, course meetings, student representatives and notice boards. There is nothing new in that. However, what often happens is that handbooks do not contain information which students need and so are relegated to the back of cupboards. Noticeboards are out of date and are solely for giving information and so are not consulted. Meetings are at inconvenient times and are dominated by the vociferous and so are not attended. The timing of information is not sensitive and is therefore not taken in or is forgotten. The overall outcome tends to be all system and no communication.

I have tried to improve our communication systems in the following ways.

1. Making the systems genuinely circular. By taking feedback from students and noting what they ask, we can ascertain what they need to know and when. For instance, I noted what people rang up to ask just before or at the start of the course. This included basic information about car parking, childcare facilities, timetables as well as suggestions for academic preparation. Such information is now supplied in a preparation pack, sent to candidates well in advance of the course. Prospective students can therefore take responsibility by planning ahead in terms of childcare, finances and study.

2. Trying not to make assumptions. I also noted things students did not seem to understand, which to us were obvious; the hidden curriculum. For example, not all students realise that a "reflective" essay will not gain many marks for a precis of the literature. This is now made explicit in the marking criteria and a description of academic terms, which are contained in the hand book, as well as being dealt with in optional sessions on course management (see separate section). This should assist students who have a view of education which is culturally different from that of the course. (See comments on adult learning above.)

3. Making the systems efficient and convenient. Staff/student liaison meetings are timetabled in to the normal working day, at convenient times, which are notified at the beginning of the year. Minutes are produced promptly and distributed widely. The notice board is updated daily. The handbook has a loose leaf format for convenient updating and is described by students in evaluation forms as "very comprehensive" and "a bible".

4. Making the systems user friendly. The noticeboard has a section for students' own notices and I try to encourage its use by sticking up less formal notices such as cartoons, asking questions and inviting replies in

notices. Students are encouraged, but not forced to chair or take minutes at liaison meetings. The time spent at a committee meeting by a student representative is credited as time on work placement and petrol money paid if it occurs during time away from college. Evaluation forms are now given out as part of an evaluation day, not thrust at students on the last day of the year with no time for completion.

5. Ensuring that communication leads to action and response. If a complaint is made, I follow this up immediately and give a prompt response. If possible, I rectify a problem even if it appears trivial. In 1970 Maslow, writing about a hierarchy of needs, stated that it was difficult for a person to "self-actualise" if more basic physiological, safety and social needs were not met. In other words it is difficult to concentrate on the finer points of Sociology if the coffee machine is broken and you are thirsty. If a problem is part of a wider problem, I encourage the students to push for change by signing a petition, using the student union etc. A balance must be kept between empowering people to take action for themselves and not wasting their time over a minor hitch in the system.

6. Getting students to see the importance of information and getting them to use it. As part of the course management sequence, we tell students that research has shown that the most successful students are those who "tune into" a course early and take control of their learning and give them exercises to help this process. (Beard & Senior 1980). For example, we give out blank year planners for students to fill in their personal, assessment, work and other commitments for the year ahead. This year we are also introducing a fun quiz on the hand book , so that students are familiar with the material.

7. Repeating and reinforcing information. Information needs to be given early to enable students to plan and to have an overview of the course. However, things may be forgotten or misunderstood. Information is therefore repeated when appropriate and is reinforced in course management sessions by expansion and interpretation.

8. Finally, we try to ensure that students feel safe to communicate. (See separate section on making groups safe).

Course Management

The course management sequence has been mentioned in relation to communication. There is insufficient space to detail its place in Equal Opportunities. However, a brief description may be helpful. Course management started as a free for all study skills sequence, focusing on skills such as note taking, but having a component of confidence boosting and course management. In order to redress the disadvantage some students had suffered earlier in education, we introduced an "add on" sequence for those experiencing difficulties with English as a second language or grammar, sentence structure etc. The sequences are now evolving to provide guidance in managing the course emotionally as well as academically. For instance, we discuss the effect of studying a discrimination which a student suffers personally. Exam preparation involves not only tips, but discussion of the effects of previous failure and how this might be related to gender, class etc. This year I am introducing stress management techniques. The sequences have been renamed "Course Management" and "Course Management Extra" partly to destigmatise them, but also as a more truthful description of their current content. Course Management is a crucial component of helping students to make use of information, understand the hidden curriculum and cope with the course. Course Management Extra aims to redress some of the additional disadvantages suffered by some students as a result of various discriminations.

Making groups safe

The literature on adult learning was silent on how to make the atmosphere in learning groups anti-oppressive. "We have described the methods, techniques and the program for a person-centred teaching approach. However, we cannot describe the more fundamental and critical interpersonal climate that must exist day by day if such a program is to succeed." (Rogers 1983)

Group work literature however has many suggestions for creating learning groups, which would provide an equal opportunity for everyone to participate as they wished, to feel safe to explore attitudes, but to be protected from discrimination. I hoped feeling safe would increase their learning and increase participation in the evaluation system.

Physical conditions

All students must be able to attend the teaching sessions offered. The day is kept within 9a.m.- 5p.m., despite the college norm of 9a.m-6p.m. In the first semester there is no teaching on Fridays. These arrangements suit the majority of our students, who have child care needs and require time to work for money.

The room must be suitable physically. "Studies in proxemics have shown that human communication is much influenced by physical spacing and distance." (Brown 1984). The room must also meet special needs; for instance, wheelchair access or a loop system. This has been possible so far by requesting rooms in the college's most modern building. However, if several courses had students with hearing problems at the same time, some would have to use the main building, which is too noisy. Besides, it is important for prospective disabled students to feel assured they will not have to spend their college career campaigning or feeling a nuisance. In the interests of Equal Opportunities, it is necessary to press for an upgrading of all the teaching rooms not just use special pleading for individual cases.

Group composition

Group composition can greatly influence group interaction. The size of the groups is largely determined by staff/student ratios, but we can influence other factors. From small group theory we know that " homogeneity is needed to develop group cohesion, and heterogeneity is necessary to produce the forces of change in a group. The emphasis will depend on whether the aim of the group is primarily change or support." (Brown 1984). We also know that it is preferable to avoid placing only one person of any "type" in an otherwise homogenous group. "..... the isolated person may be scapegoated and may feel both exposed and vulnerable. Additionally, the individual tends not to be seen as an individual but as a representative of their grouping and thus risks being stereotyped by the others." (Preston-Shoot1987).

Obviously it is not possible to organise groups to take account of all possible discriminations. Sexual orientation is an area in which the current level of discrimination is so high that it would be unreasonable to ask students their sexuality before they came on the course. This is sad, as one year, by chance, there were three gay women in a group. Only one was "out" at the beginning of the course, but gradually the others felt safe enough to challenge homophobic remarks, go on a gays in social work conference, pass on what they had learned to the whole group and start a gay and lesbian support group. No other cohort has had such good support for gay students. Other minority groups are too much in the minority to be considered in group composition. For instance, the number of students with disabilities in any one year can range from zero upwards. It would certainly not enhance Equal Opportunities if we excluded any student who was the only representative of a disadvantaged group! Careful group composition cannot answer all the potential problems of discrimination in groups.

There are two obvious minority groups in our student cohort of whom I could take account in group composition; black students and men. I ensured they were paired in tutorial groups, leaving some groups without. It reduced the heterogeneity of some groups, but I felt the needs of the minority students were more important than group heterogeneity on the grounds of Equal Opportunity. I did ensure that a group at least contained black students or men.

However, I had forgotten the effects of societal discrimination. Men come from a privileged group in society, so if a man drops out of the course the remaining male may be in a minority, but he will still carry with him the power of being a man in a patriarchal society. However, black people are an oppressed minority in a racist society, so a black student left alone in a group is more vulnerable. This year I will ensure a minimum of three black students in a group.

Every course has its minorities. Many science and technological subjects have a minority of women and for these courses it might be appropriate to group larger numbers of women into one seminar group to combat both their minority status in the cohort and their disadvantaged status in a patriarchal society. It must be born in mind that a cohort from a course which did not have anti-discriminatory practice in its content might misinterpret the manipulation of group composition on racial lines and the rationale would have to be explained carefully and be part of a wider plan.

Modular courses in which there are many optional modules would be difficult to control in terms of group composition, but attention could still be paid to it in seminars for core modules. However, group composition is not the end of the story.

Ground rules

Having created groups which have a chance of functioning in an anti-discriminatory way, it is essential to have a working agreement on behaviour and language which will make people feel safe to communicate. The Central Council for Social Work Education & Training (CCETSW) describes a working agreement as "..a means of setting the ground rules of language and behaviour for everybody associated with your programme - students, tutors, managers and visitors." They go on to specify that it should include statements that offensive language should be challenged in ways which are "constructive and enlightening" and that "racist and/or sexist comments, insults, jokes or harassment, are not tolerable".

When I first taught on the Diploma, ground rules were given considerable attention in some sequences and not in others. Where scant attention was paid to agreeing ground rules, nobody had any idea what "confidentiality" meant in this context. Did it mean the same for tutors as students? Also many people had never been trained in the art of constructive criticism, so tended to make no criticism at all leaving all challenge to the tutor. Even where ground rules were explored in depth, they were not quite the same in each subject area, which gave no overall feeling that it was safe to express yourself in the same manner, or that you would be equally protected from discriminatory remarks, across the course.

Last year, to combat these problems, I asked staff and students to formulate ground rules for the whole course right at the start and make these meaningful by exploring what difference a ground rule could make in different circumstances. I gave students practice in the skills of constructive criticism and challenge.

We carried this out in induction week and the first week of term with Year 1 students. The subject was raised first after showing the film "The story of O" which is a training film about difference in the workplace and how this can oppress people from various minority groups. Students explored situations in which they had felt powerful and powerless and the difference in feelings this evokes. They explored ways in which they were an X (majority person) in the group and the ways in which they might be an O (minority person). The examples were diverse. One student said she was an X in the group as women were in the majority, but an O because she was financially secure & the others were broke. Another student felt an O because he was a man, but an X in being in the middle of the age range. Most people commented that they were all Xs in having a common interest in the subject, which emphasised the bond making it safer to discuss difference. We then looked at ground rules which would create a safe environment where people had an equal opportunity to express themselves. The issues were recorded fairly fully.

At three subsequent sessions in different groupings, students explored the issues further. On each occasion full notes from the previous sessions were distributed. Students were encouraged to see how a ground rule might work in different situations. For example, "punctuality". I asked how students felt about a lecturer recapping for a late comer or about students sharing their notes. Very different viewpoints emerged. Some felt that a student should be punctual whatever it cost them, as they would have to do this at work. Others pointed out that when you work you can afford pre-school child care, but on a grant might have to cut it fine in order to deliver a child to school. These students said that they would therefore feel differently about someone turning up late first thing in the morning than if someone returned late after a lunch break. Some students suggested that a latecomer should give a reason for the lateness and that people could make up their own minds whether to fill them in on the session or not, but others pointed out that the reason might be very personal. Each issue was explored in depth in this way until a consensus was reached.

When discussing "challenging discrimination" we looked at whether a remark should receive the same response if it were made near the beginning of the course as it would at the end. For instance, exploring our own prejudices and place in a discriminatory society is part of the Social Work curriculum, so people need to feel free to "test the water" or admit areas they need to focus on. However, there has to be a baseline of behaviour in order for people to feel safe and students should progress to an acceptable end point.

We also practised the skill of "constructive criticism" using these guidelines.

The challenger should:-

1. Check out if the speaker's point of view had been correctly understood by seeking clarification.
2. Make it plain the criticism was a personal viewpoint, not the only possible interpretation.
3. Make it clear that the statement or performance was being criticised, not the person.
4. Make a constructive suggestion for improvement as well as highlighting any good points.

If the remark was discriminatory, the critic could also point out the possible consequences of the remark. For instance, if the remark stereotyped Asians, they could point out that this could help to perpetuate racism and that it could make Asians within the group feel uncomfortable and devalued.

We agreed a criticism or challenge should not be aggressive and that the tutor and other students should not "gang up" on the "offender". If the subject needed further exploration, the discussion should be general and used as a learning tool, not an extension of the challenge.

As well as general ground rules, we included some for special needs . For instance, there were specific rules regarding the attendance of a lip speaker in some of the seminar groups. At the end of two weeks' exploration the students' ideas were compiled into ground rules, which then went to the staff team for discussion. There was no dissension from the students' collective view and the ground rules were distributed. I have the impression that sensitive issues were explored in more depth and that I was not left to make all the challenges this year, but I have no way of proving this. With a leap of faith that it is effective, I shall try a few improvements.

1. Outside lecturers will receive the ground rules in advance and have their importance explained. I will seek their opinions about how this works in comparison to other groups they teach, where such carefully formulated frameworks may not be in place.

2. Constructive criticism and challenge will have more practice and be reinforced by including a checklist of how to make a good challenge in the ground rules.

3. Some of the second years will help at induction and hopefully will promote the importance of ground rules.

This experiment has been tried out on a group of students for whom anti-oppressive practice is a subject area. However, I think the ideas could easily be used in other arenas.

For courses which are run on strictly modular lines where students may be in a dozen different cohorts during a week, the idea of ground rules espousing Equal Opportunity principles could be incorporated into a capability module at the beginning of the student's time at college. In this way the skills of challenge and criticism could be recognised in the form of a reflective assignment with a credit rating. After all students need to know how to form non-discriminatory working relationships whatever their chosen career.

In order to make it work, the tutor needs to use examples of problems from students from similar cohorts and using the background of the subject they are studying.

Conclusion

Empowering people to use information and to feel comfortable to communicate and challenge are important components in making Equal Opportunities a reality rather than a statement. Extra help for some students should be coupled with general good practice and attention to detail.

References

Barnes, C. (1991) 'Disabled People in Britain and Discrimination'. Hurst & Company, London. University of Calgary Press.

Beard, Ruth M. & Senior, Isabel J. (1980). 'Motivating Students'. Routledge & Kegan Paul.

Brown, Allan. (1984). 'Groupwork'. Community Care. Heinemann Educational Books.

CCETSW Paper 30 (1989) in Humphries, Beth., Pankhania-Wimmer H., Seale A., Stokes, I.(1993) 'Improving practice teaching and learning' No.7. CCETSW Leeds.

Coulshed, V. (1993) 'Adult Learning: Implications for Teaching in Social Work Education'. Br.J.Social Wk. (1993) 23, 1-13.

Dominelli, L. (1988) 'Anti-Racist Social Work'. BASW. Macmillan.

Holland, R. (winter 1988) 'Visible and Invisible Curricula in Professional Education'. Issues in Social Work Education. vol.8 no.2 winter 1988 p.83-111.

Knowles,M. (1978) 'The Adult Learner: a Neglected Species'. 2nd edn., London. Gulf Publishing.

Lawton,D. (1968) 'Social Class, Language and Education'. London. Routledge & Kegan Paul

Maslow, Abraham (1970) 'Motivation & Personality'. 2nd edn. New York, Harper & Row.

Pease, Bob. (Spring 1992). 'Challenging Domination in Social Work Education'. Issues in Social Work Education vol. 11:2.

Preston-Shoot, Michael. (1987) 'Effective Groupwork'. BASW. Macmillan.

Rogers, C. (1983) 'Freedom to Learn'. Charles E. Merrill Publishing Company

Stanworth,M. (1983) 'Gender and Schooling: A Study of Sexual Divisions in the Classroom'. Hutchinson.

Sternberg, R.J. (1987) 'The Triarchic Theory of Human Intelligence', ch. 5 in 'Student Learning', ed. Richardson, J.T.E., Eysenck, M.W. & Piper, D.W. The Society for Research into Higher Education & Open University Press.

Thompson, N. (1993 + 2nd ed. 1997).'Anti-discriminatory Practice'. BASW. Macmillan.

9. Multiculturalism, Student Group Work and Assessment

Sue Ledwith and Anne Lee - Oxford Brookes University

Abstract

With the increase in student numbers, and the increase of international and multicultural students has developed an increase in the amount of work that students in the School of Business are required to carry out in groups, much of it being subsequently assessed. Concern among students and staff about the issues raised by the student mix, the criteria for assessment of group work, the nature and extent of group work and its relationship with individually assessed work and the implications of all of these for equality of opportunity among multicultural students, has led to a one-year 'pilot' research project in the School of Business.

This paper discusses the results from surveys and focus groups which centred around: student group formation: multiculturalism versus monoculturalism, heterogeneous groups versus homogeneous groups; how groups are formed, how work is distributed among group members and the subsequent group processes.

Assessment: requirements and form; individual versus group assessed work; criteria, especially the use - and abuse, of English, and how these are conveyed by tutors and interpreted by students; consistency and variation.

Student and tutor objectives: student experience of group/team working versus individual degree level achievement, and staff objectives of student development and learning and instrumentalist approaches to managing an increasing workload.

Introduction

In common with Higher Education as a whole, in recent years Brookes has seen a significant increase in student numbers. In particular in the last two/three years there has been an increase in the number of international students. This has been the case especially in the School of Business.

In response, teaching staff have developed strategies to cope with both the expansion in numbers and the increasingly multicultural nature of the student body. One of these has been a steady move towards requiring students to work in groups with their group work being jointly assessed. Another, and important rationale for the increase in group work is the experience that students are able to have in team working as a preparation for their subsequent careers in business and management.

Nevertheless group work, and especially group assessed work, is a contentious issue among students. As a student representative put it at a course committee meeting: "The average student was thought not to like group work as it might have a detrimental effect" on their individual final degree classification (School of Business 1996:3). This comment really summarises the tensions between group assessed student work and the degree classification, which the student is working for as an individual.

These tensions are the subject of much discussion between and among staff and students about group work, with the issues of mixing different cultures and of English language ability being prominent. In relation to facility with the English language, there is an allied debate among students and staff about the extent to which English spelling, grammar, syntax and fluency are influential in assessments. Students for whom English is their first language complain of having to rewrite the whole of group assignments when the group is made up of students from a range of linguistic backgrounds. This is perhaps an indication of lack of clarity about the role of English language in assessments. For example, at an International Business Management Field committee meeting a student representative questioned whether overseas students lost marks in assignments and examinations for poor English, spelling and grammar. The students were reassured that, 'as long as the meaning was quite clear, such students would not be marked down for mistakes in English language.' (School of Business 1997)

All of these are issues addressed in the study.

Two of the researchers are teaching staff in the School, having first hand experience of these issues. Indeed our concerns about these were the genesis for embarking on the study in the first place.

In the autumn of 1996 the University's Learning and Teaching Committee invited bids to support projects examining *'Using economical assessment methods to support learning and assure standards.'* A joint bid was successfully made by staff from the Equal Opportunities Action Group and the School of Business. This paper is based on the preliminary findings of the research carried out between March and July 1997 with students and staff in the School of Business [1].

The Business Studies Degrees and Courses

Students
In 1996-7 there were 1192 students on the modular business degrees. Over three-quarters of these (79%) were home students (including EU), 19% (223) were from overseas, and 3% were 'full cost' students, (mainly postgraduates).

Courses and staff

The business degrees offered in the School of Business are part of the University's wider modular degree programme. After a first year/stage of generic core modules, business students can opt to study a wide range of business subjects at the advanced/second stage. Or they can take a joint degree in a business area such as Business Administration and Management, International Business, Marketing Management, Retail Management, Economics or Accounting, which can be combined with any other field across the university. Alternatively students can follow a specialised programme within the general business degree, such as Human Resource Management, Marketing, Retail, or Tourism.

Around 70 modules were on offer in 1996-7, 94% of these ran for just one term; nine weeks. Almost a quarter were assessed through 100% coursework with the rest being assessed through a combination of coursework and exams. The most popular combination was *50/50* (31%) with a 40% coursework and 60% exam combination on a further 29% of modules. There is therefore plenty of scope for requiring coursework to be carried out in student groups.

The modules were taught by the 70 permanent academic staff with a further 39 part time tutors either running/leading modules or running seminar groups on modules with large numbers of students.

Group work issues

Increasingly the issues of group work and multicultural groups have been raised within the School of Business. For example in May 1996 staff identified: 'multiculturalism, with particular reference to teaching and learning issues, was considered to be of increasing importance as numbers of international students within the Business Fields continues to rise.' (School of Business 1996). It was reported in the minutes of this meeting that a number of the students representatives felt that there was a 'perennial problem in completing assessed group work with a mix of home and overseas students.' The general view of the committee was reported to be:

'that both students and staff need to have a greater awareness of the multicultural issues raised here and that both home and international students should work towards the ideal of learning from each other. A separation of home and international students for the purposes of assessed group work was considered to be an unnecessary and retrograde step..

A student representative went on to question the need for so much assessed group work in stage two (advanced level), *without any prior training and development activity for students,* especially on working in groups, including the multicultural dimension. [our emphasis].

Research

Research Design

The central research questions, which developed from this debate were about:

- The effectiveness of multicultural student groups on business modules.

- Equity in multicultural student group assessed work in relation to individual student performance.

- Students' attitudes about group assessed work.

- Students' attitudes when asked to work together with students from cultures other than their own.

- Attitudes of students for whom English is their first language compared to those of students for whom English is not their first language towards group working and assessment.

- Staff views about students working together in multicultural groups.

- Staff views about assessing student group work compared with individual student work.

The research programme was designed to provide a contextual background using documentation from within the School of Business, with quantitative and qualitative data to be collected from students and from staff

Research Methods

Students

The study was carried out among students on the advanced/second stage of the business studies degrees. This was to ensure that as far as possible the students could draw on a fairly wide range of experience of working in student groups. However a small number of students surveyed were in their first year at Brookes, or were only here for a year. These were exchange students, and those among an increasing number entering with credits in the final stage of a degree. The questionnaire was piloted in term 2 with a dozen students from a range of cultural backgrounds. The final questionnaire was distributed to 257 students on a range of modules in term 3. Students on these five modules were asked by the module leaders to complete and return the questionnaire, eliciting a 62% response rate.

The students were also invited on a tear off front sheet, to participate in a student focus group to explore some of the issues in further discussion. Initially three focus groups were run with students from a range of cultural backgrounds. A further seven students were invited, and participated in a further two groups, thus ensuring a representative spread of students. Altogether nineteen students participated in focus groups; seven men and 12 women, from the UK, EU countries, non-EU European countries, SE Asia and Africa.

The focus groups were facilitated by an independent consultant who had no previous connections with the School of Business. The discussions were tape recorded and transcribed.

Staff

A questionnaire was developed for staff, piloted and distributed among permanent staff via their pigeon-holes, with the part timers receiving theirs by post. Overall there was a response rate of 30% (34 questionnaires completed), with the majority being from the permanent staff group, thus moving the response rate up to around 40%.

As with the students, staff were invited to participate in focus group discussions, five groups were held, with a total of 15 staff participating. These were made up of four women and 11 men, covering the disciplines of marketing, retail management, information technology, human resource management, business and management, economics and accounting/finance. These were facilitated by an independent consultant and the discussions tape recorded and transcribed.

Main Findings

We move now to present the main findings from the preliminary analysis of the research data from the School of Business survey.

Students

Questionnaire Analysis

The majority, 75% of all the students, were under the age of 25, with a fifth being aged between 22 and 35. The balance between the sexes reflected the norm in Higher Education and was 55% women. Ninety four per cent were full time students. Ninety six per cent had experienced group coursework during their time at Brookes.

Ethnicity and language

Just over half of the sample identified themselves as 'white UK', with a further fifth identifying as 'white other'. Thus 24% were from the range of ethnicities as defined by the Commission for Racial Equality, with Chinese dominating at 10% (15 students).

Since many of the School's international students are truly that, often having moved and lived in different parts of the world and having their schooling in a multicultural environment, we asked where they had been educated at secondary level. Including the UK, 30 different countries were represented.

However, since facility in the English language is presented as a major source of tensions in multicultural student group member cooperation, students were asked what was their first language. Two thirds (67%) said 'yes' English was their first language. This included 12 students not from the UK; they came mainly from North America and African countries. Among the 33% for whom English was not their first language, 23 different first languages were identified. These were grouped together into regions which can be seen in **Table 1.**

Table 1. Students' first language, by region.

First language regional grouping	Number of students	% of students
English	104	66
European Union	22	14
European non-EU	7	4
Asia	23	15
Africa/Arabia	2	1
TOTALS	158	100

Overall the age of students for whom English was their first language were younger than the foreign students, among whom there was a higher proportion of students aged between 22-34. See Figure 1a, Appendix 1.

While the male and female balance among students was fairly even among those for whom English was their first language, among European non-European Union students 71% were male, and two-thirds of Asian students were female. See Figure 1b, Appendix 1.

Assessment and the significance of English language

Facility in the English language among students for whom this was not their first language was an issue which raised strong views among students and staff. Questions were therefore asked of students about their perceptions of the assessment criteria relating to English language, and other criteria.

Fluency of English expression/grammar was seen as not important by as many as a quarter of all the students. It came only sixth in the hierarchy of importance so far as students are concerned. However when the two groups of students; those for whom English was, and was not their first language, were examined in more detail, significant differences were found between them, as can be seen in Table 2. In particular, as many as a quarter of students for whom English was not their first language did not know whether or not their English was being assessed.

Table 2. English as an assessment criterion (percentage of students responding)

Fluency of ENGLISH expression/grammar	Is it usually being assessed?			Important to you/student		Important to tutors	
	Yes	*No*	*Don't know*	*Yes*	*No*	*Yes*	*No*
Students whose first language is English	50	35	16	75	25	82	18
Students for whom English is not their first language	61	14	26	77	23	78	22

On the other criteria there were no significant differences between the two groups of students, although it can be seen in **Table 3.** that in some areas, for example, quoting academic sources, there appeared to be a dissonance between what students thought was important and the importance they thought that tutors gave to the criteria.

Table 3. Student views of importance of criteria (percentage of students responding)

CRITERIA	Important for students	Important for tutors
Understanding	100	97
Analysis and explanation	99	99
Reading & research	88	93
Originality & creative thinking	92	87
Quoting academic sources	60	84
Fluency of English expression/ grammar	75	81
Own ideas and experience	88	76
The group process	73	87

How students are informed about assessment criteria
All but two of the students reported that they were normally given written instructions about assessment criteria, with a further 29% also getting oral instructions.

We thought that the clarity of assessment criteria to students was likely to be of central importance to the work they present to tutors for marking, and particularly for students for whom English was not their first language. So it was interesting to find that only 10% of all the students reported that they *always* found assessment criteria easy to understand and to follow, even though over two-thirds said that they always closely followed the criteria. Three quarters said that it was easy to understand and to follow sometimes, with 16% saying that it was so only occasionally. There were no significant differences however between those for whom English was their first language and those for whom it was not.

Proposals for improvements
Seventy per cent of the students said that they thought there was room for improvement. The areas which students identified for improvement were overwhelmingly to do with clarity and detail of what was required in assessments. The sort of precision students wanted was in particular 'more details'. Where these were specified they ranged from very detailed Aspecific bullet points covering every aspect of assessment for all modules' to improving breakdown of marks, and in one case a plea for word processed not handwritten criteria. One of the students identified how the subtleties

and complexities of the subject area were implicated in some of the difficulties experienced by students:

Business Studies is a broad subject therefore is very difficult to understand what is required from the student for a specific task. I would like to see tutors explain more in depth the assessment criteria and possibly advise on what the students should do, particularly the international students.

The problem of ambiguity was listed several times, with a plea for plainer English. A large number of proposals for improvement centred on two-way communication with the tutor, partly to deal with the problem of criteria being open to interpretation. This could be dealt with, several students suggested, through face to face discussion with module and seminar leaders. Here there were pleas for more time to speak with module leaders, examples to be given in lectures and seminars of staff expectations, and "clear initial written instructions to be followed by the tutor's interpretation (ie the person who is marking it)". Given that only a quarter of the students reported receiving both written and oral instructions, this is an area where significant improvements could be made.

There was a small number of proposals about helping international students which picked up the specific problems of non-UK students, and the importance of being able to clarify through face to face discussion what was required.

Throughout the study a central thread was the issue of English language, in particular for students for whom English was not their first language. For students for whom it was their first language but they came from abroad, for example North America and parts of Africa and the Caribbean, its use and interpretation was not the same as those who had lived and been educated in the UK.

In response to a question which asked whether they thought their current average mark at Brookes reflected their ability eleven students specifically identified problems with English and studying in the UK.

Tutors' feedback
The level of uncertainty expressed by students about assessment criteria could perhaps lead to a view that getting feedback from tutors was particularly important in confirming, or otherwise, how well they had understood and complied with the criteria.

Two thirds of all the students thought that tutor feedback was helpful in relation to the assessment criteria, yet a large minority, 33%, thought that it was not. The differences between those for whom English was their first language and those for whom it was not was not significant.

Working in Groups

All but seven students had experienced some form of group coursework while at Brookes, with over half of these experiencing at least three types. Over half the students had taken between 1-5 modules which involved working in groups for assessed work, with a third of the students taking between 6 and 20 modules of this kind. Four students had taken 21 or more modules involving group assessed work.

When it came to the types of assessed group work experienced by students, 89% of the students had taken part in a verbal/visual presentation in a group. The other most common forms of group work were projects/investigations (80%), case studies (47%), and essays (43%). These latter were also usually the basis for a verbal/visual presentation.

When students were asked which forms of group coursework assessment they thought best reflected their ability, 79% thought that the verbal/visual presentation did so well, but only a quarter thought that it did so 'very well'. However as many as 21% of the students who answered the question thought that the assessment of their presentations did not reflect their ability.

The anxieties that students felt about the impact of group assessments on their individual final degree grade were strongly reflected in their responses and in their written comments. See **Table 4.**

Table 4. Student views on how well assessment types reflected their ability (% of students responding)

ASSESSMENT TYPES	Individual assessment		Group assessment	
	Well	*Not well/ Not at all*	*Well*	*Not well Not at all*
Verbal/visual presentation	71%	29%	80%	20%
Project/investigation	88%	12%	74%	26%
Case study analysis	82%	18%	65%	35%
Essay	82%	18%	55%	45%
Seminar paper	54%	46%	NA	

Students consistently thought that their individual assessments better reflected their ability than their groupwork did. This was particularly the case for all the written assignment types, with only performance on the verbal/visual presentation being seen as a more positive reflection of ability in group work than as individuals, as can be seen in **Table** 4. These views were reinforced by many of the comments written on the questionnaires. In particular, the largest group of comments made about group assessment emphasised what students saw as inequity of all group members getting the same mark when not all had put in the same effort. Only two students explicitly identified problems with non UK or English speaking students in this respect. The most commonly expressed views are represented by this student:

Stronger members of groups will always carry the weaker/lazy people, and sometimes marks reflect this - which is why I generally prefer to work on my own, then I am responsible for how little/how much work I do.

Perceptions of their ability by students for whom English was not their first language were significantly different from English as first language speakers in the individual assessment areas of project/investigation, case study analysis and case study based questions, implying that there may be differential cultural experiences, understanding and expectations between these groups. See **Table** 5. There were no significant differences in the more traditional assessment methods of essays and seminar papers - although neither group thought that these two assessments reflected their abilities very well.

Best and worst groups
In order to get a better picture of the make-up and character of student groups, students were asked a series of questions about their best and their worst experiences of working in a group on business courses. The questions covered the method of forming these groups, the composition by gender, age, culture, friends or otherwise and how the work was assessed.

Table 5. Views of students in two language groups about their own abilities in individual assessed coursework (% of student respondents)

Assessment method	English first language. *Reflects ability well*	First language not English. *Reflects ability well*
Project/investigation	93	77
Case study analysis	89	67
Case study based questions	88	60
Essay	84	78
Presentation	73	67
Seminar paper	58	46

Overwhelmingly students reported that their best groups were organised by themselves (78%), 85% of best groups were organised either by themselves or jointly by students and tutors. Just over half of their worst groups had been organised by tutors and 31% organised by the students. The most common assessed tasks for both best and worst groups were presentations and project work, with presentations in particular being the main task of best groups. When it came to how the work was divided up within the group, it seemed that the same methods were applied almost equally in both best and worst groups - equal division of labour, individuals focusing on one part, with all the group members doing initial research contributing slightly more to the best groups.

In view of the findings in Table 4, it is interesting to note that only 13% of students reported that marks in their best group were allocated to the individual rather than the group, and that 22% reported that in their worst group marks were allocated individually. In best groups over 80% of the students reported that everyone in the group was awarded the same mark, and in the worst groups it was 78%.

When it came to composition of the best and worst groups, there were no significant differences in relation to gender, age, and friendship groups. As can be seen in Figure 3, Appendix 1, the majority of groups were about half and half men and women, although in more of the best groups there was a 50/50 balance between the sexes. Although not a significant difference, best groups did consist more often of a mix of ages. Again, although not a significant difference, students' preference for working with friends was reflected in the third of all students who said that this was the composition of their best group and the 45% who said that their worst group was made up of people they didn't know.

Significance of culture and difference

However when it came to cultural mix, it was found to be significant that many more best *and* worst groups were monocultural, as can be seen in Figure 3, Appendix 1.. Significantly more - almost twice as many - students reported that their best groups were culturally mixed than those who reported that their worst group was culturally mixed. When the views of students for whom English was their first language were compared with those whose first language was one other than English, significant differences were found. Many more students for whom English was their first language said that their best group was made up of students from the same culture as themselves. Conversely, students whose first language was not English reported that their worst groups were where they were together with students from their own culture and their best groups were where there were students from a culture different from their own.

Student Focus Groups.

Nineteen students participated in five focus groups; seven men and 12 women, from the UK, EU countries, non-EU European countries, SE Asia and Africa.

Necessarily these were self-selecting, and from the conversation and discussion it became clear that these students had strong views and plenty to say about group working at Brookes. It was also the case that the students for whom English was not their first language were nevertheless fluent and articulate in English. Two additional student focus groups were held with invited students from previously under represented groups.

A number of students expressed interest in seeing the report of the research, saying that this was an issue very close to their hearts.

The group discussions lasted about an hour and a sandwich lunch was provided. Students were invited to discuss in more detail some of the major issues raised in the questionnaire (which they had all completed). The focus was mainly on the students' experiences of their best and worst group experiences. So far the transcripts have not been analysed in detail. However considerable evidence emerged of a cultural divide between the UK students, for whom English was their first language, and students from other countries and cultures. An overriding view came through of foreign students perceiving UK students generally as exclusive, unfriendly and unwelcoming. This was the case whether the foreign students were from as near as the EU, northern Europe or from as far away as SE Asia. Often the foreign students emphasised that they felt that they had a better understanding of multiculturalism; they were after all experiencing it at first hand, and they were at Brookes to learn both about Business Studies and also about the UK and other cultures. On the other hand, the emphasis of the UK students was on their individual current average mark, that groupwork tended to pull this down, and the fear that this would impact adversely on their final degree classification.

The overriding concern of the students in the focus groups was that their class groups should work well. How to do that was seen as complicated and a range of strategies were developed by students, especially at the group formation stage. One foreign student's first good group experience arose from a random selection - 'we were all late for the module and we didn't have a group, so we just formed a group together. The group worked'. The five students were each of a different nationality, and were all the same sex. Finding themselves together on a subsequent module they arranged to work together again. However it is not often that modular students do find themselves on the same modules as others they have worked with before, and formation of groups was seen as a real problem, especially in the first year when no one knew anyone else. Nevertheless it was of foremost importance to almost all the students that they were able to influence or choose their co-group members. One student described how in the current term they were working in four different groups on four different modules. This student had chosen her own group members from people she already knew either directly or indirectly. 'I have found them excellent actually. I chose the right groups, which I am happy about'.

For foreign students it was often important to have English students in their group, especially at the beginning of the course. This helped with learning the culture - 'how we do things around here' as well as the language. But if there were too many students from one culture in a group, whether English, French, Malaysian or whatever, then there were internal splits with the main group speaking their own language and excluding the minority.

Both English and foreign students agreed that facility in English was a dominant issue in group work in order to ensure that 'you end up with groups of people that you pick that have English as the first language'.

A common outcome was that students without good English were ignored or excluded from the group process:

they could be super intelligent in their own country do you see what I mean, but it doesn 't come across, so we just think, 'they don 't know what they are talking about' sort of thing. [UK student]

This attitude was confirmed by several foreign students when describing their own experiences. Some also thought that teaching staff sometimes took the same view. For example this student had come through a competitive selection process in their own country, ending up in the last 10%, in order to come to Brookes:

Apparently I got the best mark for one [assignment] in the first term and the teacher was quite amazed because I was a foreigner, but why not after all?

A related source of friction was the high fees paid by international students. Students from this group felt strongly that this caused them to be more highly motivated and aim to get the most out of their time at Brookes. However, English students typically expressed this view:

In my opinion there are far too many international students... because they get the money for it and we know that, that makes us resentful. We pay for it.. .I have never heard an English student say 'it's great that we have 15% foreigners at Oxford Brookes University'. It's 'Oh God, another...'

This student thought that the University should not admit students whose spoken English was not good enough to understand; having English written skills was not enough: 'when you communicate with me I am not going to say to you 'please write it here because I can't understand'.

Since so many of the students are required to do assessed group oral/visual presentations, this becomes a very significant issue to both native speakers and especially to those for whom English is not their first language. UK and foreign students tended to think that lecturers were: 'nice about it, whereas students are a lot less nice about it'. 'I think it is partly the reason why the lecturers will just keep nodding is because they are just polite and British'. Foreign students didn't want to be embarrassed, to 'lose face'. One student whose English was good reported not feeling disadvantaged in written work, only in presentations:

I am very disadvantaged because I get, I feel a bit embarrassed or it's difficult for me to get up and stand up in front of a class with English people. Because I know that I just lose my English, I forget my English because I am very aware of what the other people will think...

Nevertheless, foreign students, and older, mature students, were especially keen to get something more out of the group process than just a good mark. As one European student articulated it:

I am really keen meeting different cultures and nationalities, so there is a unique opportunity here at Brookes, so I have rightly chosen groups when I would be with four or five different nationalities, and I really enjoy that. But at the same time it's like in one module ... we came really unstuck in many ways. Because different cultures just means so many different approaches... it is sort of different levels of confidence

Managing the group process was seen as a central issue and source of difficulty. Many students wanted more support from teaching staff. Examples were given of tutors sometimes giving support and challenging students, when asked by despairing group members. But they found this quite difficult:

You can go to a lecturer and ask, but it is more sort of a matter of bothering them, if you see what I mean.

and

It's grabbing them after a lecture and hassling them. That's very awkward. That's what it feels like doesn't it, 'excuse me for wasting your time' sort of thing.

Students on one module with a support system built in described how they especially valued this:

we have a facilitator who sits in the group meetings and takes notes and interacts with us if she thinks that.. you know .... and the group is getting on very well.

On this module student analysis of the group process was assessed as well as the group task itself. Students wanted more of this sort of differentiation, for example the suggestion that compulsory group work be a condition of passing the module but the assignment should be an individual piece of work.

Students also wanted to be able to use more seminar time for group work because of the difficulties of arranging to meet outside class and the time pressures the modular system put on assignment deadlines.

A number of the foreign students put in a plea for the English students to be more welcoming and tolerant towards international students.

Staff

Overall there was a response rate of 30% (34 questionnaires completed), with the majority being from the permanent staff group.

As with the students, staff were invited to participate in focus group discussions. Five groups were held, with a total of 15 staff participating. These were made up of 4 women and 11 men, evenly covering the disciplines of marketing, retail management, information technology, human resource management, business and management, economics and accounting.

Between them staff taught on a total of 45 second and third year modules, covering the subject range described above. The number of students taught in a class ranged from eight to 180 students. (Four staff reported teaching classes/modules of 300-500 students; these were first year modules.) Approximately a third of the staff taught classes with 25 or fewer students; another third between 30 and 50 students, and the final third between 100-180 students.

Assessment Methods Used

A quarter of the staff said that they preferred to use individual work to assess students, with three-quarters preferring a combination of group and individual work. No-one used groupwork only. The reasons for these preferences are now discussed.

Individual only

The staff who reported that they used individual assessment of students only did so for reasons falling into the following, overlapping groupings: problems with group membership, the student didn't want it; the subject matter was inappropriate for assessment by group work, and the issue of differences between group work and individual work. For example:

117

i) Problems with group membership

Students wasted time arranging meetings; lazy or coasting group members which infuriated other students and this lethargy might mean other students may fail or undertake an excessive burden of work. Cultural issues - groups not willing to address these, so seek to work with those of similar cultures to themselves, or groups became stressed; marking was difficult when some students approached the tutor to complain about the attitude/performance of other students.

ii) Differences between group and individual assessment

Difficulty in assessing individuals fairly on the basis of group work; to isolate/allocate the roles/marks of individual students; and 'I have seldom seen groupwork of as high a standard as can be achieved by some students individually', and

I believe group assessment creates the unacceptable risk that non-contributors will pass thanks to the efforts of their colleagues, and that the philosophy of working in a group conflicts as part of the learning process is, given the impossibility of effective expert support, unnecessarily harsh on some individuals.

iii) Students don't want it

Students complained of being dragged down; they didn't want it for a variety of reasons; 'students hate group work'.

iv) The subject matter was inappropriate for assessment by group work

The principle assessment objectives related to individual skills; syllabi did not lend themselves; when learning new academic areas, explanations would not be enhanced by groupwork.

Groupwork

By far the most important reasons staff gave for using groupwork to assess students fell into the category of benefits for the students as preparation for work/employment/career; pedagogic advantages and coping with large numbers of students.

i) Benefits for students

The benefits which staff said they thought students gained from groupwork were wide ranging, however they can be grouped into the following broad, overlapping, categories:

a) The development of interpersonal, group and team working skills, and opportunities for reflection and insight into themselves and for building friendships, especially in a new cultural setting;

b) Opportunities for effective collaborative working in teams, which in turn produced more effective outcomes through synergy: 'Good groups can produce really excellent work - the sum is greater than the parts, as research on groups has found'. This was in turn seen as being enhanced by the sharing of tasks in groups, enabling them to cover more issues, carry out in depth work and tackle tasks which would be too big for an individual student.

c) Mutual help and support in learning was seen as another important reason for student group work; it enabled more reserved/shy/diffident students to contribute and to get practice in presentations in a non/less threatening environment; and less able/committed students could be helped by their more able peers.

ii) Preparation for work/career

Here staff described how group work replicated the reality in the workplace and reflected the real world with its increased emphasis on task orientation in groups.

iii) Pedagogic advantages

For several staff, working in groups enabled them to ask students to carry out larger, more realistic tasks; gave scope for larger, 'more interesting/ substantive assignment topics/tasks because the workload is shared'. It also allowed for students to comment on the work of other groups, 'which I think is valuable'.

iv) Coping with large numbers of students

Reducing the workload and saving time were the two main reasons a number staff gave for coping with large numbers of students: 'It reduces the amount of marking, especially group presentations' and 'Pragmatically, with more and more students, groupwork has to feature more and more.'

Combination of individual and group assessment

About a third of the staff also commented on the relationship between individual and group marking. For example, it was seen as important to be able to evaluate both individual skills and knowledge and the ability to apply these in a group situation; to be able to compare individual and group work; different skills could be assessed in each form. Staff favoured group assignments to encourage sharing and collaborative learning and effort, but stressed that the individual aspects needed assessment in order to ensure fairness and to differentiate at the individual level of performance. One lecturer thought that in individual work only, language could often be a major inhibitor.

Group membership and group performance

Almost all (91%) of the staff thought that student performance was affected by the makeup of the group members, with three staff answering 'don't know'. when asked what affected student performance, homogeneity, heterogeneity, monoculturalism or multiculturalism, 70% replied that groups were affected by all four configurations, with heterogeneity and multiculturalism particularly being identified by 19% of staff. When asked in what ways they thought students' assessed performance in groups was affected, 25 staff made comments.

In general, staff thought that group performance was affected by the level of maturity of members and their motivation to do well, together with *previous experience* of group work (good or poor). Chance played a large part, with staff thinking for example, students could be lucky to be in a group with a bright student(s) or unlucky in ones where one or more people did not pull their weight. The proximity of students' domicile was also seen as significant.

i) Homogenous Groups
In these, students were seen to be able to bond better, but produce less effective outputs; 'Similar mindsets - easy solutions', and 'Good teamwork, but narrow perspective'. Students also had 'Less difficulty initially - but content, breadth more limited'.

ii) Monocultural Groups
There was little support for monocultural groups as an effective source of learning, For example: 'Unwillingness to look outside own culture, when really a benefit is there to gained from multicultural contacts.' By implication several staff seemed to be referring to such groups *other* than English/UK students. For example: 'If all one culture (eg Spanish) they seem to hit the lowest common denominator'. and 'Monocultural (non UK) tend to do worse.' and 'Often poor confidence in all-female Asian groups'.

iii) Heterogeneous Groups
In heterogeneous and multicultural groups staff recognised that it was far more difficult at first but with the longer term possibility of deeper understanding. The diversity of mixed groups was seen to bring both potential benefits and problems: 'Sometimes diverse groups can adversely affect the performance because they do not get on so well with each other; BUT sometimes diversity adds to their performance quality because they are able to learn from each other's different knowledge and experience

iv) Multicultural and Language issues
The combination of students from a range of different cultures and with different first languages, led to the largest group of staff comments and a range of concerns, both positive and negative. On the positive side, a number of lecturers wrote of how 'multicultural groups are probably the most important in that they bridge language and cultural barriers and lead to

more complete approaches in tackling project work. However there were more concerns expressed about the problems, such as: 'Complex dynamics, misunderstanding can occur and can sideline the less articulate and confident'.

Some students without a good grasp of spoken English may be isolated and their views given less credibility'. Where there were differences among students from different cultures in expectations, and where social conventions and education are thought to be different/inferior/superior, problems arose. For example: 'Some cultures may dominate proceedings and others may not be willing to challenge.'

The differential experiences of students from a range of cultures of their prior education and thus their expectations of what would be required of them at Brookes was an important issue raised by staff - 'Students from certain cultures are not used to or are more experienced in group working'. Also, the speed of learning can be a problem, especially with language and technical jargon.

v) Gender
A few staff also identified gender difference as being important in the balance of group make up, with an emphasis on a tendency for male students to dominate. For example: 'Sometimes a tendency for males to take the more dominant tasks, leaving females (often willingly) to undertake mundane work' and 'Men can dominate females or not pull their weight and be carried by females.' One lecturer thought that all female groups tended to do better, and another thought that 'the sex split is almost as important as the culture split - all female groups seem to work hardest!'

When combined with culture, the gender dimension became especially important for this staff member who saw 'a mixture of say Asian women and central European men' as a problem because of the cultural/male female split.

Advantages of students from a range of cultures

Lecturers were asked about the advantages and disadvantages they thought that students from a range of different cultures brought to their classes. On balance, slightly more staff gave negative reasons than positive. Some staff also differentiated between UK/English students, European students, and a more general group of 'overseas' and 'international' students.

The positive advantages centred on the richness and the diversity of student experiences, cultures, business ethics, management systems and general understanding that students from a range of different cultures brought to classes. An important aspect of this was the challenge these presented to both staff and students about cultural preconceptions, traditional ways of perceiving business and management issues. However, as one lecturer put it: 'whether the potential [this offered] is realised depends on the quality of reflection on the group process'.

Some staff compared foreign students to their UK students, and found the latter wanting. UK students were perceived by one lecturer as being insular and 'rather too self-centred', while another lecturer found them less mature and competent than European (non GB) undergraduates. Another staff member thought that overseas students set a good example to UK students of people 'committed to learning home and studying for a degree in a foreign language'.

The advantage of helping students prepare for careers in a global economy and being better equipped to understand cultural difference was seen as important, with lecturers commenting on the possible long term benefits such as improved future international trade, and world peace.

Disadvantages of students from a range of cultures

i) **Structural** Some of the disadvantages perceived by lecturers related to the structure of the modular programme, such as the limited timescale, for example the challenge of integrating different cultures; 'This is a huge subject. We need to consider much more focus on this issue. and:

> *'6-8 weeks to deliver good work is very short and leads to exclusion of international students by UK students anxious about maintaining their marks, because it takes longer than 6-8 weeks to get to maximise group members' contributions.*

The tension between this and giving adequate support to such groups was raised by some staff, and articulated thus by one tutor:

> *I think it is generally beneficial to stimulate awareness of others' philosophies, assumptions and ways of living. However I do not believe this process is beneficial (or at least it is high risk) if is not managed and supported effectively. This is very difficult in the free ranging philosophy and anonymity of the modular and I don 't believe, despite a lot of goodwill, it is really achieved.*

ii) **Language** was another major area of disadvantage as seen by the academic staff, especially where students' oral English was not felt to be up to the needs of group discussion and assessment. Language barriers in large groups meant that some students got left out/behind.

iii) For tutors this meant harder work, for example, to ensure that: 'the less linguistically able and articulate students did not become marginalised by dominant assertive individuals'. Other tutors wrote of how they had had to slow down their lectures so that those whose first language is not English were able to follow. For one tutor, this also had its advantages in making the lecturer speak more slowly and clearly which was seen as a benefit to English speaking students too.

iv) Cultural differences in expectations of the learning process and tutor and student roles were listed as disadvantages, particularly when tutors were managing multicultural groups. All of this meant a lot more time was spent by tutors, as several staff pointed out. Student antagonisms were also listed as disadvantages. These were mainly in the area of complaints from UK/'home' students about 'non participation' and 'slowing of progress' in producing work.

Some staff saw foreign students as hesitant to contribute to class discussions. In one lecturer's view this inhibited the value of both their being in the class, as well as 'short changing' other participants. One lecturer commented that some cultures inhibited participation as a rule, and especially that of women.

Organisation of student groups

Given the importance that lecturers put on the benefits of students working in groups, and the problems of group membership, it is interesting to see that only *15%* of tutors said that they organised the groups entirely. This was not without its difficulties however. One tutor wrote of the difficulties of 'breaking up multicultural classes into equal groups - I've resorted to mixing people by month of birthday'. Two thirds of the staff reported that their groups were organised by a combination of students and tutors, with 18% being organised by students. So it can be seen that students did have an input into how their groups are organised as far as 70% of the staff respondents were concerned.

Assessment Criteria

Analysis of types of assessment criteria on Business modules is currently being carried out, but not yet complete. However staff were asked on the questionnaire about the methods they used to communicate criteria to students. Almost all the staff (97%) did so formally, with 3% doing so informally. Written instructions were given by 94% of staff; with a small number, four, giving additional written instructions. Over two-thirds followed up their written information with oral instructions in the lecture and just over half also doing so in seminars, while a high proportion of the staff were clearly willing and available to respond separately to questions and queries from students both in groups (62%) and as individual students (82%), only 59% did so with all the students together in class.

Role of English in assessments

However when it came to explicitly informing students of the role in their assessments played by English spelling, grammar, syntax and fluency, as can be seen in **Table 6**, staff did this much less, with only 62% giving formal written instructions. Also far fewer staff discussed the issue with students orally in class, in groups or individually.

However, only half of all the staff respondents said that they gave marks for correct English spelling, grammar and syntax and fluency when marking written coursework, with 47% saying they did not and one lecturer saying 'it depends'. When it came to oral coursework presentations, fewer staff gave marks for correct English; only 31%, with 69% answering 'no'. Lecturers were less concerned with English when they marked exams, with 27% deducting marks for incorrect spelling, grammar, syntax and fluency.

Table 6. Lecturers' methods of informing students of assessment criteria

Methods of informing students of assessment criteria	All criteria		English spelling, grammar, syntax, fluency	
	No. lecturers	*%*	*No. lecturers*	*%*
Written instructions	32	94	21	62
Additional written instructions	4	8	2	6
Oral instructions in lecture	23	23	11	32
Oral instructions in seminar	19	56	7	21
In discussion with student group in class	20	59	13	38
When questioned by student group separately	21	62	12	35
When questioned by individual students	28	82	14	41

numbers add up to more than 100% because lecturers answered all questions

Feedback on coursework

The majority of lecturers gave feedback to students in the form of written comments, and just over half used two or more methods of giving feedback. Almost three-quarters of the tutors gave both written and oral feedback of various kinds. Oral feedback included general comments, comments initiated by staff and those initiated by student queries. A fifth gave written feedback only.

Staff Focus Groups

The focus group discussions reinforced views expressed through comments on the staff questionnaires. The two main, interrelated debates centred on:

i) Multiculturalism

The debates about the issues of multicultural students in classes and groups were long and complex. On balance staff thought that the diversity, examples and new insights offered by multicultural students were very positive for both students and staff. However there were considerable anxieties expressed about the ability of some foreign students to communicate with sufficient fluency and confidence in group work. Staff tended to differentiate between European students, who were reported as mainly having good English - German and Danish students in particular - and students from further afield. In particular students from South East Asia whose English was less good. Often these students were seen as not fluent and at ease with spoken English in particular - essential for communicating, working in groups, and making oral presentations, which were part of the majority of group work. Such students were often excluded from UK student groups. Where these students formed a whole monocultural group, the problems were compounded when the students communicated with one another in their own language. Staff felt that this limited the students' development in English and their understanding of the requirements and culture of the University was thus not good enough to perform adequately. Where such students were producing work using computing - a global language - these sorts of problems did not occur and staff reported some excellent results. Staff reported that one important effect of the issues around multiculturalism and group working was that foreign students - students from the far east, Malaysia, France and Spain, for example - often said that they didn't get to know the UK students, who were not very welcoming.

> *International students have come to see our culture, meet English people. But the average*

18-year old UK student does not see it like that.
It's just not one of their priorities. [Tutor]

ii) Group formation

Contrary to the views expressed by students, staff were equivocal about imposing group formation on students. They preferred to leave it to the students, but also were anxious about the imbalance that resulted whereby foreign students were excluded and homogenous groups resulted. In these cases staff sometimes tried to 'manipulate' groups to balance them more. Other staff felt that students would not take ownership of a group if staff imposed it - 'they blame you if they've got a duff member of the group. I've had that before: "you put them in our group..."'. Bad groups included those which failed to attend classes regularly, and as a result misinterpreted or failed to produce the work as required.

Staff commented that the best groups they had seen tended to be homogenous, but others identified multicultural groups which had produced excellent work; especially groups composed of European students from different countries. For one staff member:

> *'all the best groups that I've worked with are mature student groups with a homogenous cultural background probably. They tend to agree on the objectives and get on, with very little arbitrating by the tutor, or disagreements. I think they've got life in perspective...'*

Summary

From the data analysed so far it does seem that the issues identified in sections 1 and 2 from ad hoc evidence, are the major ones for the School of Business in relation to group work and an increasingly diverse multicultural, international student body. The research has shown significant differences between attitudes of UK students and 'foreign' students. These centred on the tensions between getting a good mark (for UK students) and taking something positive from the multicultural group experience in its own right. These concerns and views tended to be endorsed by the staff; who also offered some important critical analysis and insights to the issues.

They identified tensions for staff as well as students. For those who used group work, especially assessed group work on modules that they taught, problems with group formation, group processes and being called in to arbitrate when groups go wrong were all significant factors. Many staff saw themselves as not adequately skilled or trained to deal with group breakdown and problems, and in particular the sensitivity needed for intercultural difficulties. Such staff were also anxious about the possibly damaging impact of such difficulties on young students, especially those from overseas. Staff also found that what may have started out as a mechanism for saving time on marking large numbers of individual assignments, took up much more time in coping with student group problems.

Both students and staff expressed the need for more support and training in group skills, and in working with students from a range of different nationalities and cultures.

Students, and particularly staff articulated an underlying set of contradictions impacting on what they saw inherently as substantial advantages, rationales and ethos of group working. The structure of the modular degree, with its short, one-term (10-week) courses/modules was perceived as antipathetic to the effective development of group cohesion, ways of working together, *and* carrying out the task, all in a matter of a few weeks. This was compounded by the ethos of choice which often meant that students were working on three or four different modules in a term, in groups on all of them, but with different group members on each. This structure inhibited the development of coherent cohorts of students, let alone groups of multicultural students, who could develop a close and effective working relationship over time and several modules. The anxieties of students, especially UK students, about their marks, and subsequent degree classification, and how these can be adversely affected by group assessment, can be seen as a product of these tensions.

On the positive side, staff overwhelmingly supported the concept of group work on a number of bases; preparation for careers in business, personal and skill development of students, larger, more complex and 'realistic' tasks could be carried out, and the outcomes of good groups were usually better than those of individuals. The multicultural nature of the study body added a richness which was essential as business itself became more global and international.

There was nevertheless, a substantial minority of staff who questioned what they saw as an inexorable drive to group work. The grounds for these doubts tended to be; difficulty in establishing individual ability, that tasks were not always appropriate, and the pragmatic reasons that students 'hated' group work, and that it gave staff more problems than marking individual assessments.

On assessments, students were on the whole not always clear about what was required. This was particularly the case when it came to 'correct' English language, grammar, spelling and syntax. Foreign students especially were not clear whether or not it was being assessed. Staff were not always clear either. Fewer than two-thirds gave students formal written guidance on the issue, and in the focus group discussions several admitted to responding to the particular piece of work, or group rather than following criteria consistently. There were no clear or consistent guidelines across the business and management modular degree fields on this, or other aspects of criteria. As a number of staff commented, it was up to the module leader to do what they thought appropriate. Student anxieties about producing work to tutor requirements, finding these contradictory and ambiguous at times, led students to demand more detailed, clearer criteria and guidance on their tasks - particularly as they had to produce them in a short timescale, and when in a group each of the members may have a different interpretation of the requirements.

Staff in the focus groups discussed at length the difficulties of providing unequivocal criteria for complex subjects of business and management. The main criticism of students centred on the seeming inability of many to carry out an analysis rather than merely produce descriptions. This was seen as a particular problem where South East Asian students were concerned, as they came from a different educational culture where such an approach may not be respected.

Clearly then, there are a number of interrelated issues which arise from this research and which. staff and students will, hopefully, be able to debate, gain further insights from, and develop solutions to some of the problems identified.

References

School of Business (1996) Proceedings of the Field Committee Meeting [Joint Subject Honours Degree Business Administration and Management (BA); Single Subject Honours
Degree Business Administration and Management(13M); Single Subject Honours Degree
Business Studies (BS). May 29.

School of Business (1997) BA International Business Management field committee meeting, April 29.

Notes

[1]. The field work was carried out by members of the team; Sue Ledwith (School of Business and Equal Opportunities Action Group), Simonetta Manfredi (School of Languages and Equal Opportunities Action Group), Clive Wildish (School of Business) and Anne Lee, researcher based in the Oxford Centre for Staff Learning and Development.

Appendix 1

TABLE 1.

Language regional grouping	Number of students	% of students
English	104	66%
European Union Catalan Danish French German Greek Italian Portuguese Spanish	22	14%
European non-EU Albanian Bulgarian Hungarian Russian Turkish	7	4%
Asia Cantonese Chinese Hindi Japanese Malay Mandarin Persian Thai	23	15%
Africa/Arabia Arabic Edo	2	1%
TOTALS	158	100%

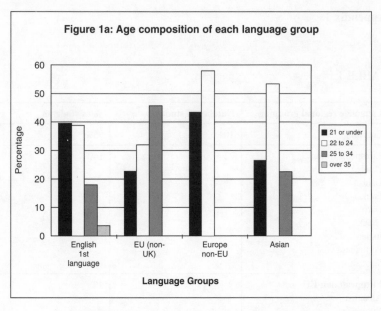

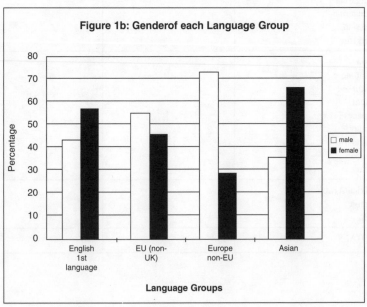

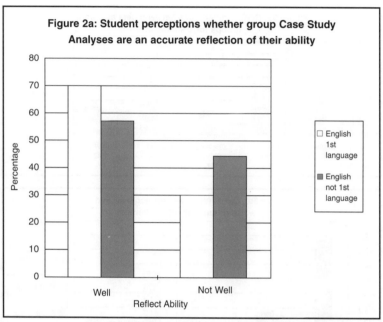

Figure 2a: Student perceptions whether group Case Study Analyses are an accurate reflection of their ability

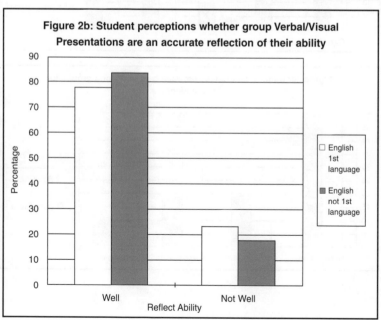

Figure 2b: Student perceptions whether group Verbal/Visual Presentations are an accurate reflection of their ability

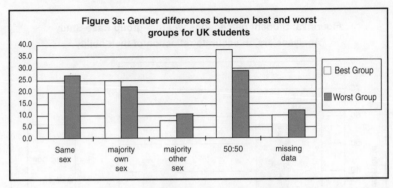

Figure 3a: Gender differences between best and worst groups for UK students

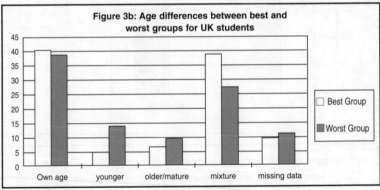

Figure 3b: Age differences between best and worst groups for UK students

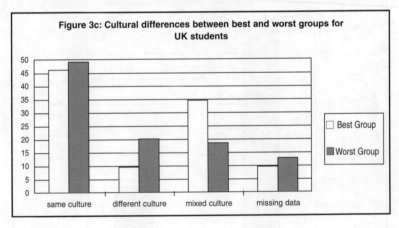

Figure 3c: Cultural differences between best and worst groups for UK students

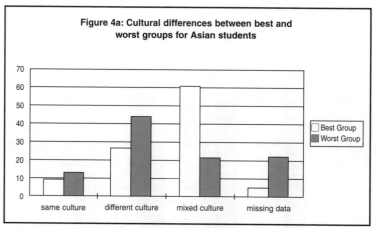

Figure 4a: Cultural differences between best and worst groups for Asian students

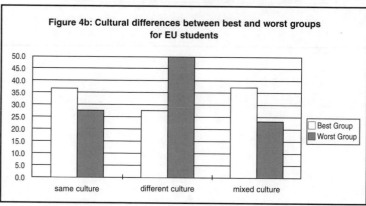

Figure 4b: Cultural differences between best and worst groups for EU students

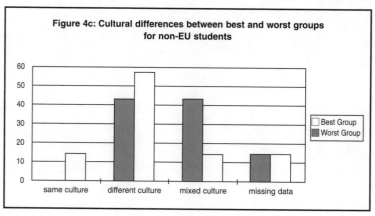

Figure 4c: Cultural differences between best and worst groups for non-EU students

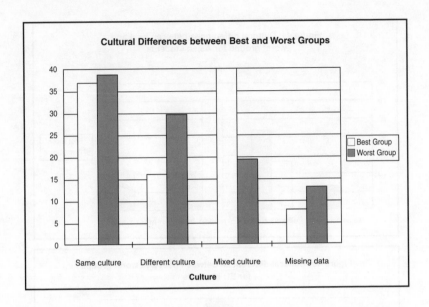

10. Equal Opportunities And The Curriculum: A teaching strategy for Self Directed Learning: Diversity and Culture

Penny Wallace and Sue Rendall - University of Sunderland

Abstract

This paper describes a teaching and learning strategy which is being developed within a professional training programme for social work. The teaching is based on a workbook which uses individual and group based activities and exercises to explore a range of equality issues pertinent to social work. The central aspect of the strategy recognises that personal experience and knowledge is important in developing professional practice; the learning is therefore based on linking own experience and knowledge through using the skills of self-directed learning. The paper explores the ideas which initiated the strategy; gives an overview of how the learning is structured, describes how we have tried to develop critical thinking, and describes the role of the facilitator. The content of the workbook is given section by section, and an evaluation plan is included to demonstrate how the strategy is being currently monitored and refined.

Introduction

The purpose of this paper is to describe how the social work teaching staff at the University of Sunderland have put together a self-directed learning workbook on the subject of diversity and culture.

We drew on a number of ideas and not a little experience of teaching on the subject of anti-oppressive practice. The term anti-oppressive practice means practice which seeks to actively challenge oppression and is used to cover general oppression conditions, structural and personal. Anti-discriminatory practice is similarly practice which actively challenges discrimination; discrimination being a term which is associated with legal concerns. Sometimes these phrases are used interchangeably, but we use them in the way described above. The question of language is an important one and is the most common way to express our feelings and ideas, as such we communicate our culture, ideology and biases. As Hugman succinctly states,

"Language is a central aspect of discourse through which power is reproduced and communicated" Hugman I 991:37

Leaving aside such a contentious issue as structural oppression for the time being, it is perhaps self-evident to state that social workers are working with people who are powerless and vulnerable, such as people with mental health problems, disabled adults and children, people with learning difficulties and so on.

This vulnerability is compounded by the disadvantage which stems from racism, heterosexism, classism and disablism.

The Central Council for Education and Training in Social work, in its guidelines for the knowledge base and practice placement also includes a section on values. (CCETSW Paper 30 revised edition 1995). These value requirements state that:-

"In order to achieve the award of the DipSW, students must demonstrate meeting the core competences and these are based on six specific values. These values must be integrated into practice and must be evident in "all assessable work". See Appendix One.

This position has not been arrived at by travelling a smooth route. Social work practice and education had been substantially criticised for not addressing adequately the effect of racism in service delivery (Commission for Racial Equality, Annual Report 1983). And in 1987, the Director of the National Institute of Social Work, Daphne Statham wrote;-

"Social work has a poor record on race and gender issues .....they (social workers) should demonstrate they can work with black people and in situations where black people are leaders"......

Statham, Community Care 5. 11. 87.

The demand for change was also being advocated by black people themselves academics, students and social workers. Dominelli (1988).

Feminism and the voice of the Women's Movement was also making itself heard and indeed, it is partly from the practice of feminism we have drawn our ideas. In the late 70s and early 80s, there grew a way of raising consciousness which owed something to Paolo Friere's concept of conscientisation. Friere's work focused on literacy as a means for people to learn and find their own voices, because, as he puts it, non literacy supports a "culture of silence", which makes "thinking difficult" and ' speaking is forbidden' . (Friere 1972).

In the second wave Women's Movement, women met together in groups, which were generally unstructured, and discussed, well, whatever they wanted to discuss. For some women this sharing of experiences brought a realisation that they were not alone in feelings of being restricted, or oppressed and stereotyped. They, (or should I say we), reflected on our experiences and from this we could construct an understanding, a knowledge of personal and structured oppression.

Reflection is an important element in this development of "deep learning". And "deep learning" was one of our goals when devising the workbook. We know already the danger of students "just using the correct words" without understanding or without transforming their world view to incorporate any new learning. Boud, Keogh and Walker (1985) see "reflection" in learning as the main component for developing a "deep approach." They define reflection as "the ability to bring ideas to our consciousness", it is seen as "an integral part of the self directed learners pursuit of meaning", (Boud, Keogh and Walker, 1985:162)

So we wanted to create learning groups for students where they could share their experience and combine it with the written information provided and work their way through exercises designed to facilitate the exchange and develop ideas. Above all, we wanted the students to be actively engaged in the process, for, as Barton suggests that tearing involves students participating in an active way to construct knowledge. Barton (1994).

If students are to have active and meaningful conversations which build on their own experiential knowledge this also means re-examining what they already "know". Some students are bringing a wealth of life experience as well as some professional experience; most of our Diploma in Social Work students are 'mature' and many have their own stories of oppression. Sharing these in a structured and safe learning environment could unlock these personal histories and bring new understandings to bear on their professional roles. However, part of the pre-workbook learning contract entails agreement about respecting individuals privacy and a need for confidentiality. The learning environment itself should ideally provide a model of anti-oppressive practice but should also encourage challenging previously held ideas if students are to develop the ability to think critically.

As a staff group we agreed on these ideas and it was a short step to divide out writing our own contribution to the workbook. We continued to meet as a writing group, reading each other's chapters and developing our ideas. We were supported by the Learning Development Unit in the University.

Structure of Learning

The Level One workbook is used in the first semester of the DIPHE / BA (Hons) in Social Work Studies programme. Introduction to the workbook materials and preparation for learning are covered in initial sessions which generally identify the content, aims, learning outcomes, and how students will learn. An overview of the workbook material is presented, layout clarified, and the general aim is made explicit; that is to develop awareness and understanding of anti-oppressive practice. Outcomes, in terms of what learners will need to do to demonstrate awareness and understanding are also made clear.

Learners are divided into groups in which they will work, the boundaries of group working defined, that is learners can choose which areas in the workbook to follow, divide tasks and exercises between them, and consult with other groups to manage the learning process. The role of the tutor is explained and other resources complementary to the workbook activities are identified. Students prepare for learning through a number of experiential activities which are designed:-

i) to introduce them to the benefits of group working, students work together to produce their own ground rules.

ii) to clarify their expectations of the learning and write down their own learning goals. Students are encouraged to share their personal objectives, but they can choose not to do so. What we do ask however, is that they keep their records for final evaluation.

iii) to identify their own learning styles, for example active or passive, rigid or flexible, holistic or serialistic as learners this can help learners to "fit" their learning style into the model of self-directed learning which we use.

These initial activities set the context for an "active" relationship with both peers and facilitators. Problems may arise through discussions, it is important that groups are encouraged to resolve difficulties themselves. These activities emphasise doing, feeling, thinking, and interacting as a valid and meaningful way of learning.

Facilitator / Tutor Role

Within the context of self-directed learning one of the main tasks of the tutor is to enable learners to make the important links between personal and professional knowledge and help them to become more aware and adept at the skills involved in this process. Learners vary in their readiness to work with their personal experiences and there will always be those who cannot explore personal experiences or share values. In managing these links, and the resulting dilemmas and conflicts between personal and professional knowledge there appear to be three interrelated tasks for the facilitator. Described by Taylor (1997) these are; establishing a climate of trust, containing difficult and conflicting feelings, and providing learning opportunities which allow for exploration and linking different areas of knowledge, Taylor (1997: 82).

Overall, we felt that the tutor needs to be sensitive to the group processes in relation to the demanding and emotionally based nature of the learning material and the impact this can have on learners current experience. It is the facilitator's responsibility to create as safe a learning environment as is possible by:-

i) Developing with learners a set of ground rules with respect to behaviour towards each other; for example how to challenge in a constructive way by challenging the idea rather than the person, and how to address confidentiality. We encourage learners to self-regulate when it comes to sharing personal issues.

ii) The facilitator is responsible for physical space and comfort, i.e. to sit comfortably, move around if necessary, privacy for groups.

iii) The facilitator must ensure that any special needs are met, for example learners with hearing, visual, mobility problems. This obviously relies on students declaring these needs.

iv) Responsibility for equipment and resources which learners may need access to, i.e. library facilities, use of video, audio.

The facilitator should provide support for both individuals and groups, by helping to develop supportive networks and making them aware of the stages of group development; forming, norming, storming etc. Facilitators should be prepared to help groups who need help with these stages. What is aimed at is a collaborative style of working, which does not impede group processes, but which provides support at an appropriate level. Creating a climate of trust means not only developing sets of ground rules with learners but also as Brookfield (1993) suggests earning the right to ask others to share themselves by being prepared to share own experiences in a way which does not burden or impose on the group participants.

"In a transactional relationship the facilitator cannot be a blank slate, reciprocity is crucial", Taylor (1997:83).

Containment, the second aspect of the facilitators role, according to Bion (1970), means actively managing the learning process so that learners do not feel exposed or vulnerable. Pietroni (1995) identifies "a state of calm receptiveness that is required for pre-conceptions to be projected, received, reflected upon and given back in an articulate form," Pietroni (1995:40). For us as facilitators this means helping learners to find the "public words" to describe their experience. When "public words" are located the experience is beginning to be understood,. Thompson (1995). It is recognised that learners take considerable risks when voicing their opinions and assumptions in the area of anti-oppressive practice. It is therefore important that facilitators act as containers for powerful feelings and demonstrate anti-oppressive principals by intervening and supporting at appropriate times. For example, learners need to know that tutors will step in if ground rules are seriously disrupted or if group members are being marginalised or oppressed. These situations are challenging for tutors as well as learners, being aware of one's own power is therefore vital.

To manage the third prime task of the facilitator, that is helping learners link different areas of knowledge, and become more "critical" in their thinking, we have devised a way of working with the whole group. To be a reflective practitioner who can negotiate and utilise the many forms of knowledge required for effective practice requires considerable skill. Without the skills of critical analysis evaluation and learning of anti-oppressive practice is very much a superficial exercise. The teaching and learning represented by the workbook begins with this crucial learning process. The facilitator therefore works with the whole group to identify a framework for critical thinking which uses the following principles:

i)   What am I being asked to believe?

ii)   What evidence is there available to support the assertions?

iii)   Are there any alternative ways of interpreting the evidence?

iv)   What additional evidence would help evaluate the alternatives?

v)   What conclusions are most reasonable?

Throughout their learning students are encouraged to use this framework when they work through the workbook materials and then present evidence to the group from their own research activities.

Figure (i) outlines the overall learning framework, and Figure (ii) the actual Workbook content.

Evaluation

The primary aim of our evaluation plan we decided was to improve the quality of learning by developing the current material in terms of accessibility and effectiveness. The effectiveness of the learning materials needed to be evaluated in terms of does it improve practice? Covering competences gained is important, but we also had to take into account for whom the evaluation will be for. In our example the evaluation techniques needed to provide information to a range of other audiences which include the monitoring processes of the University i.e. Quality Board, and Programme Management which includes outside agencies. Evaluation for the development of learners skills was therefore only part of the plan, other audiences had to be considered:- tutors, facilitators, outside agencies, placement providers, and the institution. All of these parties were fully involved in the evaluation process by being made aware of the overall aims of the materials as well as what was being assessed. The strategy therefore covered both development and accountability needs and we did this through both formal and informal modes of collecting data.

Fig (i)

Teaching & Learning Framework

	HOW/PROCESS	CONSTRAINTS	BENEFITS	POTENTIAL DEVELOPMENTS
RESOURCES	Staff Expertise. Enthusiasm & Commitment. University Support. Time to write material	Time needed for negotiation of Learning. Time to write. Appropriate Accommodation	Attending workshop for writing resource based learning. Staff Discussions. Working with practitioners.	Wider audience. Dissemination to other programmes. Uses less staff time in terms of direct teaching.
ASSESSMENT	Matched Learning Aims. ie Reflection leading to awareness & understanding of AOP. Allowed learners to manage own learning & gain feedback from activities & other learners	Need to structure criteria of Learning. Time to write. Appropriate Accommodation	Feedback to learners on an ongoing basis through workbook activities. Also at the end and during formal assessment	More flexible assessment methods to accommodate reflection - "Deep" Approach to Learning
METHODS	Through Resource based Learning - Activities, Group Exercises. Consultation with facilitators Interaction	Some learners may "hang onto" surface learning. Little tutor control.	Learning a new way of learning. Develop deep approach to learning. Peer support. Student centred.	Extend to 2nd Level workbook. Linking with outside practitioners. Wide Dissemination.
PREPARATION FOR LEARNING	Being clear about purpose. Engaging learners with own goals. Creating a supportive Environment. Developing a framework for Critical thinking. Recognising own style of Learning - Benefits of Group Learning.	Varied learning & life experience of Learners. Dominant members of a group. Oppressive behaviour "preserved" Time Needed for Preparation.	Openness to subject matter. How to use learning materials for maximum benefit.	Preparation will become more focused as staff & learners experience widens.
SUPPORT	Peer support & group learning. Facilitors support. Wider University Structures Practice Teachers	Time & availability of Peers & Facilitators. Confidentiality.	Become familiar with skills needed for self directed learning. Working in a team & in partnerships. Dealing with "own issues.	Wider resources/support from partner agencies. Involve more outside practitioners & service users.
EVALUATION	Negotiation with Learners, Tutors, Outside Agencies. Using a Questionnaire designed by students. Formative and Summative Evaluation	Resources to carry through changes. Students become more assertive	Empowerment of learners. AOP becomes more coherent in relation to course structure, for students, staff, Outside agencies. Be able to link theory to practice.	Development of staff skills & knowledge. Using Evaluation more imaginatively.

141

Informal evaluation in education is an inevitable and ongoing activity which is usually carried out unconsciously (Harris & Bell 1990). The balance of power within the informal evaluation we felt should lie with the learners. The criteria for evaluation was therefore worked out with them. They wanted informal evaluation and feedback as the sequence progressed and they agreed that informal evaluation should be by recording their responses to various sections of the workbook. Students decided that formal evaluation (i.e. summative) should be by questionnaire at the end of the module. The evaluation (both formal and informal) involved both learners and facilitators in sharing what was to be judged and how. This meant being open and honest in identifying the strengths and weaknesses of the learning materials. The key focus however in this evaluation plan had to be devising a means of gathering data which would directly involve learners but would also involve the other audiences identified

(Fig ii)	**Content**
Workbook One	**Diversity and Culture in British Context**
Introduction	**Summary Description/Objectives** **Purpose of learning, how to use the material, working in groups.** **Assessment and Evaluation Methods**
Section A Power	**Describes meanings of power, considers own experience of power and effects on others. Recognises who holds power in various groups.**
Section B Historical Perspective	**Recognises difficulty of establishing a "true" historical perspective, outlines the history of immigration, racism and discrimination in Britain. Explains how some discourses come to be privileged. Describes the influence of the myth of Anglo-Saxon superiority. Outlines the history of legislation which affects black people. Race Relation Policy.**
Section C Concepts of Equality &Justice	**Considers the various views of "truth". Identifies situations which demonstrate the different sorts of equality operating in our social system.**

Section D The Impact of Language	**Describes how language is used as symbol and source of power. Communication as a social construct. Considers definitions of oppression.**
Section E Identity	**Defines what is meant by identity and how it is formed. How oppression is internalised. Thinking about ways to break the cycle of internalised oppression.**
Section F What is Racism?	**Establishes definitions of race. Examines ideas and attitudes about race. Suggests how language underpins racism. Recognises how racism is constructed in society.**
Section G Inequality & Oppression	**Recognises the main forms of oppression. Reflects on the diversity of oppression and its multi faceted nature.**
Section H Equal Opportunities	**Identifies legislation related to equal opportunities. Relates Equal Opportunities to structural inequality.**

The questionnaire designed by learners included the following areas:-

i)   Structure of learning materials, were goals understood, was the topic covered in depth required?

ii   Evidence - is this accurate, is it logical, is it relevant to the learners experience, are sources referenced correctly?

ii   Style of writing - is it readable, succinct, is language understandable, are concepts adequately defined?

iv)   Presentation - is it legible, well set out, of reasonable length?

v)   Assessment - is criteria clear, who will assess, who can provide support?

vi)   Transfer of learning- can learning be transferred to other parts of the course, if so how?

vii)   Has self-directed learning, (working in groups, as well as individually) helped you, if so how?

What is not working needed to be addressed as well as what is working. It was made clear to learners who would have access to the data gathered through the questionnaire and who would be responsible for the changes to be made. The aim was to gather the best possible information to meet the credibility of not only learners but also the wider audiences. We negotiated with learners how we would use the results of the questionnaire and also what questions we would be asking outside agencies - for example we would need to gather evidence from practice teachers about learners competence, and the formal results from practice assessment.

The formal and informal means of evaluation in our example means gathering qualitative rather then quantitative information. The summative evaluation gathered the information from learners, tutors, outside agencies to provide a public statement summarising the workbook materials, its accomplishment and limitations. The formative ongoing evaluation undertaken by learners produced some sound data and allowed us to take a good hard look at the effectiveness of the material, but also the summative statement produced included results from all the audiences involved and was used for the quality assurance mechanisms of the University. Both formative and summative will inform decisions about the future of the material. From our experience the evaluation plan adopted served a number of clear purposes.- it gave immediate feedback which allowed for changes to be made as the learning progressed, it helped learners to feel in control of their learning as they were actively involved in designing the means for evaluation and most importantly evaluation became part of the learning process. By seeking evaluation from tutors, assessing outcomes through formal assessment, and consulting with outside practitioners in relation to learners' competence, we were able to satisfy the accountability functions required by the University.

See Figure(iii) for an overview of the Evaluation Strategy.

Conclusion.

At this stage, the workbook has been evaluated. Suggestions from students, staff, and practice teachers have been considered and the revised edition has now been printed.

Some placement agencies were not aware of self-directed learning and we need to ensure all practice teachers have this information. Students wished to know how to use the workbook for referencing, and they wanted more structured facilitation time with tutors. This comment seemed to be about needing clarification about the purpose of the workbook and pre-workbook preparation.

Fig (iii)

Evaluation Strategy

Students (were involved by)	Tutors (were involved by)	Programme Management and Practice Teachers (were involved by)	University
By recording responses to material as they experienced Group Activity.	Availability throughout the learning & responding to formative evaluation by students.	Discussion of learning objectives & content of workbook - Practice Learning Group. (Programme led)	We involved in discussion of learning objectives & content of workbook. (Learning & Development Services)
Questionnaire designed by students & shared with tutors for summative purposes.	Using questionnaire designed by students to review the learning materials.	Provided practice based assessment of learners competence in AOP.	Received summative statement of overall evaluation: - how evaluation had been processed, changes to to be made.
	Tutors accepting responsibility to make changes.	Received summative statement of overall evaluation, how their data was interpreted, & changes to be made.	

Overall the most positive aspect identified by the learners in the evaluation was the style of learning, working in peer groups, and the supportive environment. They thought they had gained a lot from this. It is perhaps too early to make any definitive statements about our goals of enabling "deep learning" to take place, of developing critical thinking, and relating theory to practice, but the early signs are encouraging. As one student commented, " I never knew I knew so much".

References.

Barton, D. (1994). Literacy: *An introduction to the Ecology of Written Language*. Oxford. Blackwell.

Bion, W. (1970). *Attention and Interpretation*. London. Tavistock.

Boud, D.J, Keogh, R. and Walker, D.(1985). *Reflection, Turning Experience into Learning*.
London. Kogan Page.

Boud, D.J, Keogh, R. and Walker, D.(1993) *Using Experience for Learning*. SRHE and O.U. Press. Buckingham.

Brookfield, S. (1993) *Through the Lens of Learning, How the Visceral Experience of Learning Reframes Teaching*. In Boud, D. J. Keough, R. and Walker, D. (1993) Using Experience For Learning. Buckingham. Open University Press.

Central Council for Education and Social Work. *Rules and Requirements in Assuring Quality in the Diploma in Social Work*. Revised Edition (1995).

Dominelli, L. (1988). *Anti-Racist Social Work*. MacMillan.

Friere, P.and Shor, I. (1972). *A Pedagogy For Liberation*. MacMillan.

Harris, D. and Bell, C. (1990) *Evaluation and Assessing For Learning*. Revised Edition. Kogan, Page, London.

Hugman, R. (1991) *Power in the Caring Professions*. Macmillan.

Pietroni, M. (1995) *The Nature and Aims of Professional Education for Social Workers; A Postmodern Perspective*. In Yelloly, M. and Henkel, M.(eds). Learning and Teaching in Social Work; Towards Reflective Practice. London. Kingsley. Statham, D. Community Care. 5. 11. 87.

Taylor, I. (1997) *Developing Learning in Professional Eduacation. Partnerships for Practice*. SRHE and Open University Press. Buckingham.

Thompson, N. *Theory and Practice In Health and Social Welfare*. Open University Press.

Appendix 1

The Values Requirements

In order to achieve the award of the DipSW, students must demonstrate in meeting the core competences that they:

- identify and question their own values and prejudices, and their implications for practice;

- respect and value uniqueness and diversity, and recognise and build on strengths;

- promote people's rights to choice, privacy, confidentiality and protection, while recognising and addressing that control of behaviour will be required at times in order to protect children and adults from harm;

- identify, analyse and take action to counter discrimination, racism, disadvantage, inequality and injustice, using strategies appropriate to role and context; and

- practise in a manner that does not stigmatise or disadvantage either individuals, groups or communities.

From: Rules and Requirements in Assuring Quality in the Diploma in Social Work. August 1995 CCETSW.

11. Teaching Equal Opportunities in a Welsh University Department of Education

Hilary Lloyd Yewlett - University of Wales, Swansea

Abstract

This paper will focus on the teaching of gender and equal opportunities in a PGCE course at a Welsh university during the period 1993-97. It will review the institutional difficulties encountered in setting up the course, together with attempts made to subvert the course contents. It will consider how far institutional hostility towards feminism and female teachers of gender studies is endemic in Welsh university culture. It will compare the Equal Opportunities Policy of t he university as a whole with that practiced in the Department of Education. It will also present external examiners' comments on gender aspects of the PGCE course. In addition, it will consider how far current research emphasis on the underachievement of boys constitutes a backlash against feminism. In conclusion, this paper will analyse students' written evaluations of the Equal Opportunities Gender course content, paying special attention to the evaluations of those students who have never previously encountered gender studies. It will also present the results of in-school investigations into gender and equal opportunities, conducted by students in selected South Wales comprehensive schools. It will seek to discover how far students' limited study of gender and equal opportunities has impacted upon their classroom practice.

Introduction

The examination of gender influences on pupils' achievement is accepted as being an integral part of the professional training of teachers throughout the University of Wales, as perforce it must be, given the legal requirements placed on educational establishments by the Sex Discrimination Act of 1975. Indeed, the assessment of Equal Opportunities teaching in Welsh UDEs is one of the tasks of Her Majesty's Inspectors.(OHMCI, 1995) However, Salisbury (1996) notes that 'a recent content analysis of a sample of OHMCI reports from inspections (of schools) conducted in 1994, has revealed a paucity of commentary on gender and equal opportunities issues generally.'

The present writer was responsible for teaching this component of the PGCE course at Swansea University from 1993-97. However, the exercise of male power and the controlling of female power in dictating the nature of the course is one of the important underlying themes of this paper.

During their thirty six weeks of professional training for teaching, PGCE students at Swansea receive three hours' tuition on the topic of Equal Opportunities. A one hour lecture at the university is followed by an hour's seminar. In addition, students usually participate in a further hour's seminar on the topic at schools in Swansea and the south Wales valleys where they complete their teaching practice. This is usually conducted by a member of the school's staff.

The lecture on Equal Opportunities is one of a series given under the overall title of Professional Studies. Other lectures in the series cover: Home, School and Community Links, Assessment, Pastoral Care, Race, etc. A four thousand word essay on one aspect of the Professional Studies course is mandatory for all students. About 25% of students choose to write on the topic of Equal Opportunities. Of that quarter, about 25% are men.

As in other university departments of education, PGCE students at Swansea come from a variety of academic backgrounds. A minority are mature entrants with varied life experiences behind them. However, the majority are young and newly graduated from conventional academic departments. The demands of the National Curriculum now require us to recruit graduates with 'orthodox' degrees. Most PGCE students know very little about developments in feminist thought and scholarship over the last twenty five years. The exceptions are usually arts graduates from universities other than Swansea.

The ratio of female to male PGCE student intake varies from year to year, depending on the state of the UK economy. Because well-qualified male scientists are offered more lucrative salaries in business and industry than they could earn in teaching, there are invariably more women than men students recruited and the majority of those women are arts graduates. Many of the men find it discomforting to learn about the gender inequalities that have prevailed in education and society over the centuries - but more of that later.

If students choose to write their assignment on Equal Opportunities, then they have a choice of two topics:

- Analyse the text and illustrative material in a small sample of books currently issued to pupils in your teaching subject. Discuss the ways in which the gender images presented in schools' books may influence the expectations and achievements of boys and girls.

- In what ways does the school in which you are currently teaching reproduce traditional gender roles? What efforts are made to implement equal opportunities for boys and girls?

Responses to both questions provided me, as examiner, with perceptive and illuminative observations. However, given the constraints of word length upon me as writer of this paper, I have chosen to present here students' responses to the second question, as these particularly highlighted some interesting and sometimes disturbing events that are occurring in the secondary schools of South Wales.

Of course, in order to respond appropriately to the second question, students must have some understanding of how gender roles have evolved. Consequently, part of the Equal Opportunities lecture which I have given in the past five years has been devoted to the long struggle for women's equality with men, particularly in the sphere of education. It has not made easy listening either for some male students - or for some male colleagues.

Answers to Assignment Two have inevitably revealed some of the changes that are taking place in social attitudes in the valleys of South Wales. Until recently, in these areas, coal mining was the chief means of employment for men. As young men are now forced to consider alternatives to 'going down the pit' in order to earn a living, traditional attitudes towards women and work are very slowly giving way to more progressive ones. For example, in some families, women are the sole breadwinners and men take on the management of the home, because prospects of full-time paid employment for them are poor. Women also found a strong voice in the running of their communities as a result of the miners' strike in the 1 980s. But the pace of change is faster in some areas than others. 'Taffy with attitude' means a very different thing in the Rhondda Valleys from what it denotes in Chelsea and other chic areas of the arts milieu in London.

There are still deeply entrenched patriarchal values in Wales (Betts, 1994, Rees, 1994) which have particular implications for gendered experiences within education at both staff and pupil level. This is evidenced in collections of studies such as *Our Sisters' Land* (Aaron et. al., 1994) and *Our Daughters' Land* (Betts, 1996). To take one example - in the Principality, women have made even fewer inroads into the higher levels of educational management than they have in England. There is no female Chief Education Officer in any of the twenty two new unitary authorities in Wales; there has never been a female Vice-Chancellor in any of the constituent colleges of the University of Wales. There has only ever been one female professor of education in the University of Wales. Less than 12% of secondary school headteachers in Wales are women and the number is decreasing. In the city of Swansea, the sole all-girls' comprehensive school has a headmaster. The all-boys' school does not have a headmistress. Proportions of men to women on the governing bodies of schools show a similar imbalance. However, for the first time in the history of education in

Wales, a woman has been appointed this year as Her Majesty's Chief Inspector for Education Chris Woodhead - take warning!

All Welsh local education authorities have equal opportunities policy statements (Salisbury, 1996) and all students completing this assignment reported that their schools had such a policy. However, not all the schools had a designated teacher responsible for its implementation Salisbury (1996) notes *the extent to which the reduction of staff in LEAs has removed or substantially reformed the role of the specialist equal opportunities officer or adviser.*

Gender imbalance in school management was pointed out by all PGCE respondents to this assignment. Female heads of departments were to be found in the traditionally female areas: English, Modern Languages, Music, Drama, for example. Maths, Science and Technology were invariably headed by men and the majority of teachers of these subjects were men. Support and ancillary staff were almost, without exception, women. All cooking, meal supervision and cleaning was performed by women, *reaffirming,* as one student wrote, *the traditional images of men in control of decision making and discipline, while women service the needs of the school.* Many students observed that, in their schools, messages were being conveyed to pupils that authority is masculine and that it *is men who are the dominant force to be reckoned with.*

Some of the schools used by Swansea University for teaching practice are on split sites. Thus they have a number of staff rooms, some of which are frequented more by one sex than the other. In the male dominated staff rooms, students often heard feminist issues being adversely commented on to the point of ridicule. In the staffrooms most frequented by the women, issues of gender divisions and inequalities were hardly ever discussed.

In one comprehensive school, segregation of pupils according to their sex was perceived to be a normal part of the everyday life of the establishment. Class registers were listed according to gender. Boys' hair *had* to be cut short and girls were not allowed to wear culottes or trousers *at any time of year.* And the winter winds are as cold and uncharitable in Wales as they are in any other mountainous region of these islands! The sporting ethos of all the schools was seen to be predominantly masculine. Welsh media attention and sponsorship are largely concentrated on the sports where men dominate. In the south Wales valleys, there is an emphasis upon more aggressive contact sports, particularly rugby. As a result, rugby and football-playing pupils, who are successful, achieve high prestige among other pupils and some of the staff Sometimes these pupils are low academic achievers, but they are often given time off lessons to practise for an important match.

Emphasis upon success in certain sports was noted as not only excluding girls, but also a number of boys who do not enjoy contact sports or excel in that area. However, many students pointed out that the changes in the local management of schools of recent years present many Welsh valley schools with a dilemma. Schools need to use every means to attract pupils, since Government legislation allows pupils and parents far more choice in their selection. Therefore, schools having a high profile in rugby (which forms the greater part of the national sporting life of Wales) are naturally going to use their success in this field to their best recruitment advantage, for that way lies an additional source of the funding.

An incident occurred in one school which illustrates the *macho* attitudes that are still unfortunately all too prevalent in many areas of school and society in the Principality. A lunch time dance club organised by the school's drama teacher happily attracted support from both boys and girls. The boys were ridiculed with chauvinist comments *from some male members of staff.* The Equal Opportunities Committee at the school circulated a memo to all staff pointing out that in addition to being professionally reprehensible, such behaviour could be classed as harassment. However, the damage had been done, for the male dancers pulled out of the club.

Another school, which in the past had boasted of a Welsh Rugby Cap among its members of staff; formed a working team whose primary purpose was to ensure that both staff and governors were made aware of the issue of Equal Opportunities. A sheet entitled 'Guidelines for Good Practice' was produced and every subject department in the school had access to a copy of Kate Myers' 'Genderwatch'. At this school, class registers are arranged in alphabetical order - the school's new computer database facilitated this task. Pupils are no longer seated according to gender in assemblies, but are arranged in year groups. Thus, from Year Seven, both sexes learn to interact with one another naturally on a day to day basis in school. There is a 'unisex' uniform. Boys and girls wear the same colour sweaters and ties; trousers are optional for female pupils though boys are not permitted to wear jewellery or their hair long.

However, in this school too, there still exists the belief that there are 'male' and 'female' areas of study. For their work experience placements, fourteen boys chose to work closely with computers, whereas only five girls made this choice. My own research (in Betts,1996) confirms this student's findings. After interviewing thirty adolescent girls in two comprehensive schools in Swansea about their marriage, family and career aspirations, I discovered that: *Many of the girls interviewed aspired to careers that were likely to reproduce not only their class position, but also their subservient gender position.*

During the period of their teaching practice, all students became aware of the boys' domination of the conventional classroom. As other more sophisticated researchers have noted (Stanworth,1983) (Mahoney,1985) (Askew,1988) (Ruddock,1994) students also commented on the extent to which boys monopolise teachers' time, attention and resources. One female student experienced at first hand the way *boys can control the women who teach them by adopting a 'male' discourse which emphasises negative aspects of female sexuality and embodies 'direct sexual insult'* (Millard, 1997). Other students observed teachers' differential expectations of gender behaviour. It was not often that they witnessed a teacher intervening and encouraging pupils to view an activity as being equally accessible to both sexes. The incident described in the paragraph above is therefore all the more disheartening for those who attempt to foster equal access to all areas of the curriculum.

In the last two years, performance difference between boys and girls, especially at GCSE level, has received attention from academic researchers and from Her Majesty's Chief Inspector for Schools in particular. Although Chris Woodhead's writ does not run in Wales, concern about the underachievement of boys now occupies the minds of the Education Establishment in Wales as it does in England. Recent press reports (The Observer,7:9:97) however, indicate that this is also a world wide problem.

Swansea's Education Authority has made the underachievement of boys an area of priority attention in its schools, with the result that some schools are organising seminars for their staff on ways of improving boys' performance. Some dubious reasons for boys' underachievement are put forward, for example:

- Adults use more complex language when talking to girls than to boys.

- As an older baby, the boy is far more likely to be smacked than a girl for doing the things which inquisitive babies do even though they have no concept of right or wrong and are not being 'naughty.'

- Girls have dolls with which they make stories, boys have cars with which they make noises.

Counsel such as the following is offered in all seriousness:

Operation Test-Ease: A Programme to combat
Poor Male Performance

Plan your lessons to be more fast paced and to include a series of peaks. Males are more quickly aroused than females but lose interest more quickly. The average secondary school boy has an attention span of four minutes compared to the average girl's fifteen minutes. Girls are multi-tasked; boys are not.

Force the pupils to work in mixed gender pairs or groups. This will have beneficial results for both boys and girls. The boys will use thirty five times more language than they would in boys only groups. The boys will be forced to speak more, the girls will be forced to be more speculative and will benefit from the risk taking approach of the boys.

Sex-role stereotyping will not be eradicated by such interventionist strategies as these.

Keele University's Centre for Successful Schools claims that 'boys' underachievement is *the* gender issue for the nineties.' Provoked into action by this claim, in 1995, the English department of one Swansea comprehensive school embarked on a project which involved segregating two Year Ten English classes into single-sex groups for a period of one week. The girls were taught their four English lessons by a woman, the boys by a man. In the boys' group, a marked change of atmosphere was recorded and thenegative ambience was reflected in poor classroom behaviour and performance. The boys were much more ebullient and were difficult to settle at the start of the lessons. Those who were normally 'quite forthcoming' in a mixed sex group were now reluctant to contribute, while the previously quiet ones tended to make flippant remarks. The student teacher at this school commented: *This seems to give testimony to the research which shows that single-sex boys' groups tend to create inferior sub-groups and that some are reluctant to be seen to be working hard, for fear of censure of 'feminine' behaviour.* She noted that the girls were noisier than had been anticipated, but were very willing to contribute ideas to discussions and to share examples of their written work.

The post-project questionnaire responses showed that 32% of the girls saw 'having more confidence to contribute' as one advantage of a single-sex classroom. Astonishingly, 76% of them thought that the class 'wouldn't share as many ideas', since 'the boys aren't afraid to speak up.' Again, the student-teacher remarked: *This finding seems to reflect the research on boys' domination of teacher time and attention, suggesting also that girls' confidence is lessened as a consequence.*

Sufficient evidence has been presented here to show that male power and female subordination to it is still a live issue in the schools of Wales, as it is in the university department of education where I taught this course. At the beginning of this paper I indicated that some male students and staff felt uncomfortable when confronted with the facts about the unequal treatment of women in all societies. In the post-lecture seminars, a few of them took the obvious line: *But there is no problem here.* However, some students were sufficiently disturbed by my lecture on *Equal Opportunities: Gender* to raise the following points at the Staff-Student committee in January 1997:

- The overly historical background material was unnecessary

- The relevance of the lecture to the seminar was unclear

- Direct links with the current school situation should have been made more explicit.

According to the Minutes of that meeting, the PGCE Secondary Course Director agreed to take up these matters with the lecturer concerned. It is interesting to note here that in the Minutes of the Staff-Student Consultative Committee meeting of October 1996, the following point was made about Professional Studies lectures:

It was also felt that some lectures were politically biased, but one purpose of seminars is to challenge and present alternative views.

No such advice was proffered to students who were unhappy with the content of the *Gender* lecture. As the Spring term of 1997 progressed, I received, without a covering note, from the PGCE Secondary Course Director, several press cuttings and book reviews on the subject of underachieving boys. Then, on March **5th,** the following hand-written memo came, quite by accident, into my possession:

W-,
PS. <u>Gender</u> <u>Issues</u>
A- came up with some names, and some very interesting ideas for replacing HY's contribution with one on 'Underachieving Boys"

Names:	BC (female) M.Ed. on subject at D- School
	EF (female) doing M.Ed. at G- School

There is also HI (Female) (3-School).. ask KL (female member of staff) about this. I suggest you have a chat with A about his ideas.
Given that, based on the above, you can put something in place, then we (Head of Department, me, you (!)) can explain to HY why she is being replaced.
Keep me in touch.
S.

I sent a sharply worded memo to the Course Director and received an equally tart response. I quote from it here:

You will be aware that a programme such as Professional Studies is kept under review so that it meets students' needs, course requirements and quality assurance measures. To imply that a change would be made because an offering puts forward 'controversial or unpopular opinions' is as insulting as it is wrong.

I considered, and explored the possibility of replacing your session on 'Equal Opportunities-Gender' with one on 'Underachieving boys' for two reasons:

1. this is THE most important and relevant aspect of gender issues in secondary schools today;

2. not for the first time, there were adverse comments from students about the content of the Equal Opportunities - Gender session.

I had previously spoken to you about this and sent you various materials and suggestions. Having had no response from you to this, or from you about the concerns minuted in the Staff-Student consultative committee, I then initiated an exploration of other possibilities...

My concern, as always, is for the quality of the course and the best interest of the students.

It is clear from the Course Director's hand-written memo that his intention was not merely to ensure the treatment of the currently topical issue of boys' underachievement, but also to remove *Equal Opportunities: Gender* from the curriculum, without any prior consultation with me. It is evident that a clear attempt was being made to eliminate this material from the course and to present me with *a fait accompli.*

Even Chris Woodhead (1996) acknowledges that:

The issue of boys' achievement must, however, be seen within the context of the overall issue of the provision of equality of opportunity for boys and girls. Girls currently achieve relatively well at age 16, but we have concerns about some aspects of their education too; not least the serious fall-off after 16 in their participation in subjects which could lead to careers in science, engineering and technology. Any national debate about education and gender must take continual account of both sexes in an attempt to ensure not that they achieve equally, but that each has equal opportunity to reach their full potential. Girls and boys need an education which prepares them equally for the challenges and opportunities presented by the changing world of work. The evidence suggests that though some schools demonstrate very good practice others have a considerable way to go.

At the end of *The Gender Divide* (1996) appears the following: *The inspection evidence tends to suggest that girls' schools in average and disadvantaged areas, and **boys' schools more generally, do relatively little to broaden pupils' horizons beyond traditional and often stereotypical expectations...Boys' schools should pay** particular attention to...boys' perceptions of themselves, their future roles in life, and the skills they will need if they are to fulfil their potential... Girls' schools should look at girls' selection of subjects and future destinations, and plan ways of raising **standards and aspirations further and counteracting any residual stereotypical attitudes.***

Stereotypical attitudes towards gender issues continue in some faculties of the University of Wales as they do in Welsh society as a whole. However, if the concept of a university is to mean anything in the twenty first century, then such attitudes must pass away as completely as the first millennium. For what is clear from the evidence presented in this paper is that, at present, female subordination remains intact in some areas of the education system. It is time that our society acted upon the words of the gentle, German poet, Rilke: *Men and women should be united by their humanity and not divided by their sexuality.*
We must teach that precept to *all* our children.

Acknowledgements:

I would like to thank those students who, over the past four years, have furnished me with some of the material presented in this paper.

References:

Aaron,J.,Rees,T.,Betts, S. and Vincentelli, M. (1994) *Our Sisters' Land The Changing Face of Women in Wales,* Cardiff University of Wales Press.

Askew,S. and Ross, C. (1988) *Boys don't Cry: Boys and Sexism in Education,* Milton
Keynes: Open University Press.

Betts, S. (ed.)(1996) *Our Daughters' Land,* Cardiff: University of Wales Press.

EOC, OFSTED (1996) The Gender Divide: Performance Differences between Boys and Girls at School, London: HMSO

Mahoney, P.(1985) *Schools for Boys?* London: Hutchison:

Millard' E.(1997) *Differently Literate: Boys, Girls and the Schooling of Literacy,* London: The Falmer Press.

Myers, K (1992) *Genderwatch!* Press Syndicate of the University of Cambridge.

OHMCI (1995) *Inspection in Initial Teacher Training,* Cardiff: OHMCI.

Ruddock, 3. (1994) *Developing a Gender Policy in Secondary Schools,* Milton Keynes: Open University Press.

Salisbury, 1 (1996) *Educational Reforms and Gender Equality in Schools, Cardiff:* Equal Opportunities Commission

12. 'Mathematics is Mathematics': An Analysis of the 'Gender Dimension' of the Curriculum in Higher Education

Barbara Bagilhole and Jackie Goode - Loughborough University.

Abstract

This paper draws on data from a qualitative research study undertaken in an old UK university. The main aim of the study was to measure the impact of gender issues on the university campus, an important part of which was the issue of the curriculum. A total of 37 academic, academic-related and technical women and men staff, at all levels and across all schools, were interviewed in depth using semi-structured interview schedules. Individuals were found to operate either a 'narrow' or 'broad' definition of the term 'curriculum'. In either case, there was found to be a 'gender dimension' involved. In male-dominated disciplines a 'narrow' definition of the term 'curriculum' was predominantly in use - appropriate discipline content and an unproblematic body of knowledge, which is to be transferred to students largely by lecturing. In the broader definition of the curriculum, the gendered division of labour in the domestic sphere was repeated in the university, with the result that the division 'rational/emotional' became an aspect of the masculine/feminine divide in a way which disadvantaged women.

Introduction

Most of the debates about, and research on the operation of gender factors in the educational curriculum have been school-based. The focus has been on what constitutes appropriate subject content, on physical provision, on the gendered construction of knowledge, on classroom interaction, and on appropriate assessment methods. Such questions are on the agenda in a number of countries:

> *In France the very term 'pedagogy' has been taken as the symbol, if not the scapegoat, of the controversy between those who hold that schools should concern themselves exclusively with instruction and those who hold that schools should also have an educative role which includes instruction but which also takes responsibility for the conditions under which one learns and the civil, social and moral aspects of education.* (Best, 1988)

Pedagogy is of course only one aspect of education. As Martin (1995) observes, pedagogy is embedded in a larger educational system consisting of curricular goals and subject matter, institutional forms and structures, definitions of the functions of the institution, and conceptions of an educated person. To treat issues such as low female self-esteem, male harassment of females, and curricular misrepresentation of girls and women as unrelated phenomena is to ignore the connections between knowledge and power, and between gender and education. It allows the underlying beliefs and practices to remain hidden and go unchallenged, and perpetuates the status quo of the male structuring and shaping of knowledge.

As Gipps (1995) documented, recent work in cognitive and constructivist psychology showed learning in terms of an organic process of reorganising and restructuring as the student learns, rather than of an external map transposed directly into the student's head. Cognitive theory suggests that learning is a process of knowledge construction that is context-related. Teaching is therefore an intervention in an ongoing knowledge construction process, where students learn best by actively making sense of new knowledge, making meaning from it and mapping it into their existing knowledge map or schema. Head (1995) catalogued a number of gender differences which affect learning style, and concludes that those who teach 'should be eclectic in their choice of teaching and assessment methods,' whilst Schulman (1987) promoted a repertoire of strategies for providing effective curricula to all students, including preparation of texts, the representation of ideas via appropriate analogies and metaphors, a selection of teaching methods and models, an adaptation of these to the particular group being taught, and formative assessment - or assessment which supports learning.

If, as Ausubel (1968) suggested, 'the most important single factor influencing learning is what the learner already knows,' the operation of gender in learning becomes crucial. It may be, as Gipps (1995) suggested, that girls' lower take-up of science and mathematics careers is to do with 'ownership' of the subject area, which encompass defining and legitimating the knowledge, as opposed to simple achievement within it. If girls are achieving but not really engaging with such subjects, there is less likely to be the motivation to overcome social and cultural pressures to break the norms.

The curriculum in Higher Education has received much less research attention, especially in the area of 'equal opportunities' (EO) implications or innovations. One exception is Becher (1989) who has looked at the ways that academics defend their disciplines, and de Groot (1997) who describes academic work as 'gender-blind/biased and masculinist scholarly theory, method and practice' (p.131). It is seen that knowledge hierarchies, with the denigration of 'soft' female-identified subjects below hard disciplines where men predominate, favour the concerns and interests of men (Smith, 1992; Spender and Sarah, 1980). Despite this, Bird (1996) points out that there has been a general national and international growth in the numbers of Women's Studies courses, and hence the numbers of students studying this discipline. Stiver Lie *et al.* (1994) showed this in their study of 17 countries. In fact in countries where there is governmental involvement in curriculum design, there has been direct encouragement for its establishment (Bird, 1996). However, some have argued that Women's Studies incorporation into academia has diluted and tamed its radical roots (Richardson and Robinson, 1994; Bagilhole, 1995).

Driven by both feminism, and by changes from an elite to a mass system of Higher Education, re-evaluation of curricula is now underway. Innovation now taking place in universities seems to have come from three directions. Firstly, EO specialists are now beginning to undertake EO audits of the curriculum. Secondly, where women scholars are themselves represented, *completely new curricula* have appeared as a result of feminist endeavours. And thirdly, in the traditionally male-dominated science and engineering disciplines, concerns have centred around *access to subjects* where female representation is poor.

All three dimensions have been at work in the university used as a case study in the research reported here, and have resulted in mixed responses from different disciplines. The male-dominated disciplines of Science and Engineering have largely maintained a 'narrow' view of the curriculum, and in disciplines where a 'broader' view has been taken there still remains a gender dimension to it.

The Study

In 1992, a study was commissioned of EO issues for women, ethnic minority and disabled academics at the University (Bagilhole, 1992). At the time this was a relatively new area of interest and development in the University. An EO working party had led to the establishment of the EO Committee, but no formal procedures had been introduced. The study highlighted both structural barriers to EO and informal cultural issues. Subsequently, the University appointed a half-time EO Officer. It adopted formal procedures and codes of practice in the areas of recruitment, selection, probation, promotion, appraisal, and careers guidance, set up a sexual harassment panel, and joined Opportunity 2000. The present research was intended to chart the progress made since the study. The research project focused on gender divisions within the University and examined a series of research questions including the appropriateness of curriculum design.

Methodology

The study used a combination of analysis of available quantitative and qualitative data and the collection of additional information through interviews with key informants. Thirty-seven semi-structured interviews were conducted across the whole university and were analysed using the Nud*ist software package. The interviews included women and men, lecturers, heads of departments, Deans, the Vice-Chancellor, personnel, training andtechnical staff.

Findings - the 'narrow' and 'broad' definitions of curriculum

The term 'curriculum' was not seen as problematic by respondents, although it became apparent in interviews that individuals could operate either a 'narrow' or a 'broad' definition of this term. The curriculum might be taken as simply referring to the topics to be covered in a particular course or module, rather than the whole process of teaching and learning and all the activities in their various contexts which take place during that process.

Gender and the 'narrow' curriculum

In the Science and Engineering faculties in particular, the nature of the curriculum itself tended to be seen as uncontentious and unproblematic - 'Mathematics is Mathematics,' as one senior academic commented, when asked about gender and the curriculum. A 'narrow' definition of the term 'curriculum' was predominantly used, as referring to an unproblematic body of knowledge which is to be transferred to students largely by lecturing. Adherents to this definition apparently had not engaged with broader definitions of curriculum, which include the 'informal curriculum'. Concerns in these departments centred around access. In practice however, this referred to access to courses, in terms of recruitment of undergraduates, and did not encompass access to the curriculum itself, or considerations of how far there are differentiated curricula and therefore differential access to and engagement with particular aspects of the curriculum.

Interviews showed that both awareness of issues, and activity in curriculum innovation, was highest in the Social Sciences and Humanities where a gender dimension has been introduced into the curriculum. The response of students varied:

> *Because I've taught feminist courses, there sometimes have been challenges from both men and women to this, but they've been intellectualised rather than personalised, and that has sometimes been very rewarding to have that brought out into a class.*

Senior academic, female.

The popularity of such courses with students allayed early reservations, and paved the way for a gender dimension to many other courses:

... until a few years ago, issues of gender were not raised in the undergrad. programme ... and I can remember with many students, their response was, What's this all about? They thought it was unimportant - both the women students and the men. I can remember this very clearly. They just thought, Oh dear! This is crazy feminists. And that's not the case now. I think it's just the general raising of awareness of gender issues. I think it's very important, because I can remember being one of the ones who lectured on this issue, and I did it with a degree of trepidation, especially with the first year students because the response could be very varied. But it's not the case now. I feel that that is real evidence of change ... which I think is very important, and I can say that with authority simply because I was in on it in the early days, and I see the difference now.

Senior female academic.

However, forays into departments with few women students or staff, by visiting staff who gave gender-related lectures or presentations, had on occasion elicited a hostile response. The difficulties to be overcome in order to undertake a gender-sensitive evaluation of the curriculum in these departments stemmed from the evaluations of the staff themselves of what the problem was and where it was located. Distinct positions could be identified, each with its own implications for gender and the curriculum, and for necessary action.

The first was the continuing view that any 'problem' lay 'out there' rather than 'in here':

I think we have to be careful not to imply that we are currently doing something wrong. I don't believe we are doing something wrong. Maybe we're not doing everything we could be doing, but I don't know of anything that we're doing wrong ... sometimes I think ... they imply that because we have for example low participation rates in women, we're doing something wrong, and that we need to put it right. Well, we need to put something right but not because we're doing anything wrong. We just need to do more, we need to put more effort in.

Senior male academic

This position led to the view that the further action which was required was simply a better selling job, and therefore there was no need to examine current curriculum practice:

In Engineering (poor representation of women) is a battle that needs to be fought in the schools ... Engineering has a reputation of being low-grade dirty work, its a status thing ... so its a PR job I think we've got to do much more in terms of selling Engineering as an enjoyable and challenging and exciting and creating thing to do ... more of the same I think, these visits that we have ... both school students and careers officers to come, and we try to sell what's done in Engineering

Senior male academic

Another aspect of the view that the problems lay 'out there' was that what we did 'in here', in terms of the curriculum, was seen as dictated by the demands of industry. The engineering industries were perceived to be hostile to women, and to judge women students more harshly than male students, but the function of the curriculum was seen to be to equip women undergraduates to operate in the 'real world' The University was seen to serve them best therefore by equipping them to cope with, rather than to challenge discrimination, when they leave:

In this department where we send students out into quite difficult environments, we send them out to factory floors where they're supposed to be in charge - the first job our students will get quite often, the manager will say, 'There's your production line, there are 12 people working on it, you're now in charge of it - get efficiency up by 20%'. We have to have a fairly robust attitude to learning here, in order that they can react to that in a positive way. We can't spoon-feed them here and then expect them to go out in to the real world.

Senior male academic

The fact that the 'real' engineering world discriminated against women was recognised, but once again the change that was seen to be required was in the women themselves - they must learn to adjust to it, cope with it, become fitted to it:

Basically I think industry has an attitude that, if they're a male graduate and they're not performing, its because they're not very good. If it's a female graduate that's not performing, it's because they're a woman ... 'she's no good, she's a woman', or 'he's no good because he's stupid' ... I think the average female graduate has to be a little bit better than the average male graduate to be treated equally ... because there's a very strong body of prejudice in the engineering world among employers and employees ... I think all that we can say is that we look at it as part of life and we recognise that men and women experience different problems in life and therefore that the

163

problems that they will have on this course reflect real life ... I'd say life is unfair to women ... in the industrial world, it's either neutral or unfair, it's very rarely positive ... are you asking should we be preparing female students for the roles or the experiences they will experience in industry? I think at the end of the day we try and treat every student as individual but at the same time we give them the same training. We wouldn't sort of tailor what we do here specifically for females or males - they go through exactly the same process.

Senior male academic

In the same way that Willis' (1977) male working class school students were 'learning to labour,' women Engineering undergraduates at the university would appear to be learning to be discriminated against. The role of the University was seen by staff in senior positions simply to prepare them for 'real life,' and anything else was seen as unfair. Both the formal and the informal curricula remained gender-blind in their operation, and in the name of equality it was seen as necessary to treat all students 'the same'.

The third obstacle to gender-sensitive curricula was to do with the kind of Engineering courses offered, and the kinds of students attracted as a result. In interviews, comparisons were made with other institutions, which attract more women. These offered courses which could be used as 'stepping stone' to other occupations:

Engineering is seen as a stepping stone. Engineering is the classics of today - people use Engineering as a way of getting a degree from a good institution which they then go into all kinds - accountancy, management - you're numerate, you're good at solving problems, you're IT literate to a good degree. So an Engineering degree can be used as a stepping stone, rather than as a training and an education for a job and a profession

Senior male academic

This university on the other hand was seen as offering training for those who were looking to pursue a professional career in engineering. This meant that the teaching group was more homogeneous, and by implication a narrower range of teaching methods were employed, from the more traditional position of 'expert' whom one cannot question:

I'm not a stepping-stone person. I like Engineering, I want to do Engineering ... so I enjoy working with the students - there's a contrast, more of our students want to study Engineering because they want to do Engineering as a profession ... and its easier to teach, because you're of a like mind, whereas if you're talking to someone who is only doing it so he can apply to a different job, there's a different relationship there: they question why you're teaching them.

As above

Women Engineering students at the university who experienced limitations on access to the curriculum as currently designed and delivered found the homogeneity of a predominantly male group, the teaching style, and the compatibility between the two, difficult to question. It was even difficult for women students to challenge male academics over matters of language. A senior female academic argued that women students found 'steering a middle course' difficult:

I think they lack a certain kind of confidence which is valued highly in professional life generally. I see this even in the good women students. They are rarely the people who will speak out in seminars and make their own space, and make themselves known. I almost want to push them and say, 'go on, get in there'. You've really got to risk a lot. They lack a kind of audacity sometimes, and I think this does tend to carry on, and if they are assertive and audacious this can have a backlash effect on them as well. You're in a bit of a no-win situation really. You're diffident and you get overlooked and you're the opposite of diffident and you're seen as shrill, strident, you know all those other terms that are given to women, so its difficult. It's possible, but I think it's difficult to steer a middle course between those.

Senior academic, female.

The unwillingness of the Engineering faculty to conceive of the problem of the under-representation of women *in these terms* with all the implications for curriculum change, may represent a continuing obstacle to a gender-sensitive curriculum, and to the further recruitment of women. Nevertheless, such recruitment represented a continuing objective, albeit for reasons which included the stereotyped view of women students as exerting a variation of the 'civilising influence' theme:

[Do you think it matters?]
I do. I actually think the atmosphere changes ... you don't need 50 per cent for the atmosphere to change. But you need a critical mass as it were, 10 or 15. And the atmosphere in lectures changes, the atmosphere in group work changes. You get less silliness, you know, joking, and you get more, it doesn't become more formal, but it becomes more a workaday-type atmosphere.

Senior male academic

However, it may be that the reverse is true - in order successfully to recruit and retain women, Engineering departments themselves may have to become more 'civilised,' and this will involve some more radical self-evaluation than they appear at present willing to undertake.

The 'broad' curriculum: but still a gendered division of labour

To make a revolutionary feminist epistemology, we must relinquish our ties to traditional ways of teaching that reinforce domination ... we must focus on the teacher-student relationship and the issue of power' (Hooks, 1989, 52).

Early on in the research the question arose of how far the gendered division of labour, which remains the dominant pattern in the domestic sphere, was repeated at work, including the 'emotion-work' typically done by women. James (1989) drew parallels between divisions of *emotional* labour in the home, and at work. She showed how the division 'rational/emotional' became an aspect of the masculine/feminine divide: women exercised greater *skill* in recognising, anticipating and empathising with the moods of others, and they also undertook a form of *work* in trying to bring those moods into line with the image of happy family life. However, in a male-dominated society, such 'emotion work' or 'emotional housework' remains virtually invisible and goes largely unrewarded. The same can be true of women's emotional labour in paid employment. The parallels between the nurturing aspects of the parenting role which have been found to be more central to women's performance of it than to men's (Lewis and O'Brien, 1987) and the teaching and pastoral care of students, are obvious. As West and Lyon (1995) commented, 'at times it seems that women provide the substructure of collegiality, while individuals, individual men, excel.'

Interviewees in this study felt that there were gender differences in the way pastoral duties were undertaken. Men as well as women felt that men were less inclined to undertake the emotion-work involved in supporting student learning:

... it manifests itself I think in two ways - firstly, one is given administrative duties that involve pastoral care, but also, other male members of staff make no secret of the fact that they try and distance themselves from students - don't want to get involved in pastoral care - things like 'I don't expect to see my personal tutees from one year's end to the next, and make a virtue out of not knowing who they are. So one feels obliged as it were to pick up the pieces. You get it coming through from students - you ask them who their personal tutor is when they come to you with a problem and you recognise that that isn't the kind of person who is going to be able to help them ... (they come) often

under the guise of coming to see me about academic work to do with the kind of stuff that I teach, and then it transpires that there's other things going on

Female Lecturer.

The women who found students at their door did not necessarily see themselves as having particular strengths in this area, but neither did they feel able to turn students away:

I don't think of myself as a terribly caring, sympathetic sort of person. I'm always amazed at how many of these people end up on my doorstep. I don't think I've got particular strengths in that regard - I think I've got quite good problem-solving abilities and I know where to send people for better advice than I can give them ... I always say 'Well you really ought to be talking to your personal tutor about this'. But I wouldn't turn somebody away.

Female Lecturer.

I see it absolutely everywhere, women looking after the students and doing the student liaison, and looking after the difficult ones and the lost ones ... women get trapped into the caring roles - the students who need cosseting, and the 'Oh well, you're much better at that so you can do this'. The male gets on and writes the paper that gets him the promotion. while the woman's still stuck doing the supporting-the-students ... women can very easily find huge amounts of their time mopped up in supporting - student supervision for example - huge amounts of efforts into supporting the not-so-able student, whereas the male project supervisor will take the much more hands-off, 'Well if they're drowning, let them drown' kind of thing

Senior academic, female.

Formal systems of allocating teaching and administrative loads were essential, but they did not typically address the thornier issue of informal mechanisms such as stereotyping which led to women undertaking work, aspects of which were intrinsically more labour-intensive if performed well - such as relationships with students as part of the broader 'informal curriculum'.

You can either change the system or you can change the characteristics of the female members of staff. Changing the system's fairly difficult ... It would be unfair of me to have an internal performance measure which told people to do certain things which then wasn't rewarded by the external University-

wide system ... but should I accommodate the fact that female members of staff have different ways of working to males, then I think that would be seen as favouritism, and it would be seen as a style of positive discrimination and I certainly couldn't initiate that, I'd get ripped to pieces.

Senior academic, male.

Conclusion

There would appear to be two definitions and interpretations of the term curriculum in action in Higher Education: the 'narrow' and 'broad' definitions. This research indicated that this definitional split lay largely along discipline lines. In male-dominated disciplines the idea that the curriculum is 'the delivery of traditional facts to students in traditional ways' held firm. In other disciplines, where women were present in greater numbers, gender dimensions had been considered, seen to add depth to academic pursuits, and been well received by students. However, a note of caution must be sounded, even when the 'broader informal curriculum' is recognised. It may be that when the 'softer' approach to teaching, which recognises individual student needs, is adopted, it falls disproportionately on women to undertake this role. In other words, there appears to remain a gender dimension to both 'narrow' and 'broad' interpretations of the curriculum.

References

Ausubel, D.P. (1968) *Educational Psychology: A Cognitive View*. Holt, Renehart and Winston, New York.

Bagilhole, B. (1992). *On the Inside: Equal opportunities in Academic Life. A Research Report on Women, Ethnic Minority and Disabled Academics*, Department of Social Sciences, Loughborough University.

Bagilhole, B. (1995) 'Can Women's Studies affect change in universities? Some views from women academics on the inside', Bradford University Women and Society Seminar Programme (February) Bradford.

Becher, T. (1989). *Academic Tribes and Teritories: Intellectual Enquiry and the Cultures of Disciplines*, SRHE/Open University Press, Milton Keynes.

Best, F. (1988) The metamorphosis of the term 'pedagogy' *Prospects*, Vol XVIII, no.2, pp157-166.

Bird , E. (1996). 'Women's Studies in European Higher Education', *European Journal of Women's Studies*, 3, 151-65.

de Groot, J. (1997). 'After the Ivory Tower: Gender, commodification and the "academic"', *Feminist Review,* No. 55, Spring, 130-42.

Gipps, Caroline (1995) *Towards appropriate and effective pedagogies.* Institute of Education, University of London, April 1995.

Head, John (1995) *Gender Identity and Cognitive Style,* UNESCO/Institute of Education Colloqium, London.(see 86)

Hooks, B. (1989). *Talking Back: Thinking Feminist - Thinking Black,* Sheba Feminist Press, London.

James, N. (1989) Emotional Labour: Skill and Work in the Social Regulation of Feelings. *The Sociological Review,* Vol 37.

Lewis, C. and O'Brien, R. (eds) (1987) *Fatherhood Reassessed.* London Sage.

Martin, Jane Roland (1995) A Girls 'Pedagogy In Relationship', paper to UNESCO colloqium, reported in Gipps, Caroline (1995) *Towards appropriate and effective pedagogies.* Institute of Education, University of London, April 1995.

Richardson, D. and Robinson, V. (1994) 'Theorizing Women's Studies, Gender Studies and Masculinity: The Politics of Naming', *European Journal of Women's Studies,* 1, 1, 11-27.

Schulman, L.(1987) Knowledge and Teaching: Foundations of the New Reform, *Harvard Educational Review,* Vol 57, no.1, pp1-22.

Smith, D. (1992). 'Women's perspective as a Radical Critique of Sociology', in Humm, M. (ed.) *Feminisms: A Reader,* Harvester Wheatsheaf, Hemel Hempstead.

Spender, D. and Sarah, E. (1980). *Learning to Lose,* The Women's Press, London.

Stiver Lie, S., Malik, L., and Harris, D. (eds.) (1994). *The Gender Gap in Higher Education,* World Yearbook of Education , Kogan Page, London.

West, Jackie and Kate Lyon.(1995) The Trouble with Equal Opportunities: the case of women academics. *Gender and Education,* Vol 7, No.1, 51- 68.

Willis, Paul (1977) Learning to Labour: how working class kids get working class jobs. Farnborough, Hants. Saxon House.

13. "I don't want to be empowered, just give me a reading pack!": Student Responses and Resistance to Different Forms of Teaching and Assessment

Gayle Letherby and Jen Marchbank - Coventry University

Abstract

In this paper we address the practical problems of student-centred and feminist pedagogical approaches to teaching and learning in Higher Education. We are concerned with reflecting and discussing our experiences of introducing feminist pedagogy and new methods of teaching and assessment to all the classes that we teach. In doing so, this piece focuses specifically on our perceptions rather than those of our students. We discuss the methods we have developed to address issues of equal opportunity in the classroom and the curriculum and consider students' negative and positive responses to these methods.

Introduction

Empowerment has become something of an educational and training 'buzzword', a fashionable concept which has been institutionalised within non-traditional educational environments such as youth and community work (Morley, 1995). In this context it has been taken to mean the promotion of equality of opportunity and participation. Similarly, empowerment has been used in other contexts to imply the development of individualism and the skills required for self assertion and advancement rather than any analysis of the roots of powerlessness and the structures of systemic oppression (Lather, 1991 cited in Morley, 1993). The definition that we employ both in this paper and in our pedagogy in akin to the latter analysis and to the concepts held dear to youth work. This is not simply a political position that we hold but a position that has developed from our respective experiences of research, teaching and community work.

This paper reflects our teaching autobiographies, it is written by 2 female 30 something senior lecturers who teach in the same subject group in the School of Health and Social Sciences in a Midlands 'New University'. Jen, a political scientist by background, researches and writes on the policy making process, in particular how marginalised groups and interests within communities get their voice heard in political bureaucracies (Marchbank, 1994, 1996). She also has experience of both state and voluntary sector youth and community work, specifically with girls and women. Presently she is Course Leader for the Women's Studies and Social Science degree in the University where we work and teaches (and is developing further modules) on all three levels of the degree. Gayle is a sociologist with a research background in motherhood/non-motherhood, family, health and methodology and epistemology (Letherby 1994; Cotterill and Letherby 1993,1994; Letherby and Zdrokowski 1995). Until recently she was Project Tutor for the Applied Social Science Degree and Women's Studies and Social Science Degree but is now Course Leader for the Single Honours Sociology Degree plus Course Leader for several joint programmes. Gayle teaches a range of modules over all three levels in both Sociology and Women's Studies.

Although we come from different academic backgrounds and teach different specialisms we have many academic interests in common (particularly in relation to feminist theory and epistemology) and we share a commitment to developing/helping to create teaching and learning practices and spaces which are non-hierarchical (as far as possible) and empowering. As part of this project we are currently engaged in a piece of research with 'our'students entitled *'Why do Women's Studies'*. At present there is a fair amount of autobiographical writing by, and research on, women who work as teachers/tutors in Women's Studies in particular and HE in general (eg Barnes-Powell and Letherby 1997; Davies et al 1994; Morley and Walsh 1996) but little on student experience (the exceptions being Griffin 1994 and Coate-Bignell 1996). Coate-Bignell (1996, p315) advocates that a feminist praxis which can inform the wider practices of feminist scholarship "..could be built from the experiences within the Women's Studies classroom". From our research we hope to add to the facilitating of this student voice and experience. Coate-Bignell argues that, due to this omission of student perspectives, it becomes apparent that the principles of feminist pedagogy may themselves need to be subjected to a process of reflexive, critical thinking(Coate-Bignell, 1996, p323).

As such we are concerned here with reflecting and discussing our experiences of introducing, and attempting to introduce, feminist pedagogy and new methods of teaching and assessment to all classes that we teach (be they Sociology, Social Policy or Women's Studies). In doing so this piece focuses specifically on our perceptions rather than those of our students, and our responses to the reactions, comments and critiques of our students. We discuss methods which we have developed/are developing both individually and together to attempt to address issues of equal opportunity in the classroom and in the curriculum. In particular we consider students positive and negative responses to these methods.

Practicalities and Philosophies

The relevancy of our feminist philosophies and pedagogies for equal opportunities practice is great. We realise that not all those aiming to increase access, equality of opportunity and treatment will work within such a philosophical framework but we believe that feminists have been fundamental to the development of non-hierarchical and non-exclusive theories of education. In the thirties, and before, Virginia Woolf(1938) was arguing the value of a separate women's college as a means by which the values of a patriarchal society (primarily militarism and authoritarianism) could be refused. In the 1970s Adrienne Rich (1986, originally 1973) continued the case for an educational environment which replaced hierarchies and power structures with collective work and research focused on community and health issues. Such an environment requires the creation and process of knowledge to focus on women. Thus, the catalyst for this liberating and empowering education is seen to be Women's Studies. This is more than a simple theoretical challenge. Although both the political climate and the structure of educational institutions have made the models of Rich and Woolf virtually impossible to create on the scale advocated it is clear from the writings of Women's Studies practitioners that innovative work has been attempted, challenged and has succeeded in this area (see for example, Aaron & Walby 1991, Morley and Walsh 1995,1996, Davies et al 1994). Within the Academy, Women's Studies is where critical examination of the sexist and racist structures of society can, and does, occur. Therefore, for us, it is the fundamental starting point for discussing issues of pedagogy and student empowerment for all our students.

It has been well documented elsewhere that HE like many other areas has been affected by 'New Right Ideology' (Epstein 1995, Skeggs 1994). The result is that lecturers and support staff in Universities are now (perhaps above all) expected to provide a service. Perhaps in part because of the emphasis on service and indeed, because of the structure of the labour market there is an increased stress on the 'teaching' and learning of transferable skills. Despite the fact that we sometimes resist the service culture, particularly when students insist that we are constantly available for them, we are not against the stress on learning new skills and on the empowerment of students. Indeed, we are aware of the value of these for the individual women and men that we teach: sometimes mature, sometimes non-traditional entrants, often individuals who would not have been at University in the academic climate of 15 years ago.

Given our commitment to feminism and the 'Women's Studies Model', where the teacher is not an expert and all experiences are valued, we are particularly interested in developing methods of teaching and learning which emphasise self development. Our commitment to feminist theory with its emphasis on difference, diversity, oppression, exclusion etc. as well as the value of subjectivity, emotion, biography and self also means we look to classroom and assessment experience which encourage consideration of these issues.

We also believe that it is not necessarily what we teach but HOW we teach that is important. However, this is limited within an academic framework by what is acceptable to university hierarchies. Attempts to follow good feminist practice by utilising small groups, fewer lectures, more workshops and project based activities and team staffing (Lubelska, 1991, p45) from which the students benefit most are restricted by the demands of mass teaching (over 100 in some modules), timetabling conventions and the refusal of educational managers to register two staff members against one teaching slot. So, due to our commitment to such practices we end up teaching more hours than we are recorded as doing - a wonderful incentive to return to more structured and hierarchical 'talk and chalk' approaches which, we believe, is just the educational environment which marginalised and excluded many people in the past.

Placing a high value on experience has long been an important factor of empowerment work with women(Hamner, 1991) and, likewise, Women's Studies, should include a focus on women's experiences (Evans 1995; Humm 1991; Lubelska, 1991). Lubelska(1991) argues that we need to examine the experience of women, in particular women's experience of oppression, as comprehensively as possible and to try and explain the differences and similarities which are revealed. As such we seek to apply and analyse the theoretical framework presented to actual experiences of actual women and to encourage students to do likewise. This may involve students in listening to other people, to hear what they say about how things have affected them and to theorise from that experience - this is virtually impossible in large groups.

Other structural matters are of concern to Women's Studies, for example, the continuing influence from the world of Adult and Community Education and, in particular, from Women's Groups and Radical Community Work. A hallmark of women's groups is learning to frame, enquire about and reframe ideologies and forms of knowledge. Yet one of the many legacies which some women bring to groups and to university is a negative experience of formal education where they were taught to accept the underestimation of their skills and knowledge. Women's Studies, like Women's Groups, relies on a radical and inspiring definition of education which should allow a process of empowerment to begin (Stanko, 1991).

Such a stance has strong links with the 'Process of Conscientisation' described by Paolo Freire (1970). Through his work in Brazil and Chile,

Freire sought to increase peasants' literary skills, whilst at the same time opening up their perceptions of social, political and economic conditions. Freire wrote that the educational process transmits both objective knowledge and a hidden curriculum which supports the dominant culture and class and, like Rich (1986) he attacked the use of education as a weapon of colonisation. Also, like Rich, he wrote that change can be made. Working with poverty stricken South American communities, Freire found that it is possible to develop approaches by which people can voice their feelings and experiences. Despite the inherent sexism in his language, his focus on class and not on other social divisions and criticisms for not properly acknowledging his wife's influence, his methods and theories have been of great use to women - and other oppressed groups in developing education for empowerment. That is what we are trying to offer, but in a limited way as we are housed within a traditional academic mode.

Freire characterised the traditional education process as oppressive and hierarchical, a 'Banking System', where knowledge is a commodity to be accumulated in order to gain access to positions of power and privilege. Instead Freire proposed an 'Education for Liberation' where learners and teachers are engaged in a process in which abstract and concrete knowledge together with experience are integrated as praxis. This is a daily aspect of our teaching for, as Lubelska describes, we "regard ourselves as participants in the learning process" (1991, p47).

Critical thinking and dialogue are fundamental features in this educational process which seeks to challenge conventional explanations of everyday life while considering the action necessary for the transformation of oppressive conditions. Like Freire, we advocate beginning from people's own understanding and valuing their knowledge as part of a process of empowering pedagogy. As such the environment of learning, which we are trying to create, where students are actively engaged in the creation and description of that knowledge, is a fundamental challenge to the mainstream.

This is very different from what Silverstein (1974) describes as the 'masculine model' of teaching and learning. He suggests that all that this model requires - ie texts, tests, papers are designed so that a student succeeds or fails dependant on her/his ability to understand, interpret and work within the teacher's definition of reality. Within this model academic 'freedom' requires that students have the right and are even encouraged to evaluate ideas independently BUT only after they have understood the official interpretation thoroughly. Emphasis here is on 'abstract theory' not experience. As Collins writes: Much of my formal academic training has been designed to show me that I must alienate myself from my communities, my family, and even my own self in order to produce credible intellectual work. (Collins, 1991 pxiii)

So, as already stated, our 'model', which, we accept, is sometimes hard to operationalise both in terms of time, effort and emotional labour (for us and for students), is concerned with sharing and listening, student centred learning, the use of experience (as previously noted). This often involves the move away from traditional 'exams' and 'essays' towards presentations, group work and individually constructed assessments which is aimed at changing the learning experience of students. In the next section we explore some personal implications of putting this 'model' into practice.

Teaching and Learning Experiences

Following on from the above we would argue that our politics run through what we teach and the way we teach it: both in Women's Studies and elsewhere. Yet evidence from our own experience suggests to us that although students perceive us as approachable and (generally) find what we teach interesting and challenging the masculine model of how to teach and how to learn has continuing superior status, we have several examples here.

With all cohorts of Women's Studies students there has been evidence that unless (continually) encouraged/persuaded otherwise many third year students will 'abandon' what they learnt (and received good marks for) in 'Feminist Research Methods' (a second year module on which we both teach) and begin to do 'proper research' for their final year project. This is despite their own political commitment to and enjoyment of feminist methodologies (we know this from what they have told us and from module evaluation forms). Words like 'sample' and 'objectivity' begin to creep into their qualitative research reports, within which some of them, if not persuaded by us, separate their data from their discussion (inappropriate in qualitative and/or feminist epistemological terms). Also having spent a considerable amount of time with us in the second year considering the value of auto/biography in feminist theory and research, and the feminist critique of the masculine model they ask if they will be marked down for inclusion of the self. In extreme cases they even refer to themselves in their projects in abstract terms such as 'the author'.

Similarly in terms of the devaluation of feminist work both male and female students (sometimes Women's Studies students) in Gayle's first year module concerned with the methodologies and philosophies that underpin all social science research are keen to stress that social science really wants to be objective and value free and can be if researchers try hard enough. What is perhaps even more frustrating here is when students (again sometimes Women's Studies students) do refer to feminism, they commonly use textbooks written by men to summarise feminist methodological and epistemological thought.

175

This leads us to consider complaints about the ways we 'expect' students to learn as well as what we 'expect' them to consider. On the same first year module, and others on which we each teach, students complain that reading lists are too long and that a reading pack containing the specific articles that they need for their assessment would be better for them. This occurs even after group discussions on the importance of independent thought and commitment and on the fact that the teacher is not the only expert in the room. We find that many students want the information they need to answer the question, pass the module, get a degree.

Students complain about Gayle's first year module arguing that it is too hard, not introductory, too theoretical - we think because there is no introductory textbook - no easy way through. This is supported by the fact that for one of the assignments about 70% of them answered the one question that could be (though not very well) answered from an introductory textbook. Gayle's second level module *The Sociology of Crime and Deviance* has been criticised (though this time only by part time students who were taking the module alongside full-time work) because Gayle does not indicate when teaching exactly which piece of information the students 'need'. As one student said: couldn't you sort of indicate when you say something that is relevant to our exam?

Similarly in Gayle's third year module *Feminism, Health and Caring* (FHC) it is clear from evaluation forms that some students (again largely professionals taking the module/degree to further their careers) want "more handouts, more overheads". Here we think the New Right marketisation of education with students expecting 'service' and 'value for money' connects well with the 'masculine model' of individualism and the striving for objectivity. The 'Women's Studies' model within which there is an acknowledgement of subjectivity, the time for reflection and a commitment to others rather than just to one's own degree takes more effort. Many of our students find it too much of an effort. They prepare for their own presentations but do not come to or contribute to those of their colleagues and only come to the lectures/seminars relevant to the essay they are writing. There is a clear tension then between the development of student centred learning and what students want - 'quick easy knowledge'.

Even though these modules have met with some criticism and resistance for not being 'traditional' enough nothing really revolutionary in terms of teaching and learning methods is being tried here. In her second year module *Feminist Theory and Action* (FTA) Jen does try something more challenging both for herself and for students. At the beginning of one particular academic year she talked to the group about how they wanted the classes to work and suggested various ways in which students could have control over their learning. A format which included peer teaching and a considerable amount of individual work for 'oneself' was agreed upon. Jen then spent a considerable amount of time with students considering 'how we learn' eg:

- through experience/knowledge of others
- through active listening
- through doing
- through teaching others
- through discussion, debate and 'finding out'
- whether we learn best that which is of interest and/or use and/or relevance to us
- by becoming conscious of our own skills/knowledge needs

There was also consideration of how do we develop knowledge? And finally discussion about/on problematising education as empowerment.

Although there were not too many moans about the time this took at the beginning and regular student surveys revealed that this was the preferred method, once the pressures of coursework and examinations from other modules began to impinge the requests, nay pleads, for lectures became very strong. As we believe that expecting too much work from students can be as disempowering as other practices, a negotiated degree of lecture material was agreed upon to ameliorate the complaints about the time that active and participative learning takes. This is doubly disappointing given that, as FTA underpins everything else that they do, work for this module is work for all modules which seemed not to be realised by the majority of students. Even though we (especially Jen but we) explain and emphasise this, students continue to compartmentalise 'subjects' in the traditional way, which is not surprising as this is the message they often receive elsewhere in the University and carry forward from school or college.

The control that students had over the format of their coursework assignment received a degree of criticism, but only after the complaining students received their results and never during any of the assignment tutorials. The assignment stated:

Feminist campaigns have focused on a variety of areas of male control/oppression of women. Select ONE or TWO of the following:
- *equal opportunities in education*
- *equality at work*
- *child care*
- *abortion and reproductive rights*
- *women's safety*
- *sexuality*

Outline the major theoretical debates and actions around your selected issue, drawing links between the two and critiquing the various positions.

The criticisms which ensued from students who perceived themselves as performing less well than they had expected were focused on the lack of a question and the lack of information concerning what exactly to do:

"You did not set us a question"
"You did not tell us what to do",
and this from a class which had discussed, debated and negotiated feminist pedagogy as part of the module!

Similarly in *Feminism, Health and Caring* for their second assignment students were required to critically consider the relationship between

(a) politics, morality and medicine OR

(b) the pervasiveness of medicalisation OR

(c) whether health is an individual responsibility (or not).

They were expected to do this with reference to any issue(s) covered in the module (or indeed any other issue which they were interested in). The module included consideration of health promotion, women and men as patients - generally or specifically in relation to particular illnesses and diseases, the bio-medical model, alternative approaches, addiction, sexual health, pregnancy, pregnancy loss, infertility, dying and death (and more). Yet on module evaluation forms there were some complaints about little choice of essay questions.

We think that both in FTA and FHC it is not that there is not enough choice or enough material but that there is in fact too much. However, what there is not is clear directional instructions in the 'traditional' style: ie 'here is the question which must be answered in this way'.

It seems though that the main problems that students have is not with us or with our teaching and learning styles but with each other. Interestingly, one feminist strategy which we both advocate and facilitate is peer teaching and the sub division of work amongst the class. Despite spending hours on group work within class any group work set for preparation outside of class is fraught with difficulties. The majority of complaints at the course consultative meetings that we have attended this year have been about other students - "not turning up", "not sharing the work in group projects", "not contributing in class", "hoarding books and journals in the library". Indeed, we have seen this and similar in action - students not working for and not turning up for group presentations[1], students not returning articles to the 'Resource Boxes' that we have established for *Feminist Theory and Action* and *Feminist Research Methods*, students not offering each other feedback following presentations, students very definitely concerned about what **they** are going to get from the module rather than being concerned about the group as a whole.

The old established masculine model of competition fits very nicely with a political emphasis on individualism. Also as the "common cultural senses" of most of our students "would have been constructed almost entirely within or against the dominant discourses of the New Right" (Epstein, 1995, p59), what more can we expect from Thatcher's 'children'.

It was only very late in this last academic year that the value of the concept of sharing reading and discussing material with peers really became accepted amongst first, and particularly, second years. Not unsurprisingly this occurred around examination time when the activity was restricted to group revision and examination preparation. It was obvious from the examination papers which students had prepared together, in their exclusive sub-groups, that still, a true sharing and dialogue did not develop amongst the students.

All this, of course, appears very negative and we would like to stress that we are generalising here. Indeed, some of the students we teach and learn with are very interested and committed to what they learn and to developing different approaches to learning. Some produce excellent work. Also, some students are very supportive of their colleagues and of us.

Certain techniques and styles appear more popular too. In Gayle's first year module the 'sociological autobiographies' that students worked on in seminars seemed to be enjoyed by many and were often very thoughtfully prepared and presented. In *Feminist Research Methods* after we had each spoken about the relationship between our autobiographies and our intellectual and personal development and interests students (generally) carefully and fruitfully did likewise.

---

[1] Jen is currently attempting to employ the advantages of new technology to the learning environment to ameliorate these complaints - using e-mail (available to all students) to devise 'virtual groups' and to deliver module information, exercises and tutorials. At present there has been support only from academics with technical support being wholly absent. This probably is a further indication of the hierarchical divisions within educational institutions and is yet one further block to overcome.

Other positive experiences include the first year module *Women in Society*. Here the student evaluation forms indicate that the group work exercises which are necessitated by the large size of seminar groups (20 students) are viewed as productive and engender quotes such as "at least we learn something and have to think in these seminars unlike in other subjects". These exercises are based on dividing the seminar into four or five small groups and being somewhat prescriptive about what has to be achieved by the end of the session - though how they wish to achieve that end is not prescribed. The first few weeks of this course were spent discussing group dynamics, the rights and responsibilities of group members and the need for us not to repeat the established hierarchies within society within our groups. Once this was established it was possible to begin to get students (both male and female) to discuss their experiences, ideas, knowledge and arguments on a whole range of subjects.

We are encouraged by this support and interest but discouraged by the fact that students did not (always) rate other first year modules, within which there is a considerable amount of group work and tutor feedback, as highly. It is important to note here that we do acknowledge that what we refer to as the 'Women's Studies' model is, at least in part, recognised by many of our colleagues. Indeed, empowering teaching and learning methods have been used by many of our colleagues for many years.

Despite these positive reports our experience still contrasts greatly with Jen's history of teaching Women's Studies in a different institution and under different criteria. As Co-ordinator for an University Diploma in Women's Studies (at a Scottish university) which was wholly taught at night and on weekends Jen witnessed the relationships, trust and sharing which developed amongst students over the two years. In this, a sharing and supportive environment, it was possible for the students, all women, to discuss their personal experiences including abusive situations and other traumatic and very personal matters in a responsive group behaving much more like those women described by Louise Morley who:

> ..appear to move away from attacking, blaming and holding others responsible for meeting their needs. (and) There is a marked interest in the ability to appreciate themselves and other women (Morley, 1993, p123).

The main differences between these situations is not the fact that the Scottish women were 'mature' students (as many of our current students are also 'mature') but that they were a much more cohesive group, whose whole university experience was centred around the one Women's Studies course. Divisions were not able to develop due to experiences in other modules, or reactions of other members of the University as this was a very self-contained course and, as such, probably came closest to Rich's(1973) and Woolf's(1938) notions of separate education challenging patriarchy. Although the women in Scotland faced patriarchal, and heterosexist structures in their everyday lives and work situations the structure of the Women's Studies course was able to offer a place where such forces were kept at a minimum and, this insulation served the students well, permitting a truly empowering environment as well as a place to discuss the effects of marginalisation and oppression elsewhere in their lives. By contrast, our current students who often face racist, sexist and ageist attitudes and institutions do not find a haven in even their Women's Studies classes and marginalisation continues: Sikh women claiming to speak for all 'Asian' women which silences and suppresses Muslim women, heterosexual women speaking in ways which silence lesbians. It appears that in "an increasingly competitive, individualistic culture" students find it hard to engage in dialogue (Walsh, 1996, p187). As Walsh adds:

Dialogue involves disclosure/exposure, and the attendant risks of conflict, hostility, even abuse. Yet without dialogue from different class, ethnic, religious, or cultural backgrounds; between disabled women and non-disabled women; between younger women and older women; between lesbians, bisexual and heterosexual women; between child free women and mothers, and without alliance women remain dispersed, strangers to each other: potential enemies.

Women's Studies students are clearly not protected and often do not overtly challenge the dominant ideologies of the era.

Some Reflections

Despite our commitment to feminist and empowering pedagogies we have found that some of our students still appear to be oppressed. This is primarily due to university structures but also to attitudes of classmates. Like Coate-Bignell (1996) we believe it is necessary to examine this student experience for:

'to ignore the times when a feminist process is inhibiting would be in danger of building a feminist praxis based on a dishonest feminist scholarship' (Coate-Bignell, 1996, p323).

However, we would argue that such oppressions are not so much due to feminist practice but to the artificial constraints put upon both students and staff by the structural limitations of the institutions in which we work. If a small, community education styled course can succeed in Scotland then that indicates that our aims are possible, just not perhaps within the present structure of HE. It seems that we are back to the ideas of Woolf and Rich.

Finally, we would like to consider if mass HE is the place for the development of empowerment. In our classes we can address the issues of disablism, racism, sexism and homophobia - and we can even require our students to indicate their knowledge and understanding via assignments and assessments. However, perhaps the ethos and ideology that shaped mass HE in its current form automatically militates against a truly empowering understanding of these issues for as many of our students suffer the disempowering effects of poverty and harassment and oppressions due to their own identities (perceived or actual) in the hours when they are not in our classes just how empowering can we be? This is the same ethos which has made students treat their education as a service and in our own personal resistance of the standardisation and marketisation of education, we as staff come to resent the demands made upon us by students purporting to express their empowerment but really exercising oppressive behaviour.

Stanko (1991 p2) argues that:

> ... *I do think it is possible to be a feminist within academia. But to do so one must be prepared to cry alongside one's students; to take the time one's colleagues do not to challenge oppressive administrative policy; and to face the ire of fellow academics because you confront their institutional sexism, racism or classism. To do so we must be prepared to be constantly aware of our own power, of our ignorance, or our restricted views, fed by the benefits of being employed (often on a lifetime contract).*

We do accept this but with qualifications. We would argue that it should not be and indeed is not exclusively academics who identify as feminist those who challenge oppressive practice and policy. Also, although we do accept that we objectively hold powerful positions in relation to our students, within the institution we have little power and in day to day University life the subjective experience of power is constantly shifting. Simply as people we feel hurt when working hard to develop equal opportunity in both our curriculum and practice we are criticised despite and indeed sometimes because of our efforts. We open up a critical space whereas some of our colleagues protect themselves behind hierarchy, closed doors and closed minds.

References

Aaron, J and Walby, S (1991) (eds) *Out of the Margins: Women's Studies in the Nineties,* Falmer Press.

Barnes-Powell, T and Letherby, G (1997) 'All in a day's work : gender and care in HE' forthcoming .

Burgess, R (ed) (1994) *Studies in Qualitative Methodology Volume IV,* Jai Press

Coate-Bignall, K (1996) 'Building Feminist Praxis out of Feminist Pedagogy: the importance of students' perspectives in *Women's Studies International Forum* 19: 3 pp315-325

Collins, P H (1991) *Black Feminist Thought: knowledge, consciousness and the politics of empowerment* London: Routledge

Cotterill, P and Letherby, G (1994) 'The Person in the Researcher' in Burgess (1994)

Cotterill, P and Letherby, G (1993) 'Weaving Stories; personal auto/biographies in feminist research' in *Sociology* 27: 1 pp67-80

Davies, S; Lubelska, C; and Quinn, J (eds) (1994) *Changing the Subject: Women in Higher Education,* Taylor and Francis

Epstein, D (1995) ' In Our (New) Right Minds: The Hidden Curriculum and the Academy' in Morley and Walsh (1995)

Evans, M (1995) ' Ivory Towers: Life in the Mind' in Morley and Walsh (1995)

Freire, P (1970), *Pedagogy of the Oppressed* Harmondsworth: Penguin

Griffin, G (ed), (1994), *Changing Our Lives: Doing Women's Studies,* Pluto.

Griffin G, Hester M, Rai S, and Roseneil S (eds) (1994) *Stirring it: Challenges for Feminism* Taylor and Francis

Hamner, J (1991) 'On Course: Women's Studies - A Transitional Programme' in Aaron and Walby (1991)

Humm, M (1991) 'Thinking of things in themselves: Theory, Experience, Women's Studies' in
Aaron and Walby (1991)

Kennedy, M Lubelska C and Walsh V (eds) (1993) *Making Connections* London and Washington: Falmer Press

Letherby, G (1994) 'Mother or not, mother or what?': problems of definition and identity' *Women's Studies International Forum* 17:5 pp

Letherby G and Zdrokowski D (1995) 'Dear Researcher; the use of correspondence research' in *Gender and Society*, 9:5 pp576-593

Lubelska, C (1991) 'Teaching Methods in Women's Studies: Challenging the Mainstream' in Aaron and Walby (1991)

Marchbank J (1996a) 'The Political Mobilisation of Women's Interest Issues: The Failure of Childcare' in *Politics* 16:1 pp9-15

Marchbank J (1996b) *'Going Dutch or Scotch Mist?': Making Marginalised Voices Heard in Local Bureaucracies'* Bradford and Ilkley Community College: Papers in Community Studies

Marchbank J (1994) 'Nondecision-making: A Management Guide to Keeping Women's Interest Issues off the Political Agenda' in Griffin et al

Morley L (1993) 'Women's Studies as Empowerment of "Non-Traditional" Learners in Community and Youth Work Training' in Kennedy, Lubelska and Walsh (1993)

Morley, L (1995), 'Empowerment and the New Right', *Youth and Policy*, No 51, Winter

Morley, L and Walsh, V (eds) (1996) *Breaking Boundaries: women in HE*, Taylor and Francis

Morley L and Walsh V (eds) (1995) *Feminist Academics: Creative agents for change*, Taylor and Francis

Peck, J H and Sawyer, J (eds) *Men and Masculinity* New Jersey: Prentice Hall

Rich, A (1986) 'Towad a Woman-Centred University' in *On Lies, Secrets, Silence: Selected Prose 1966-78* London: Virago (originally 1973)

Silverstein, M (1974) 'The history of a short, unsuccessful academic career' in Peck and Sawyer (1974)

Stanko, B (1991) 'Angst and Academia' *Trouble and Strife* 22 pp19-21

Walsh V (1996) 'Terms of engagement: pedagogy as a healing politic' in Morley and Walsh (1996)

Woolf V (1938) *Three Guineas* Harmondsworth: Penguin

14. Degrees of Deafness: the Match Between Requirements And Provision for Deaf Students in Surveying Education

Lewis Anderson - University of Greenwich

Abstract

This paper considers the tutoring and learning requirements for deaf students in general, and for those in surveying education in particular. Current educational good practice is noted and explained, and the varying degrees of handicap associated with the term deafness are considered.

The provision available at Accredited Centres for Surveying Education is established, by survey questionnaire, and the data analysed to establish general patterns. Specific issues arising are identified and, where possible, relationships between Equal Opportunity Policies, University Mission Statements and local provision are considered.

The paper concludes by identifying and describing appropriate further areas for study and investigation, particularly concerning deaf applicants' perspectives, and graduate employment.

Keywords: handicap; deafness; deaf awareness; communication.

Introduction

There are approximately 67,500 deaf children (aged 0-16 years) in the United Kingdom (NDCS, 1995). This figure is replenishing at an annual rate of 6 : 1,000 (OPCS, 1989). There is, therefore, a significant pool of deaf potential applicants for Further Education (FE) and Higher Education (HE). Deaf applicants will have particular needs and will enter FE and HE with varying backgrounds of preparation. The common factor within the pool is a level of IQ comparable with their hearing peers.

The first part of this paper seeks to explain, briefly, what is meant by deafness, and what the implications of deafness are, for both the deaf and the hearing. The legal context for dealing with deafness is noted, in particular by references to the Disability Discrimination Act 1995 (DDA).

The paper examines HE provision for deaf students from a general perspective, exploring particularly the different kinds of support which is available, financial and technological.

Good practice in communicating is the fundamental requirement for HE providers, and deaf/hearing communication is explained in some depth. In particular, the paper looks at the difficulties hearing tutors may have in understanding the basic needs of deaf students.

The second part of the paper looks at all these issues in the context of provision in Accredited Centres for Surveying Education. A sample survey (Appendix 1) has provided some basic data, which are analysed to indicate any relationship between Equal Opportunities Policy (especially as articulated by Mission Statements), and provision. It is very important to note that the questionnaire survey is not intended to provide robust data for statistical analysis. The purpose of the survey was to gauge the spectrum of possible responses and to influence the direction of subsequent research.

The Handicap of Deafness

General Perspective

The term "deaf" is not clearly defined, nor can it be. Organisations such as the National Deaf Childrens' Society (NDCS) use the term "deaf" to embrace "the full range of hearing loss" (Talk, 1997). Various terms are in common use to cover a similar range: hard of hearing; partially deaf; moderately deaf; severely deaf; profoundly deaf; and even the much less scientific, stone deaf. Audiologists tend to use the three terms only; moderately deaf, for all hearing loss that has a measurable impairment; severely deaf, for hearing loss which is short of total; and profoundly deaf, which is reserved for total hearing loss.

There are regular discussions about these rather unscientific divisions, but there is not great purpose to such debate. The significant factor associated with deafness is the degree of handicap or disability which results. This is a complex, and emotive, area for discussion. The Law recognises disability (as discussed in a subsequent section) but there is a body of opinion which prefers deafness to be considered in terms of handicap, rather than disability. The arguments are based on the notion that (where a deaf person retains all other faculties, including normal IQ) there are few activities where that person would be *disabled* (ie "prevented from doing"). Examples of such activities could be using a standard telephone, hearing the sound on television, listening to a speaker whose back is turned. However, there would be many activities where that person would be *handicapped*, (ie "would have a disadvantage to make up") but would not be prevented from doing. Examples of this category are too numerous even to indicate. They are, in fact, all aspects of a full life other than those where the person is disabled. The list would be very, very extensive.

Viewed from this perspective, with deafness treated as a handicap, the attention of both deaf and hearing communicators can be focused on "making up the disadvantage", with the objective that the deaf person will not miss out on the experience of any activity, either as a recipient or, even more importantly but frequently overlooked, as a contributor.

Deafness and lower intellect are not linked. The IQ of hearing groups and deaf groups is comparable in all its ranges. This is highly important because the mannerisms and communication style frequently associated with deafness are incorrectly but regularly misinterpreted by hearing people as indicative of some form of mental handicap. For those infants who are either born deaf, or become deaf before they are 36 months old, the most significant difficulty is that they are pre-lingually deaf. Becoming deaf before the acquisition of language is a huge handicap to overcome. Deafness after the acquisition of language, at any time through early or middle age, is significantly different form of handicap.

Legal Context

The Disability Discrimination Act, 1995 (DDA) provides legislation covering deafness, together with many other forms of disability. In the Act, disability is defined as "a physical or mental impairment which has a substantial long-term adverse effect on a person's ability to carry out day-to-day activities." This definition applies to hearing impairments, and speech impairment (which may be linked together) which, by their very nature, will reflect on day-to-day activities.

Under the Act, discrimination means "less favourable treatment without justification". The justification for any discrimination must be both "material to the particular circumstances and substantial". Although the Act is an enforcement, the enshrined concepts of positive treatment of all individuals regardless of disability is a sound basis for determining an approach to these issues even where they are not legal requirements. The Act clearly sets out to change our perceptions of disability, from an excuse culture (of why a disabled person could not do a particular job) into an action culture (of what adjustments could be made to enable a disabled person to do a particular job). This is a fundamental, and very forceful, change and is likely to have a significant impact on perceptions of disability within society in general.

In this regard, HE provision is significant; because it is more of a controlled environment than society at large, the opportunity to effect changes and to influence activity and perceptions are more focused. There is also the potential for a much more productive confluence of needs and provision. Students in HE, whether hearing or deaf, have ultimately identical ambitions in terms of their studies, and educators have, in some regard, a similar unitary goal of enabling learning, detached from the particular circumstances of their students.

HE Provision and Deaf Students

General Perspective

It is again useful to remember the notion of the handicap of deafness as requiring the "making up of the disadvantage". Deaf and hearing students in HE have similar aspirations, similar needs, and similar responses to provision. A deaf student, additionally, has certain requirements to enable fulfilment of these goals. It is too easy to look to the disability as an excluder, rather than to look to the individual requirements of a particular student. HE provision is a particularly good example of where the concept within the DDA of positive treatment of an individual is so valuable.

Financial Support

Financial support is a fundamental requirement for mitigating the handicap of a disability. There are numerous grants and allowances, in addition to the mandatory maintenance grant, although many are means-tested and therefore highly discretionary. The Disabled Students' Allowance (DSA) is available for those students whose disability makes it more expensive to undertake a HE course. It is available for any additional disability-related costs of study, in 3 different categories. There is a General Allowance (maximum ,1,215 pa), intended to cover any costs related to disability and study that are not covered by other specific allowances (eg extra books or extra photocopying). The Specialist Equipment allowance (maximum ,3,650 over the whole course) is self-explanatory, as is the Non-Medical Helpers' Allowance (maximum ,4,850 pa).

The Disability Living Allowance (a state Benefit) is not income-related, and so it is possible to continue claiming it in addition to the mandatory grant and the DSA. In addition to general access funds and student loans, several trusts disburse discretionary awards to deaf students. Of course, none of these grants and awards reduce the level of deafness, their purpose is to facilitate, with their buying power, the positive adjustments that can be made to enable the student to benefit from the HE provision on offer.

Technological Support

There is a significant amount of technological help available to achieve the positive adjustments. Computers, text telephones, induction loop systems, radio aids and captioned videos can all be deployed to facilitate learning. Other technology embraces living and, in particular, living safely, including vibrating alarm clocks, doorbell and telephone linked lighting, vibrating pad smoke detectors and vibrating alarm pagers. For many students, these securities will be available in their home environment and it is even more important to have them available in the unfamiliar and potentially threatening new environment away from home.

Communication Practice

Allowances and grants may help fund the purchase of technological aids but technology itself is nowhere near being the most important part of the process of reducing the effect of the handicap. Without question, the human dimension is the most significant factor, and in HE provision this means primarily the tutors and educators. It is not possible in this paper to cover in any depth the full range of teaching strategies for use in HE with deaf students. This information is, in any event, comprehensively published elsewhere and widely available. The following salient points have been distilled from excellent literature published by the Royal National Institute for Deaf People (RNID, 1994).

Good practice for teaching deaf students is likely to be good practice for teaching hearing students also. The distinction is that hearing students are more able to make allowances for bad practice than are deaf students. There are 2 core areas to consider: content & delivery, and timetable & venue.

1.   Content and Delivery

A large proportion of deaf people rely heavily upon lip-reading, which is an extremely difficult and very tiring skill, requiring a huge amount of concentration. Lip-reading also relies on a large proportion of guesswork, and is dependent, therefore, on clear speech and contextual clues. To lip-read, a student must be able to see the tutor's mouth, and preferably make eye contact. Lip-reading requires clues, and switching topics rapidly lays a false trail that easily confuses. Similarly, the guesswork involved means that a clear logical structure is essential. Visual aids such as overhead projectors (without fans) are excellent, but tutors must avoid darkened rooms when using slides. Lip-reading is difficult in good conditions, but it is impossible in the dark.

Handouts give the deaf student real assistance, because the activity of studying them can be undertaken at an appropriate pace. Carbon-copied or photo-copied contemporary notes from hearing peers allow deaf students to lip-read whilst the tutor is talking (deaf students cannot lip-read if they are looking at what they are writing).

2.   Timetable and Venue

Empathetic timetabling can make an enormous difference to a deaf student. Lip-reading is tiring and cannot be sustained for long periods throughout a day. Regular breaks, and a timetable over different days is a great benefit.

Timetabling classes in the appropriate rooms is important, as it may often be possible to allocate the most acoustically friendly rooms to those classes which a deaf student will attend. This is not the "tail wagging the dog", but would be a clear example of what the DDA refers to as a "reasonable adjustment". In this case, as so often, the most appropriate learning environment for a deaf student is, coincidentally, probably the most pleasant learning environment for a hearing student.

Needs and Awareness
The human dimension is paramount, and it is not productive to describe the needs of deaf students solely in terms of their own requirements. Only when the needs of deaf students are addressed in terms of awareness by others can a real start be made in eroding the barriers of handicap. This approach could be described as holistic and, in many aspects of HE, would show positive benefits for deaf and hearing students alike.

Deaf and hearing students will be alike in-so-far as they have aspirations, expectations and motivations. The aspiration to read for a degree, to gain useful employment and to develop socially are a common bond amongst most students. To talk of a deaf student in terms of needs is possibly to disregard the potential for fulfilment of these greater objectives. It can lead to an addressing of the issues in mechanistic terms, seeing a deaf student, for example, as needing a radio aid. What the deaf student needs is the ability to be involved without handicap in the complexities of classroom and social communication. This could happen, with or without a radio aid, if awareness levels of hearing people were high enough to make communication a proper two-way involvement. Without this level of awareness, the radio aid can become merely a palliative.

Awareness begins with the conscious effort of individuals and becomes, eventually, second nature. It is easier to raise awareness in a formal classroom setting, where the active co-operation of the tutor and the deaf student can be harnessed. This can then be extended to the less formal seminar/project settings, where awareness amongst the tutees generally needs to be encouraged and developed (no speaking without prior sight indication, etc). Finally, the heightened awareness levels will transfer, through empathy, to social settings. In a social environment, many of the protective aspects of the classroom are lost, and social environments can be much more hostile for deaf people (compare the orderly calm of a semi-circular seminar arrangement in an acoustically friendly room with the social hubbub of a darkened dance floor).

Regardless of the extent to which a tutor manages to heighten deaf awareness amongst a group, there will inevitably be a resource demand (either physical or human). In its simplest terms, a tutor preparing a self-explanatory handout for a hearing class is able to concentrate solely upon the content and presentation of the handout, and its position within the teaching programme. With a deaf student in the class, there are the extra considerations of distraction, explanation and reading/concentration time. However, the good practice deployed to assist a deaf student in these circumstances will inevitably be good practice for the rest of the class also. Deaf awareness should lead to clarity of communication, leading to the main objective - the surmounting of handicap.

Deaf awareness also has a further benefit - the development of an environment in which the deaf student can contribute. With any handicap (and deafness is no different) the first objective isoften to enable the handicapped person to *receive* on more equal terms. The subsequent stage is often not achieved, but is *essential* in HE - that is, generating the opportunity for the deaf student to contribute. Just as a hearing student who has not completed preparatory work is unlikely to make a worthwhile contribution to a seminar, so it is with a deaf student not being likely to make a contribution if the previous discussion, or peripheral questions and answers, have not been heard. The contribution of a deaf student in a class often proves invaluable. Not only is a deaf student more likely to have read recommended preparatory texts, but the opportunity may arise for comments filled with the insights of a different perspective.

The Survey of Accredited Centres for Surveying Education

Surveying is a graduate-entry profession and the Royal Institution of Chartered Surveyors (RICS) grants approval to appropriate degree course through an accreditation process. Since 1993 , several universities have been designated Accredited Centres (ACs), allowing the accreditation process to be devolved.

As a focus for this paper, surveying HE provision available in the ACs has been sampled (see Appendix 1 for Questionnaire). All United Kingdom ACs were contacted and 24 completed responses were returned. A summary of the responses is included as Appendix 2.

The questionnaire was designed, as stated previously, to "gauge the spectrum of possible responses". The responses appear coherent enough to allow this to occur. There were five sections to the questionnaire. The first section concerned teaching accommodation, and answers provided information on the physical provision which might be available to accommodate a deaf student. The second section, on teaching resources, reflected the notion of "reasonable adjustments" from the DDA. The third section was to enable a judgement to be made on institutional commitment to the provision of minority services. The fourth section was designed to sample levels of deaf awareness. The fifth section was designed to sample self-perceptions of adequacy on the part of respondents. A brief general analysis of each of these sections follows.

Section 1: Teaching Analysis

The analysis reveals quite clearly a greater ability to provide standard furnishings such as carpets and suspended/low ceilings, than non-standard soft furnishings such as curtains. This is quite understandable, and possibly reflects the usual accommodation improvements that would be made for general use.

Similarly, radio-mike facilities are now common in large-group teaching areas, and are often seen as a standard improvement for all users.

Section 2: Teaching Resources

The "passive effect" of enhanced facilities for all students being of benefit for deaf students is clearly indicated in responses to Questions 4 and 5. A high proportion of respondents confirmed their ability to provide written handouts and other material, and confirmed that tape recorders could be permitted. Both these examples could be of use to all students. However, where an "active effect" would be required for the benefit of deaf students, the responses to Question 3 showed that classroom activity could take place with no possibility of full involvement by deaf students (although the affordable technology exists to remedy this in many cases).

Question 6 showed a willingness to accommodate the needs of deaf students, but a significant number of respondents indicated that they would not be able to make this basic facility available to deaf students.

Where the resource demands were indicated as being significant, as in Question 7, the positive response rate dropped sharply. This would be expected, and Question 6 and Question 7 together begin to indicate the differing perceptions of what constitute "reasonable adjustments".

Section 3 : Mission Statement and EOP

The responses to Question 8 support reasonable supposition - that it, Mission Statements embrace broader issues such as equal opportunities, but do not explicitly mention more specific issues such as degrees. This is understandable as Mission Statements, by their nature, are short and generalised.

Within EOPs, however, there should be opportunity to be explicit about some of the more specific issues which they cover. The responses to Question 9 revealed a dominance within EOPs of racial, sexual and colour issues, and a similar explicit concern for physical handicap. It may be significant that these four areas have a visual element of distinction to them. Dyslexia, blindness and deafness are much less distinctive and in the case of dyslexia and deafness are almost fully internalised.

There is a logic to the possible reason for this. A student with a physical handicap, (if the EOP had resulted in affirmative action), would find access to a lecture theatre being provided. Failure of an EOP to provide this would leave the very tangible result of a wheelchair-user outside a classroom, and physically denied entry, which would be a wholly unacceptable scenario.

However, the deaf student would find access to any lecture theatre no problem, although once in the lecture would suffer all the educational shortfalls explained earlier in this paper.

Section 4: Deaf Awareness

Questions 10 to 18 were included to sample issues of deaf awareness, and are not deemed to have any level of statistical significance. However, they are probably the most challenging questions in the survey, and it is likely that all respondents would wish to be in a position to give correct answers. There are no such answers although, as a generalisation, the response should generally be FALSE to all questions. Questions 10 and 14 are linked and both show a significant TRUE response. In fact, lip-reading is a skill which is very difficult to acquire and to become proficient is unusual. Slow speech may aid audibility, but it makes lip-reading even more difficult. This is because deaf people, when lip-reading, use key words, body language indicators and other devices to make proficient "guesses" at the structure and content of the full sentence. Abnormal speech patterns, such as speaking slowly, detract from this.

Section 5: Adequacy of Provision

Understandably, no respondents considered their current level of provision to be excellent, but there were some surprises. A small number of respondents who were unable to offer access to a fax machine (Question 6) considered the level of provision for deaf students to be adequate. Similarly, a number of respondents who were able to indicate YES to Question 7, claimed "very inadequate" provision in response to Question 19. There may be a simple desire here to accept the inevitable, on the one hand, and to always want improvements on the other. The pattern of spend in Question 20 was consistent with expectations from previous responses.

Further study

There are two additional areas which require investigation, and several aspects covered by this paper could provide the basis for a proper research project.

The two additional areas are deaf applicants' perspectives and graduate perspectives. For applicants there are significant problems associated with both the initial contact with an HE provider (minicom available?) and with published supportive information about particular special needs. For graduates, especially vocational HE courses such as surveying, there is the difficulty of employment, and also Health and Safety issues associated with property and construction.

From this paper, the areas covered by the questionnaire could be fully researched, and the cost of adequate provision could be quantified. The relative difficulties for deaf students on different courses could be explored. The passive/active effect of the influence of formal statements of intent (enshrined in EOPs) could be explored in some detail, and could lead to positive conclusions for the enhancement of provision generally.

References

NDCS   Statistical Sources of Information About Deaf Children, NDCS, March 1995.

OPCS   OPCS Survey of Disability, HMSO, 1989.

TALK   Magazine of NDCS, Spring 1997.

RNID   Fact sheet: Teaching Strategies to Use With Deaf Students, RNID, 1994.

15. Becoming a Nurse: the Experience of the Black Student

Linda Waterworth - Leeds University

Abstract

Melia (1987) described nursing as an organisation which presented considerable problems for those attempting to gain acceptance to its ranks. The black student may have to overcome the additional problems of racism within society, the NHS and the educational setting. This paper explores this issue. It places racism within the NHS within an historical perspective. It considers recent evidence of racism in the NHS. It provides a description of black nurses' experience based on interviews with four student nurses in the third year of a Dip HE (Nursing) Programme. The black nurses reported experiences are considered within the context of existing research on the process of becoming a nurse. The findings must be of concern to both providers of nursing care and nursing education, not only for the individuals concerned but because this is the environment in which the next generation of nurses is being socialised. Racism is being reproduced. The NHSME (1993) has set the goals of ensuring that the NHS workplace is free from racial harassment and that the identifiable needs of people from ethnic minority group may be met. Appropriate multi-cultural care can not be provided in a racist environment.

Note: In this paper the word 'black' is used to refer to any person whose skin colour renders them liable to being treated in a racist manner.

Introduction

Racism is an aspect of British society. The National Council for Civil Liberties (1993) stated "Reports from monitoring groups, advice centres, and legal officers... told of increasing racist vandalism, graffiti, and personal abuse in the streets, estates and schools" (NCCL London 1993 p33). Virdee (1994) found that one third of the black population studied felt constrained in the way that they lived their lives because of fear of racial harassment. The NHS has a legacy of racism and this is the environment in which the next generation of nurses is being socialised. It is essential to understand the processes by which racism is reproduced if effective remedies are to be pursued.

NHS: Historical Legacy

The NHS has always been reliant on ethnic minority workers. In the early days active recruitment from the colonies was organised by a centralised recruiting system with selection committees in sixteen countries. Colonial immigrants provided a source of cheap labour when workers were in short supply (Pearson 1987). Staff recruited into the NHS from the colonies were mostly placed in lower status occupations. They were predominantly female. Black overseas applicants for nurse training were more likely to be offered enrolled nurse training even though they often had the entry requirements for registered nurse training. Enrolled nurse training was not only a shorter, less academic, course but led to a qualification not recognised outside Britain. The early exploitation of black workers within the NHS established practices which have become institutionalised.

Some hospitals did not recruit black workers from the colonies, these were usually the more prestigious teaching hospitals. Some gained local reputations for not employing black staff; remnants of these reputations remain to this day. A Commission for Racial Equality survey (CRE 1987) found that 3% of recruits to schools of nursing came from ethnic minority groups, whereas approximately 5% of the working population had ethnic minority status. The CRE (1987) gave the example of three London hospitals which had only 1% of black trainees when the local average was 15%. A Leeds hospital had only two black trainees out of a total of 425, the local black population averaged 4% (CRE 1987). The reasons given by the hospitals was suggested to be a lack of applicants. Pearson (1987) suggests that racism within the NHS has tested the endurance of black nurses and that young black school leavers are reluctant to expose themselves to the humiliation and degradation that they have seen their parents and relatives endure. It seems possible that this may affect student nurse recruitment.

NHS: Present day

The Policy Studies Institute study "Nursing in a Multi-ethnic NHS", has clearly demonstrated that racism continues to be a problem (Beishon, Virdee & Hagell 1995). The study showed that ethnic minority nurses were disadvantaged in career progression above grade E posts. For example, black nurses could expect to reach sister grade five years later than their white colleagues. Racial harassment was identified as an ongoing problem. Nearly two thirds of the black respondents reported racial harassment by patients and one third reported racism from colleagues. Racist verbal abuse was considered to be the norm in some areas. The report established that most incidents of racism go unreported. Black respondents anticipated that management would be unsympathetic.

The process of becoming a nurse requires time in practice arenas. Students are thus exposed to an environment in which racism has become institutionalised and is overtly expressed both in the order of the staffing hierarchy and in unrestrained harassing behaviour by both patients and staff.

NHS: The educational setting

The King's fund (1990) suggested that nurse education should equip nurses to practise effectively and sensitively in a multi-racial and multi-cultural society. Many nurse educators have only recently come to acknowledge the existence of racism in society, and the NHS. This recent acknowledgment has in part been brought about by the introduction of Sociology into the Dip HE (Nursing) courses. Racism is an uncomfortable subject. Sometimes it may be side-stepped and replaced by the topics on multi-culturalism. In mainstream education this was found to increase cultural stereotyping and support racist backlash (Rattansi in Donald & Rattansi 1992). Alleyne, Papadopoulos & Tiki (1994) emphasise the importance of an understanding of racism and anti-racist strategies as a prerequisite to consideration of multi-cultural issues. Studies on racism within educational settings have demonstrated that it is endemic (CRE 1988). Racism in nurse education settings has not as yet received much research attention. To increase understanding of this issue a small study of black students' perceptions was undertaken, the findings of which are reported below.

Rationale for the study

Little is known of black students' perceived experience of undertaking a nurse education program. The CRE report (1989), referring to mainstream education suggest that it is important to establish what is experienced by students once admitted to an educational institution. This study attempts to do this.

It is not thought that the findings from the study could in any way be generalised, but it is hoped that they may serve to increase insight and understanding.

Method

The size of the study was limited, only 8 students were identified as being both black and having experience in both practice and educational settings. All had completed a common foundation program and were undertaking specialist branch studies. Only 4 students responded to the request for interview - 3 females and 1 male. The students were interviewed at a time and setting of their choosing. The interviews were recorded from which detailed notes were made. The interviews were semi structured by using open ended questions. It was suggested to the students that they start by talking about life before entering the college, then describe settling into college, and experience of the course. The students were not asked directly about racism. The interviewer endeavoured to encourage student flow by use of non verbal behaviour and verbal prompting. The students were asked on occasion to elaborate on how they felt or how they had coped with a particular circumstance.

Three of the interviews lasted over one hour and the fourth 35 minutes. On completion of the recorded interviews the students continued to talk with the researcher in an informal way, this information was not used. The student was then thanked for participating, and offered future support if required.

Ethical issues and validation

The students were given the assurance that their anonymity would, as far as possible, be safeguarded. Their names were only known to the researcher. Passages selected for quotation or comment from the tape recording would be presented in a way that would make identification unlikely. A write up of material used was sent to each individual concerned for validation. It was considered possible that students may reveal information that was upsetting to them, or that they may reveal incidents that they felt required college intervention. Prior to the interviews, these potential issues were discussed with a member of the college executive and it was agreed that if the student so wished the researcher would provide continuing support. The decision was made that action would only be taken if the student indicated that this was required. This opened the possibility that the researcher may gain information on unacceptable practices and not intervene. It was felt that this may be in part resolved by less specific intervention at a future date.

Findings

Reoccurring themes were identified from the detailed notes taken from the interview recordings. These include "making friends","culture shock", "experiences of racism", "academic issues", "stress and coping mechanisms".

Student's own words will be indicated by the use of inverted commas, omissions will be indicated by (...), and ... will be used to indicate a pause.

Biographical Background.

Two of the students were born in England but had spent a large number of years in their home country as well. One of these had English as a first language. The other had been brought up to be bilingual including English. Both had A-level qualifications. One had relatives near the college. The other had friends in a nearby city. The other two students had been born abroad. One had studied A levels in this country at a private boarding school in an environment she described as "protected". The other student came to England for the first time for the interview. One of these students had English as a first language but spoke with a marked dialect. The other student had learned English as a second language as an adult. Neither of these students had friends or family in the vicinity of the college. One of these students had O levels. The other had A levels.

Making Friends

The two British born students settled into college and soon made friends. One suggested that this was helped by the "nice teacher" who had made "everyone comfortable". Changing group membership for the specialist branch program was less comfortable. The student now feels that the "English are difficult to get to know ... people in my class ... very difficult ... sometimes I hesitate to think it's a black problem ... avoiding you because you are black". The student now felt "really nervous" in the branch group and felt that they were "waiting for me to make a mistake". The student said that white students from the original group appear to have been accepted in the new group.

Three of the students were disturbed at the small number of black students at the college and that there was no-one from a similar ethnic background. One student said, "by being the only coloured person in the class ... not able to express my will ... it would be different". This student did not feel safe in class and during the early part of the course had felt vulnerable.

One student described embarrassment in class when the subject of race was brought up, and said, "I always keep my mouth shut." This student had on one occasion been asked in class by the teacher "What do you think about being black?".

One of the non British born students had found it very difficult to make friends in the college and felt that her behaviour was misinterpreted and repeatedly referred to having been "very lonely" "extremely lonely" "wanting some friendship" and said that there had been a lot of "heart ache". This student received some support from a black English student, but this was limited and the student explained "she had to portray being against me ... she needs support also". This student said that the students were "very negative".

Culture shock

The two non British born students had experienced what may be described as culture shock. One student described the main difficulty as the "NHS meant nothing to me ... the old history didn't make any sense" This student was also unfamiliar with everyday life and had to learn to fend for self for the first time.

One student felt that many of the problems were related to cultural difference. This student said "I discovered that the English were very different ... not as expressive (...) you would not know how different another country is if you have not been there (...) because my interactions are very different (...) white students didn't understand different cultural backgrounds ... a lot of people don't know the vast cultural difference ... one country to another". Students took offence and said so. It was "very stressful not getting on with classmates".

One student described experiencing cultural difference on placement. Break-time discussions of "boyfriends, sex , drinking and holidays" were not what was always wanted. Taking breaks away from the ward led to suggestions of unfriendliness. This student was aware of conflict between self and nursing culture. This was described as "some things I want from you ... some things I don't want from you"

Experiences of Racism.

All students described experiences related to racism.

One student stated a reluctance to believe that different treatment experienced was based on being black and said " Its very difficult when you are black ... if you go through college or life thinking I'm black ... and expecting to be treated this way ... almost in a mysterious way these things happen (...) I just try to brush things off ... that's me that's them... and don't think its happening because I'm black (...) sometimes its happened ... being funny towards me ... that's them ... probably not very nice people (...) tried not to think it's because I'm black (...) make the best out of life ... go for what you want."

One student described being confronted by overt racism from patients on the ward, " a few times patients have said they don't want a black nurse attending to them...". A student had learned to deal with this in a diplomatic way. The student would get someone else to attend to them and explain "she doesn't really like me, not because of something I have done but ...". The student did not complete the sentence. The student was aware that such patient behaviour did restrict ability to practise. This student described ward experience as being a positive enjoyable learning experience most of the time.

Another student had also been rejected by clients but suggested that this could be part of someone's illness. This student then stated "I can tell who doesn't want me to go near them ... just the way they react." The student was aware that some patients would be compliant to other members of staff and concluded that there was "something that person doesn't like about me". This student suggested, "if you can't speak English that well you are going to get discriminated against".

One student described rejection by ward staff which appeared to have a racist basis, "picking on me ... made life very difficult (...) I know that they really did not like me from day one ... whatever mistake I make they are ready to pick on me and laugh behind my back". The student said " I know my English is not as good as normal people." The student had difficulty with long jargon words. The student described hating that experience from beginning to end. For ten weeks, "Every day I prayed that I would be ill. I wanted to phone in sick." The experience was stressful in other ways. The student had twelve "really poorly" patients to look after. The ward was short staffed and the staff were "not happy ... bitching amongst themselves". The student felt that there was no-one to turn to. Time and energy was taken up by academic study and a tiring workload. On other wards this student had found the mentors very supportive and helpful.

One student suggested "some wards and some staff are really different with white students than with me ... as though white students are superior to me ... I can't say it's racism ... could be racism, could be my personality or combination of both. It's there but underhand". This student said "it hurts, it really hurts if you are in a group and they don't value you", and felt that ward staff "wanting to show what I can't do rather than what I can do".

One student on placement had witnessed ill treatment of a black client and felt that if there were more black staff this would be less likely to happen. The student was aware of the dilemma of suggesting changes in treatment and the possibility of unpopularity, the student did nothing about the incident. A black student may feel more vulnerable in this situation.

One student described a situation where a patient had developed a rapport with them in which the patient was "taking the mickey ... not racist". The student had obviously remembered the incident and considered it worthy of relating. The patient had asked how the medical staff had reacted to a black nurse in theatre and had apparently said to the sister "don't forget to give that black kid loads of food". The sister had interpreted this as a good patient/nurse relationship. It perhaps demonstrates a racist undercurrent that is so prevalent it is seen as normal.

Academic issues.

Three out of the four students had been referred on an assignment/examination.

The student with English as a second language had been referred on an open book examination. The student had been awarded 39% (40% is the pass mark). On resitting the examination, extra time had been requested for reading and access to a dictionary. These were refused by the exam board. The student described how it took her longer to understand the meaning of questions and her reading speed was slower than other students. The timing of the resit examination required the student to cancel a visit to her parents. She has since tried to negotiate a further three week holiday but this has been refused by the college. This student has felt that she was "fighting against a brick wall".

One student described problems with meeting the academic requirements. The student felt that this was related to the stress of settling into the college. The stress was compounded by teachers and students whose advice was to give up the course, saying "you are not right for this course". This students family had provided financial support. The student described that they were not rich. This student had paid for private language tuition. The students described problems with English the "simple things - like getting tenses right".

One student described initial problems with essay writing and described finding the first assignment "really difficult ... I've never done such a thing before ... I went loads of time for supervision ... so many times." This student was grateful for the support given.

Two students described the experience of failure as "heartbreaking"

Stress and coping.

One student described episodes of extreme distress, and described feeling so ill on one occasion and telling a teacher, and was told, "no you're just stressed, go and have a cup of tea". The student said "I actually brought everything up".

One student described episodes of depression. "I got depressed ... and called in sick ... all I did was sleep". The student felt that the college did not handle the situation well. This student went for counselling but did not find it helpful and described feeling "negative vibes". The student would have appreciated a black tutor to talk to.

One student suggested that more consideration needs to be given to the needs of all students. In particular support from tutors, not just personal tutors, because sometimes it is others that give support. This student described "mumbling to some of the tutors" to relieve stress. These students all described getting support from some mentors on the wards as well as some tutors.

Summary of findings

The students described difficulty with making friends with their peers, and feelings of vulnerability in classroom situations. They all described experiencing various degrees of being excluded and isolated. They had all experienced racism both from colleagues and patients, although one of them described a reluctance to accept that the problems were related to racism. The students did appear to be having more academic problems than might have been expected from their entry qualifications.

Discussion

Research on the process of becoming a nurse has identified that it is stressful (Melia 1987, Bradby 1990). In the initial stages many students have to contend with being away from home and having to fend for themselves. The new recruit to any organisation may have feelings of bewilderment and being overwhelmed (Louis 1980). The situation may well be more extreme for students who lack local knowledge, local family support, and have to cope with the experiences of racism. Bradby (1990) found that the majority of students soon fitted in. The black students in this study seem not to have done so.

Bradby (1990) described the process of becoming a nurse in terms of a "status passage" involving a change in personal identity. She described how many students appeared to deal with this by going home at every opportunity in order to reinforce their personal identity. It may be that the change in personal identity required in becoming a nurse is greater for the black student. Students who do not have accessible family and friends may lack an important avenue for stress release.

Melia (1987) identified "fitting in" as a central concern for student nurses. They were aware of the pressures to conform and the need to "learn the rules". The rules were not spoken or written but were, it seems, conveyed by non-verbal behaviour. It may be suggested that becoming a nurse requires much informal learning. It seems likely that informal knowledge is shared among a peer group. Students who do not fit easily into peer group networks may have less access to informal knowledge. Black students may have increased needs for this informal knowledge and yet may have less access to it.

The students' experiences of racism are supported by the findings of Beishon, Virdee & Hagell (1995). It seems that subtle and overt forms of racism are commonplace within the NHS. It also appears that it usual for black nursing staff to make excuses for racist patients on the basis of their illness, and not expect management to take any action against racism. Tomlinson (1990) describes the experience of racism as being extremely hurtful and deflating. Experiences of racism must be damaging to self esteem and increase black students' anxiety. Bradby (1990) described students who had problems as seeming to be vulnerable individuals demonstrating lower self esteem and higher anxiety. It may be that black students have a higher risk of falling into this category as a result of their experience of racism.

The increased risk of isolation, loneliness, whilst at the same time having to survive in an often hostile environment may explain in part black students seeming academic underachievement. Black students may feel more vulnerable in classroom discussion. Teachers need to be particularly sensitive to the black students needs when issues related to race are discussed. The need for extra time for written examinations for students with English as second language requires further consideration.

Bradby (1990) describes nurse education as a serial method in which skills are passed from one generation to the next. She suggests that this may result in the transmission of poor practice. It does seem that student nurses are being prepared for practice in environments where not only racism exists but where it remains largely unchallenged. This process must result in the reproduction of racism.

Teaching and nursing staff need to be more aware of appropriate ways of dealing with racism. Tomlinson (1990) advocates the open identification, discussion and dealing with all racist incidents, as this reduces the isolation for the black nurse. To achieve this the NHS must put in place an active training programmes to support anti-racism.

References

Alleyne J. Papadopoulos I. Tiki M. (1994) Anti-racism within transcultural nurse education British Journal of Nursing 1994 Vol 3 no 12

Beishon S. Virdee S.& Hagell A. (1995) Nursing in a Multi-Ethnic NHS PSI Publishing London

Bradby M. (1990) Status Passage into Nursing: another View of the process of Socialization into Nursing Journal of Advanced Nursing 1990 15 1220-1225

Commission for Racial Equality (1987) Ethnic Origins of nurses applying for and in training - a survey.

Commission for Racial Equality (1988) Learning in Terror

Commission for Racial Equality (1989) A Review of Equal Opportunity Policies in Higher Education.

Donald J. & Rattansi A.(eds) (1992) Race Culture and Difference Open University Press.

Louis M,R, (1980) Surprise and Sense Making:what newcomers experience entering unfamiliar organisations. Administrative Science Quarterly 25 (2) 226-251

Melia K.(1987) Learning and Working the Occupational Socialization of Nurses Tavistock Publications.

National Council for Civil Liberties (1993) Racism: the Destruction of Civil and Political Liberties (London NCCL)

Pearson M (1987) Racism Nursing Times 17/6/87.

Taylor P. Minority Ethnic Groups and Gender Access to Higher Education New Community 19(3) 425-440 April 1993

Tomlinson C.(1990) Biting the Hand, Nursing Times September 26, Vol 86, No 39, 1990.

Virdee S. (1994) Racial Violence and Harassment, London Policy Studies Institute 1994